Joe Karam was born in 1951, the only son and eldest child of six. Raised on a farm near Taumarunui, he rode horses to the small country primary school he attended before becoming a boarder at St Patrick's, Silverstream. At seventeen he was the youngest player selected to play rugby for Wellington; by twenty he was in the All Blacks. After touring the UK and France with the team, Joe took time away from the All Blacks to live in France and travel around Europe for six months before returning to New Zealand to take up his place in the team again. After ten test matches, frustrated with rugby administration and determined to go his own way, he switched to rugby league at the age of 24.

Since leaving full-time sport, Joe has had a variety of business interests, including a jewellery shop, property development and franchising companies. He was involved in Radio i and Radio Hauraki in the early 'post-pirate' days, and his early love of horses evolved into owning racehorses, including Wellington Cup winner Flying Luskin.

Despite having no previous legal experience or connection with the Bain family, Joe became interested in David Bain's plight when he discovered that several of David's friends were attempting to raise funds for an appeal to the Privy Council. That interest has since become a passion, and Joe Karam is now seen as a crusader on David's behalf.

Joe has three children, Richard, Matthew and Simone, and lives in Ardmore.

DAVID AND GOLIATH

THE BAIN FAMILY
MURDERS

JOE KARAM

REED

Published by Reed Books, a division of Reed Publishing (NZ) Ltd, 39 Rawene Rd, Birkenhead, Auckland. Associated companies, branches and representatives throughout the world.

ISBN 0 7900 0564 6

First published 1997
Reprinted 1997

Printed in New Zealand by Brebner Print

Love, compassion and understanding
Peace, purpose and integrity
Like ripples on a pond
From pebbles beyond

JFK

CONTENTS

ACKNOWLEDGEMENTS

To everyone at Reed Publishing. If these people and this company represent the legacy of A.H. Reed himself, then without doubt he rests very peacefully.

To Colin Withnall QC, for his prudence, perspicacity, courage and comradeship; and Steve O'Driscoll for his efforts and support.

To the 'Friends of David' for their faith and patience.

To Mike Turner, who has the intelligence to match his heart; and Melanie Reid for 'taking no shit'.

To the management and staff of the Southern Cross Hotel in Dunedin, my second home in 1996. It's lucky room 691 can't talk!

To 'Holmes', for breaking the suppression order and giving me a fair platform.

To the staff at Paparua Prison, for their courtesy, co-operation and care for David.

To all of those police staff throughout New Zealand who selflessly do an honest hard day's toil in a most difficult arena.

To a 'Doctor of the Desert'; charming company and delightful cuisine.

To all of those who offered their unsolicited support to me by phone, fax and post.

To David for his trust.

And finally, to Richard, Matthew and Simone for their unwavering support and encouragement during a difficult time.

PROLOGUE

Monday 20 June 1994. Deep dark hours of the morning. Mid-winter in Dunedin. A cold and unwelcoming dawn is just hours away.

In the very old house at 65 Every Street, Andersons Bay, the Bain family sleeps. Well, five of them do. The sixth, David, 22 years old, marathon runner, student of classical music at Dunedin University, is stirring already. It's about 4 a.m.

For the first time in almost a year, seventeen-year-old practising prostitute Laniet has stayed at home, sleeping in a room used as a study, opposite Margaret's bedroom. Margaret Bain, Mum, sleeps soundly in the main bedroom, having been out to the bank ATM machine late the previous evening. The $200 cash she withdrew is on her bedside table. Stephen, a lean and strong fourteen-year-old, sleeps in a room just off her bedroom, probably the original nursery in this old house. Arawa, a twenty-year-old trainee school teacher, beauty pageant winner and former dux of Bayfield High School, is in the downstairs bedroom, accessible through a pokey hall from the old kitchen.

In a derelict, filthy caravan at the back of the section, about twenty metres from the house, Robin Bain, Dad, is sound asleep. He has been ostracised by his wife, and during the week lives at the Taieri Beach School about 45 kilometres south of Dunedin. On weekends however he returns to Every Street, in his barely roadworthy Commer van. His alarm is set to go off as usual at 6.30 a.m. He needs to leave at about 7 a.m. to be back at Taieri Beach in time for work. He always leaves on Monday having already eaten breakfast, showered and dressed to go straight to school.

David's alarm clock is set for 5.30 a.m. He has a large paper delivery run around the Andersons Bay hills which he has been doing for about five years. Sometimes he takes his dog, Casey, with him. The run keeps him fit, as part of his training for running, and earns a few extra bob for a young student. David has always loved to run, right from the time he was a youngster growing up in Papua New Guinea.

Today he doesn't require the alarm though. He has a busy morning ahead of him, aside from delivering the papers.

He wakes up. It's getting on for 5 a.m. Pitch black. Very cold in the old ramshackle house. No heating. No insulation. Weatherboards rotten and missing. Spouting rusty, ungracefully degenerated.

He goes to the wardrobe in his bedroom. Some of his dad's clothes are in there, along with his own. At the back is his .22 rifle, which he bought about a year ago to shoot rabbits and possums. Dad had long been into shooting and had shown David how to use the rifle and set the sights. It is fitted with a silencer so the neighbours won't be disturbed when he shoots possums on the overgrown section around the house.

There's a whole pile of ammo in the wardrobe, which Mum had given to David for a Christmas present. The trigger lock is fitted, as usual. David wears the key, along with other bits and pieces, on a string around his neck. But it isn't there – not just the key, the whole necklace. Not to worry, though. The spare key is in a jar on the dressing table.

The old house creaks and groans as David moves around in the early morning silence. It's very dark, and he can't afford any lights on with what he is about to do. He mustn't disturb anyone. He has work to do.

Unlock the trigger guard and leave it on the floor with the key in it. Load the magazine; ten .22 soft-nosed bullets. Click, and the magazine is in place. No trouble to David; Dad has taught him well. A couple of other details, for his work is well planned. He goes to his clothes drawer and gets out the white gloves he purchased a few weeks ago to attend a ball at Larnach Castle. He silently slips them on.

But what about glasses? David is short sighted. His own glasses are away being repaired; he had broken them a week or so ago. He hasn't worn any glasses for the past few days, but decides he must wear them for what he is about to do, despite the dark. He takes a pair of his mother's old glasses and puts them on. One lens is no use, but the other is similar to his own.

He is now ready to execute the plan. Gloves on, rifle loaded and cocked, he stealthily creeps into Laniet's room. The floorboards creak of course, but she doesn't stir. He puts the rifle to her head, pulls the trigger. With the silencer on the gun there's just a *phut* noise like a slug gun. *Give her another one, just above the ear, that should do the job.* Blood spurts out; her hand shoots to her cheek in a reflex action and gets blood all over it. One down.

Into Margaret's room; the mum he loves. She too must die. Poke the rifle right up to her forehead. One tiny pull of the trigger. *Phut* again. Two down.

Stephen is just through the doorway behind him. He's sound asleep. *This killing is easy!* There are still seven rounds in the magazine. Put the rifle to Stephen's head; squeeze the trigger. But Stephen wakes, grabs the silencer with his left hand and pushes upwards. His right hand is in front of his head in a reflex defence action. The bullet goes through his hand and rips along the top of his scalp. Blood is gushing everywhere. Stephen scrambles free from his bedding. In his underpants and a tee-shirt he tries to fight David off, but is gradually overpowered; he is losing strength as the blood pours from his wounds. David pulls the tee-shirt tight around his brother's neck to strangle the remaining life from him.

There is a lot of noise during the struggle. Stephen has kicked, swung and fought desperately for his life, smashing his body and limbs into bedroom furniture. At last he subsides, slumping to the floor. Now to finish him off, before Arawa wakes up downstairs. The rifle jams. *Free the bullet.* The damned gloves get in the way. Rip them off and tear away the offending bullet. Click – in goes another one. Stephen is cowering and gasping his final desperate breaths. David points the gun at the top of his head and *phut* again. Three down.

Now David has blood all over the green jersey he is wearing. The gloves are soaked too, but he has taken them off. He reverses out of the gory scene of Stephen's dying moments. Blood from the jersey wipes onto the door frame.

It's still pitch black, but David realises his glasses have fallen off in the struggle. He turns on the light, manages to find the frame and one lens, and carefully takes them to his bedroom where he puts them on the chair.

Downstairs now. Into the narrow entrance to Arawa's room. The struggle upstairs must have woken her. She's dressed in track pants and top, kneeling on the floor right in front of him. Begging for sanity to prevail. He fires and misses. He is at almost point blank range, but still misses because he can't aim without his glasses. The second shot – *phut* – goes straight through her forehead above the right eye and she slumps dead to the floor, legs folded beneath her like a fallen angel. Blood splashes all over the bed, floor and walls. Amazing how much of it there is from such a small entry hole. Four down.

David returns upstairs. His clothes are covered in blood, as are his hands and head. He has grazed his knee and banged his head. He hears Laniet making gurgling noises. He must finish her off – a third bullet will do the trick. This time in the top of her head. *Phut* again. Still his father sleeps in the caravan.

About 5.15 now, maybe 5.20. David has to do his paper run. It's all part of the master plan. He goes to the washing machine, which is in the bathroom, and strips off his gory attire. He puts the bloodied clothes in the machine. Not being in a hurry, he sorts out the rest of the family's dirty clothes into 'whites' and others. He leaves all the whites in the wash basket and puts the rest in with the murder attire. In with some laundry powder and on with the washing machine.

Back to his own room, and into his running gear. On with a white tee-shirt and a red sweatshirt. Leave on the white socks he's been wearing as he goes about his morning's business, and put on brand new running shoes. Grab the yellow *Otago Daily Times* paper carry bag and sling it over his shoulders. Walkman headphones on and he's ready.

'Come on, Casey. Here, Casey, Casey, we're off now boy, off we go now.' The obedient dog joins as he often does and out to work man and dog go.

They head off up Every Street and along to the corner of Aytoun Street. Mrs Rackley collects her paper at 14 Aytoun Street at 6 a.m. Mr Warrington sees David and Casey about 6.10 a.m. further along on Somerville Street. And so it goes on as it has six days a week for years. He knows the run like the palm of his hand. And Casey, a bit overweight and unfit, trots slowly and a little grudgingly behind him.

The last papers are delivered on his way back up Every Street. He's covered a few miles now and this is a very steep road. Steep, cold and slippery. A bit tired too, are the dog and his owner. They drop the last paper where they always do, each one delivered just as required. Some in the letter box. Some to the door. You know how it is. Corner of Heath Street and Every, about 350 metres from home now, away down the hill. Pause for a rest, and Casey needs the power pole. Look at his watch, about 6.40. No hurry.

Mrs Tania Clarke is on her way to work at the rest home next door up the hill from the Bains' place. She sees David and Casey at Heath Street at 6.40 a.m. Up the hill they go. Another rest home worker, Denise Laney, sees David just entering his front gate. She knows it is about 6.46, as her shift starts at 6.45 and she is slightly late for work this morning. David is in no hurry, and old Casey is finding the last few hundred metres up Every a bit of a struggle. It has taken about five minutes to get from Heath Street to 65 Every Street. Home.

But now he must move quickly. He has unfinished business – Dad. He always gets up at 6.30. Still, he is unlikely to notice that the rest of the family are dead. If he should go into the bathroom, which he will do first, he won't see the bloody mess left there.

David goes into the house through the front door, which is upstairs. Directly on his left is his bedroom, and opposite that is the lounge with a sun room off it facing down to the front gate. The sun room is used as the family computer room.

David rushes directly into the computer room and switches on the old Philips PC, which rumbles into life. 'Boot time' is the jargon. Later, the police would say the computer was turned on at 6.44 a.m. He types in Dad's suicide note: 'Sorry, you are the only one who deserved to stay.'

He runs down to the laundry, puts his red sweatshirt in the washing machine and turns the machine on again. He still has on the white socks that he has worn throughout the whole episode. The red sweater has only been worn during his paper run.

Finally David gets the rifle for the last time, the blood-smeared murder weapon that has proved four times already its effectiveness. He hides behind the curtains in the computer room alcove; he knows his father always comes and kneels directly beside these curtains to pray in the morning. David waits and waits. *Dad must have slept in, or perhaps he has discovered the other bodies and gone for help.* But he can't come out from behind the curtains lest his father sees him and is on guard.

The plan is rid to himself of his whole family but at the same time to set it up so that the cops will think Dad did it and then shot himself. So he waits. Dad finally comes into the lounge and kneels just on the other side of the curtains, only an arm's length from David. Robin Bain doesn't sense anybody there, nor does he hear the whirr of the computer fan.

No mistakes now, David thinks, as he carefully pokes the rifle between the curtains. Just as it touches his father's left forehead, he gently squeezes the trigger. *Phut* for the final time. Five down – they're all dead! Mission accomplished.

Now, just place the rifle carefully beside Dad. Perhaps I should put Dad's fingerprints on the gun? Oh, there's no need. This looks pretty much like suicide to me. Shift his leg a little, leaving a smudge of blood on his tracksuit pants to enhance the appearance of suicide. Where's the ejected shell? Oh, that doesn't matter. The Dunedin cops are pretty dumb; they'll never link me to this. Wipe the rifle for fingerprints? No need – I had gloves on for the first two killings.

Oh – the gloves. I left them in Stephen's room. Does that matter? And the glasses? I've just killed three people, done my paper run and put a message on the computer without any spectacles. One lens must still be in Stephen's room and the frame and other lens are in my room on the chair. Oh to hell with it, they'll never suspect me. All that remains is to ring 111 feigning shock and pretend I came home from my paper run and found them all dead.

At 7.09 a.m. 111 emergency services receive a call.

The police make entry to the house at about 7.33 a.m.

David is on the floor of his bedroom semi-conscious, still talking on the phone to the 111 operator.

The residents of Dunedin were chilled and horrified by these killings, which took place just a couple of years after David Gray's massacre at Aramoana. This is the version of events as told by the prosecution. The chilling rendition of motiveless horror, of cold-blooded intentional slaughter and attempted deception has stood the test of a depositions hearing, a High Court jury trial, High Court appeal and an appeal to the Privy Council.

Since the trials many people have asked the question, 'How can it be?' The case made by the police, as presented to the jury, is so fraught with inconsistencies that, for many people, grave doubt exists that in fact things happened as they say.

The life of a young man, reliant upon a system of justice designed to give the defendant the benefit of the doubt, already ruined by the horrific deaths of his family, has the final screw turned on it by the very people charged with maintaining law and order. The sad fact is that justice is a game, to be won or lost. And for those involved in the case against David, they would stop at nothing to win.

INTRODUCTION

During the Christmas break of 1995-96, I reread two books that have held a prominent place on my bookshelf for many years. They were *Beyond Reasonable Doubt*, David Yallop's account of the facts surrounding the Arthur Allan Thomas case, and *Verdict on Erebus*, Judge Peter Mahon's account of his role as the Commissioner of Inquiry into the Erebus disaster. At the same time, Ian Wishart's *Paradise Conspiracy*, explaining his version of events surrounding the winebox saga, was in the bookshops.

It struck me that the common thread linking all three of these extremely controversial affairs is that each of them involves an attempted cover-up by establishment authorities. In the Thomas case, it was the police and judiciary under the spy glass; in the Erebus case, it was Air New Zealand management along with Civil Aviation authorities; and in the winebox, big business figureheads, the Inland Revenue Department and the Serious Fraud Office. In each instance, a well-established government-operated bureaucracy was alleged to be attempting, by the power and weight of its authority, to railroad the citizens of this country into accepting a proposition which defied common sense and logic, aided by propaganda, political manoeuvring, benign press and collusionary tactics. But, as I said on the 'Holmes' show, July 1996, in my first public statement on the Bain case, 'The truth has a strange way of revealing itself.'

Fortunately, in the first two of the cases above, despite the combined efforts of the perpetrators to mislead and cover up the facts, truth did eventually prevail, and in the third case Justice Sir Ronald Davison has yet to bring down his verdict.

A few weeks after that Christmas, about mid-January 1996, I was reading the *New Zealand Herald* early one Monday morning as I often do, and casually read an article headed up 'Bain supporters seek funds'. It was a small report stating that following the failure of David Bain's High Court appeal the previous month, his girl friend, former music teacher and a couple of other friends were considering launching a plea for help to raise funds to have his case taken to the Privy Council in London. What struck me most was that the people involved could have no possible motive except for their belief in David's innocence. I had not fol-lowed the case any more than is normal; in fact, apart from remembering the obvious details like the house being burnt down, and the hazy image portrayed of a strange, rather nerdy sort of a paper boy being convicted, the only significant matter I recalled was Cate Brett's assertion in *North and South* that no satisfactory motive or reason had ever been advanced for this brutal slaying.

For some reason, possibly stimulated by the recent reading of the books I mentioned earlier, something kept nagging away in my mind. About lunchtime that day, I decided to put a call through to Dunedin to see what was going on. I didn't know who David's lawyer was, but thought that he would be a good place to start, so I rang my local lawyers, and found out that it was Michael Guest, Dunedin barrister.

I phoned him, and he gave me quite a long run-down on the case, and then faxed up about a 20-page resumé from his perspective. He was extremely keen and enthusiastic in providing me with information about the case and helping me to understand what had happened. Over the next few days there was quite a raft of phone calls and faxes between us.

I had imagined that an appeal to the Privy Council would be extremely costly, in the hundreds of thousands of dollars, and had thought that if the cause turned out to be a deserving one that I might have been able to assist David's selfless friends in fund-raising, and make a donation myself. As Michael Guest explained to me though, the first step when going to the Privy Council is actually to seek 'leave to appeal'. This means that the appellant is granted a very brief (usually about one hour) hearing before the Lords, with the opportunity of making a case to convince them that his or her situation warrants the Privy Council granting a full appeal hearing. Hence the term 'seeking leave to appeal'.

Guest explained to me that the odds of a successful appeal were not good – only a small percentage of attempts from New Zealand in respect to criminal cases this century have been successful. He, however, felt extremely strongly that evidence that was suppressed should not have been, and that it would have made the difference in David's trial. He was prepared to do all legal work for the leave to appeal at no cost, and believed that, should he be successful, legal aid funds would be available for the full appeal. Thus the costs for the leave to appeal were reduced to his airfares, accommodation and expenses, along with fees for the London legal agents required to process the appeal. This amounted to just $12,500, a far smaller sum than I had been imagining.

Guest then invited me to meet with David Bain at Paparua Prison in Christchurch, where he is imprisoned. On 25 January 1996, at about 6 p.m., Michael Guest and I went to meet with David. It was an enthralling and engaging meeting. All three of us chatted for a while and then I had about an hour alone with David, during which we discussed

David's life and plight.

Later that evening Michael and I had dinner and talked about nothing except the case. Guest is very much a sales-person type of guy — witty, demonstrative and garrulous — and I had no trouble in eliciting information from him. What struck me was that, if what he told me was true, it seemed incredible that David could have been found guilty. But then, I reminded myself, two juries had found the inno-cent Arthur Allan Thomas guilty.

The following morning, I agreed to foot the bill of $12,500 for the appeal; my only requests in so doing were that I could have the file documents to study and read, and that I was to remain anonymous until I agreed otherwise. Guest, in response to this altruistic gesture (motivated only by com-passion for David's plight and a natural intrigue to study this mysterious case), said that I should at least have a chance of recouping the money at some later date. This was entirely his suggestion and finished up in a short agreement between Michael, myself and David. Guest wanted to offer me on David's behalf all rights to any books, magazine articles and the like. The final agreement, at my insistence, was that if I should have these rights then David and I should share equally in any proceeds that might arise. The agreement, including a clause that from then on I was to be a part of David's defence team (included to allow me full access to David and the file documents), was duly signed that morn-ing. I had another much longer visit that day with David and posted the cheque off to Guest upon my arrival back in Auckland.

And so my involvement began. What caused me to do it? Above all else, it was sitting face to face with David himself. Through my involvement in team sports as a player and coach, and through having directly employed and trained people for many years, I have developed a confidence in my intuitive judgement of a person. If there is one word I would use to summarise my assessment of David Bain, it would be 'guileless'. And yet, from the facts I had by then discovered from Guest, the case against David was that he meticulously planned the murders, in an attempt to escape detection. He is an intelligent guy, with a natural youthful sense of humour. He has an innate sense of responsibility and, borne out by his behaviour since being in prison, clearly is a caring, selfless bloke. I could not under any circumstances reconcile the case against him with the person I had met. My overriding motivation then, was that he had been served an enormous injustice. He had to deal with not only the loss of his entire family but also the burden of being the finder of them in such gruesome circumstances, the injustice of being convicted of their murders, and coming to terms with the knowledge that his own father was the likely perpetrator.

As for Guest, I believe he was compelled by three things. Firstly, that he too believed David had suffered miserably at the hands of the justice system. Secondly, that he was sufficiently touched by David's plight that he could not rest until he had pursued every legal avenue open to him, and the Privy Council was the last. And finally, his sense of the epic dramatic opportunity that the whole case had been and the Privy Council would be.

I realised at the time that I really had no idea of what I was getting into, but little could I have known the course that events would take over the following year or so.

I have been afforded the opportunity as a reasonably literate, well-read layperson of discovering from the inside, without any prejudiced viewpoint, how the wheels of justice really turn. I have become very close to, very friendly with, and developed a wonderful regard for the young man convicted of New Zealand's most serious ever defended criminal case. I have read and reread many thousands of pages of police and court documents, until I nearly know them off by heart. I have burdened my closest family and friends with little else except 'The Bain case' for over a year, and have met face to face with some of the key people who built the case against David. In David's interest, I have had to replace Michael Guest with legal counsel of my own to fight David's battle. I've invested thousands of dollars and hundreds of hours of my own time to seek and establish the truth. I've had to face the cameras and the press in the face of enormous doubt and speculation as to my motives. I've become friendly with many of David's supporters. In short, I have devoted nearly every waking moment since I met David to seeking the truth about what happened at 65 Every Street, Dunedin in the early hours of 20 June 1994.

For a long period in 1996 I spent more time in the South Island on the case than I did at home. I went to London to hear the Queen's Lords pass their judgement. I have visited David probably twenty-odd times and felt the weight of being the only person standing between him and his misery.

On many occasions I have woken in the depths of the night in a cold sweat over his possible deceit, over a piece of evidence that doesn't seem to fit, over a casual statement made, thinking, *What the hell have I got myself into here?*

From the very start I have endeavoured to do nothing more nor less than seek the truth. The jury did not hear the truth – certainly not 'the whole truth and nothing but the truth' – of the facts of this case. Even after I funded David's appeal, I was intent on remaining objective in an attempt to unravel the mess of contradictions which the police case seemed to be, and I told David so. I told him that if it became apparent to me that he was lying or guilty, I would say so. He has never wavered. His conviction and integrity as much as anything else have sustained me through the past year.

At the end of the day, I have been confronted with two questions to resolve.

Firstly, does all of the evidence (note I say all of the evidence) lead to the conclusion that David Cullen Bain is *guilty beyond reasonable doubt*, that being the standard of proof required under New Zealand law?

And secondly; do I think David 'did it', or 'didn't do it'?

The judge's summing up in this case started with the following words. 'Madam Foreman, ladies and gentlemen: who did it? David Bain? Robin Bain? The real issue in this trial is whether you are satisfied beyond reasonable doubt that David Bain killed his mother, sisters, brother and father. On the one hand the defence has said to you that you cannot be so satisfied . . .' and later '. . . on the other hand the prosecution says that the case against David Bain is overwhelming and that his guilt is the only reasonable conclusion *on all of the evidence*'. (My emphasis.)

Two significant events led to the writing of this book. In the later months of 1996 I was also troubled by some of the evidence put forward in the case against David. Two matters in particular stood out: the time at which the computer was switched on; and photographic evidence in relation to a lens from a pair of spectacles.

Colin Withnall QC, now barrister on the case, applied to the police for access to the computer. This became quite an exercise, as it had been disposed of to one of David's uncles after the trial. For my part, I thought that perhaps our concerns could be resolved by 'going straight to the top', so to speak. To this end I arranged a meeting with Peter Doone, the Commissioner of Police, and Assistant Commissioner Ian Holyoake in late October 1996. After this meeting, Colin and I concluded that any methods to resolve our concerns which the police might find agreeable were unlikely to assist David.

As a result of the failure of the meeting to establish common ground, Colin and I, after consulting with David, decided that this book should be written, and I wrote to the commissioner advising him of our decision.

This book then is my account of my search for the truth in this most bizarre of nightmares. It is a sincere attempt to put the facts as they are, as I have found them.

It answers those two questions that have haunted me since my involvement began. I trust too that it will assist in seeing a dreadful wrong righted, and that it will answer the prayers and hopes of those many thousands of people who have expressed their support for David and for my efforts.

I make no apologies to those who may be offended by the book's contents, for I have not found it possible to become so deeply involved in such a controversial conflict as this without taking a stand for what I believe to be true. Ultimately, my satisfaction will be gained by seeing the courage and faith of David Cullen Bain rewarded.

AND SO IT BEGAN

INVESTIGATION AND ARRESTS

Day 1. 20 June 1994: 7.09 a.m.

Fran Edwards and Sandra Bampton, 111 emergency operators working at Telecom in Christchurch.

Detective Chief Inspector Peter Robinson and Senior Sergeant Jim Doyle, Dunedin CIB.

Police Pathologist Alec Dempster.

ESR scientists, Cropp and Hentschell.

Senior Detective Milton Weir, Dunedin CIB.

Kim Jones, police finger print expert.

Peter and Jan Clarke, David's uncle and aunt.

Michael Guest, Dunedin barrister, and ex-Family Court judge

Bill Wright, Crown prosecutor.

Families and friends of the Bain family.

None of these people had any idea of the impact on their lives that the 111 phone call 22-year-old David Cullen Bain was about to make would have.

More than anything else, the actions taken or not taken, as the case may be, over the next few hours and days by some of the central figures listed above would set the scene for the mystery and intrigue that this whole bizarre affair has become.

For as horrific as the scene was it was also a relatively simple situation to investigate. In contrast, consider these facts from that other controversial and notorious New Zealand murder enquiry, the Arthur Allan Thomas case of 24 years earlier.

In the Thomas case, the bodies of Janette and Harvey Crewe were not found for months after the deaths. When they were located, they were badly decomposed having been submerged in the Waikato River, and therefore were of little evidential value. There was no murder weapon to be found. The time of death could not be established accurately. The scene of the murder was not discovered until five days after the deaths occurred.

Notwithstanding some of the incredible similarities in these two cases which I shall refer to throughout future pages, one of them being the inexplicable deficiencies in some aspects of the police enquiry, the one outstanding difference is that in the Bain murders, the case to be solved was in itself not complicated.

Accepting that the scene was like something from a horror movie, which even the most hardy and experienced of police officers would seldom if ever encounter, nevertheless everything was there.

Each dead person was in exactly the position in which they had died. The bodies were still warm to touch when the first officers arrived. The murder weapon was lying beside one of the bodies. The one live member of the family, David, had called the police, and was still talking to the 111 operator when the police arrived. He was fully co-operative and so there was no further danger to anybody. Therefore unlike most crimes, we have the body (bodies in this case), we have the murder weapon, we have a co-operative scene witness, and we have a fresh crime scene less than an hour old.

The task confronting the Dunedin CIB, therefore, was merely a matter of systematically and professionally going about their job. Or at least, one would think so.

Let's look first at what actually happened. At 7.09 a.m., the emergency call centre at Christchurch took a 111 call from David Bain. The operator was nonplussed, as David was so agitated and incoherent. She said, 'I thought I had a right one here – drugs or booze or something.' She called her supervisor to assist with the call. David could not tell her what he wanted, so she put the call through to the St Johns Ambulance in Dunedin. The first twenty seconds or so of David's conversation with the ambulance personnel are recorded, presenting an extremely distressed David saying, 'They're all dead.' An ambulance was dispatched to the scene, and the police were notified. The first ambulance arrived about ten minutes later, followed over the next ten minutes by more ambulances and police cars. It was still dark at this stage. The first four policemen to the house were officers Stapp, Stephenson, Wylie and Andrews. They were able to see both the father's dead body through the window of the computer alcove and David sitting on the floor in his room beside the window still talking on the phone. When they asked David to open the door, he refused saying that he couldn't because his father was 'dead in there'. Although the door was unlocked, the police could not work the latch, so they broke a glass pane beside the door and unlatched it from the inside. Once inside, Andrews maintained watch over David while the other three, guns in hand in classic 'Miami Vice' style, went through the house to see what they could find.

They made entry to the house at around 7.30 a.m., approximately 25 minutes from the time David made the call.

Within minutes they determined that there were five dead bodies, along with David Bain, in the house. Sergeant Stapp, who was the senior officer at this stage, and was conducting proceedings, had notified police headquarters of his findings by 7.45. Detectives Robinson and Doyle of the CIB were appointed to head the investigation, Robinson being in charge and Doyle his deputy. They called a meeting at CIB headquarters for 8.15, by which time they were fully aware not only of the scene situation, but also of the names of the six family members. At this meeting were Robinson and Doyle, along with the police pathologist, Alec Dempster, and Detective Milton Weir, who was appointed officer in charge of the scene (O/C Scene). There may have been others, but these four were to be the central figures.

Throughout this first day of the enquiry, every police job sheet was headed up 'Operation Every – Murder/Suicide'. If David had set it up to appear this way, then it seems he had done a convincing job!

By this time police cars and officers were swarming all over Every Street, and the street had been cordoned off. At 8.11 a.m. Sergeant Kevin Anderson was the first CIB detective to arrive at number 65. It would be over half an hour before he entered the house, having first had a discussion with Stapp and taken over for the meantime as officer in charge of the scene. Constable Van Turnhout had arrived at Every Street at 8.03 and had been directed by Detective Sergeant Roberts from CIB headquarters to go inside and 'stay with David Bain'. He took up his post in David's room a few minutes later and stayed with David until he was eventually taken off to the CIB by ambulance at about 10.19 a.m. During the intervening period, four ambulance officers in attendance had been admitted to the house. Two of them stayed with David and Ambulance Officer Wombwell, the most senior, had been taken around each of the dead bodies to test them for signs of life, of which there were none. At about 8.50

a.m., Anderson entered the house through the front door upstairs, along with Detective Sergeant Robertson, Detective Chief Inspector Robinson and Sergeant Jim Doyle. A few minutes later senior police staff Hill and Soper again made a tour of the house. At 9.00 a.m., as Peter Robinson, officer in charge of the enquiry, was about to leave the premises, he went into David's room where Van Turnhout was stationed and an interesting exchange took place, augmenting an inauspicious start to the case for Robinson. In the first instance, Robinson asked Van Turnhout how he knew David's name; in reply Van Turnhout pointed out to the Chief Inspector that his name was pinned on the bedroom door. Of far greater consequence was the following discussion, recorded in Van Turnhout's notebook.

'They [Det. Chief Inspector Robinson, Dist. Commander Hill and Jim Doyle] left the room shortly after 8.50 a.m. and at 9.00 a.m. I recorded in my notebook that they had left the house. I went to the front door as they were leaving, and asked if a firearms residue kit was being obtained. I had been asked to go to the front door. At this stage I was advised to stay with Bain, observe him, note and record anything he said.'

The issue of a gunpowder residue test is of vital consequence and, I believe, is one of the prime failures in this investigation, which will be covered in depth. Suffice it to say that at 9.00 a.m., less than two hours after David had made his panic-stricken call, the officer in charge of the case was made aware by a junior constable that this seemed to him to be a matter of some importance. My reading of Van Turnhout's notes and trial evidence suggests that he handled his assignment with true professionalism and integrity. There is no recorded reaction to his query about gunpowder residue tests.

But back to the 8.15 meeting at CIB headquarters. We now know that top brass left that meeting to go to have a look over the scene. We know for sure that by 9.45 a.m. at least eleven police staff and four ambulance officers had to varying degrees walked, poked and prodded their way around the house. We also know that apart from the very first officers to arrive, who clearly needed to secure the scene, and an ambulance officer who needed to attend to David, none of the rest of these people should have been allowed access to the house. It seems to me that, in contrast to specific experts who were available then, none of these people had any contribution to make that would be enhanced in any way by their having a 'Cook's tour' through the house at that time.

What makes this all the more remarkable is what happened to the two other participants at the 8.15 a.m. briefing. Remember, Robinson and his second-in-command Doyle along with other top brass went straight from that meeting to the house. But it was Detective Sergeant Weir and Alec Dempster who were the two people who were most needed at the scene as early as possible. Weir, because as officer in charge of the scene it was his responsibility to preserve the evidence in its original form from any possible contamination and then to direct the course of the scene investigation. Dempster, because a pathologist is the expert designated to establish likely cause, time and means of death. Astonishing as it may seem, Weir did not arrive at the scene until 9.45 a.m., after the various top brass and others had made their tour of inspection. Where Weir was or what he did during the intervening period is unknown. Alec Dempster also did not arrive until about 10 a.m., and there is no record of what he did from 8.15 to 10 a.m. Yet another person whose early attendance at the scene should have been vital was police photographer Trevor Gardiner; he was also at the scene by 10 a.m.

What took place over the next two hours is even more astonishing. Weir had a meeting with Anderson, who had been acting scene controller when he arrived, and then assumed command. Having assumed control, Weir went into the house through the front door, as everyone else had done, and looked into David's room where, he notes in his evidence, were David, ambulance officer Wombwell and Van Turnhout. He then inspected all of the other dead bodies. On his way out Weir spoke to Wombwell and Van Turnhout about having David taken from the house. He then carried out an inspection of the outside of the house and looked into the caravan where Robin Bain slept while he was at home, before arranging for David to be taken by the ambulance staff and Van Turnhout to the CIB headquarters. David was carried out on a sort of stretcher-type chair at 10.19 a.m., after he had been left lying on the floor of his bedroom under observation for nearly three hours.

Weir then re-entered the house with police doctor Pryde at 10.35 a.m. Weir stated in evidence that 'the purpose of this visit was for Dr Pryde to confirm life extinct'. These five bodies had already been visited over the previous three hours by ambulance officers and whole array of policemen including the District Commander and Detective Chief Inspector Robinson – and of course none of them had moved a muscle for the whole time. Well, you don't with a bullet or two or three in your head.

Bear in mind that at this stage we know for sure that the following people had been through the house, totally without supervision, control or protective wear: police officers Stapp, Stevenson, Andrews and Wylie; ambulance officers Wombwell, Scott, Anderson and Dick; Detective Kevin Anderson; senior police staff Soper, Hill and Robertson; Detective Inspector in charge of the enquiry Peter Robinson and his assistant Jim Doyle; Constable Van Turnhout; Weir himself; and now Dr Pryde. A total of seventeen people! In the meantime, the two people who really could make a difference to the enquiry, Alec Dempster and Trevor Gardiner, were twiddling their thumbs out on the street.

I now quote from Weir's evidence given to the court. This part of his evidence immediately follows the previous statement regarding life extinct, and must rate as one of the most astounding statements of the whole trial.

'He [Pryde] didn't go right into the scene referred to in the plan as scene F. Dr Pryde was happy to stand at the doorway of that scene. I didn't want him to go into the room; he went into all of the rooms where there was a deceased body. As officer in charge of the scene *I wasn't happy with people walking in and out. At that stage it was important that the scene was not contaminated and disturbed as little as possible.*' (My emphasis). He continued: 'I asked for a roll of plastic which I wanted to put on the floor and items in the house so they could be protected once scene examination staff moved into the address. People then walk on plastic and don't disturb what's underneath, as best as possible.' How can this statement justify leaving Dempster and the photographer on the street when seventeen other people had been in the house in the intervening four hours?

Meanwhile, it had reached 11.00 a.m., and Dempster (the pathologist) and Gardiner (police photographer) were still waiting outside; apparently Weir was holding up proceedings waiting for the plastic sheeting to arrive. Interestingly, he was the only person in the house for the intervening hour from the time Dr Pryde finished his inspection until the plastic did arrive at 11.40 a.m., when Detective Kevin Anderson joined Weir in laying out the plastic.

This is the investigation, remember, that the two officers in charge, Robinson and Doyle, have since referred to repeatedly as a copybook enquiry.

Late morning/early afternoon

At 11.40 a.m. literally dozens of officers were out on the road, including the photographer and the pathologist.

Anderson was on the verandah of the house waiting for the plastic to arrive, and Weir was inside. We have no record of what he was doing. Three and a half hours after David had phoned the emergency 111 and the police were notified, at an address only minutes from the CIB office, not one useful thing had been done in an attempt to preserve evidence or investigate the scene confronting the police enquiry team, despite the presence of the necessary expert personnel.

In addition to the human foot traffic throughout the house, the Bain family dog and cat were present. The dog was caught and tied up on the verandah fairly early on – Stapp called in Newbury, another officer, from the street, found a leash, called the dog, which had been in Margaret's bedroom, and tied it up. This was at about 7.45 or 7.50. The cat features in the police video of the scene sitting on David's bed; according to the police this video was not started until some time in the afternoon. So now we have seventeen people, a cat and a dog parading uncontrolled throughout the house during the morning.

The significance of this will become apparent as the tale unfolds. Suffice it to say at this stage that the house was splattered with blood on bedding, floors, walls and clothes. Also, the shell cases from the bullets were all over the house as they ejected when each shot was fired. The location of some shell cases and the analysis of blood samples were to be two of the primary cannons in the police assault on David. Add to that the mayhem that the house was in and the total darkness when the first officers went through, along with the state of shock they were in (evidenced by the fact that they required trauma counselling in the following days) and we have a picture not of a copybook investigation at all. Rather, I would suggest the investigation was seriously deficient for the reasons I have already mentioned, which will be analysed in greater detail in later chapters. If this sounds too strong, then put it in perspective with the fact that neither the dog nor the cat nor any of the foot traffic's footwear, bodies or clothing were checked in any way whatsoever for blood stains! The dog had been in David's lap, and a minute smudge of blood on his black shorts, alleged to be Stephen's blood, was asserted as being proof of David's involvement in the struggle with his brother. Who is to say that the dog did not transfer the blood from Stephen's room onto his shorts while sitting with David waiting for the police to arrive? Similarly, a speck of blood was found on David's duvet cover, and put forward as prosecution evidence in the trial. It was the same duvet that the cat, which had ranged freely about the house all morning, was sitting on at about lunch time. (Van Turnhout says 'the dog did not come into the house while I was there. The cat was moving around the house.') Some footprints in blood undetectable to the naked eye were alleged by the police to form a further part of their case. They were never proven to be David's, but the Crown case made it clear that as far as they were concerned, they could be no-one else's. Those matters and more will be dealt with in more depth at the appropriate time.

At 11.40 a.m., as the evidence that might have been gained by an early examination of the bodies was becoming less useful, with Dempster and Gardiner still waiting at the roadside, things were happening. Weir and Anderson were rolling out their protective plastic floor covering. David was at the CIB, having arrived about 10.30. Van Turnhout and David had been met there by Detective Sergeant Dunne, who had been assigned as officer in charge of suspect/witness. David was offered a warm drink by Dunne and accepted a glass of warm water. He was wheeled into the office in the ambulance chair. According to Van Turnhout he was showing little emotion and appeared tired and withdrawn. Dunne interviewed David from 10.30 till 11 o'clock. Then Dr Pryde arrived and David agreed to a full medical although he was advised that he did not have to. Pryde noted in his evidence that David was quiet and subdued, that he didn't talk spontaneously but answered his questions and was fully co-operative in every way. Pryde's examination of David was completed at 11.40, the same time as Weir and Anderson were rolling out their plastic mats. Van Turnhout notes that he left David at 11.55 and was replaced by Detective Lowden. That was the last David was to see of Van Turnhout until the trial.

At almost exactly the same time as Van Turnhout was leaving David, another detective at the scene (it is unclear from the job sheet who it was) rang Environmental Science and Research Ltd (ESR) to speak to forensic scientist Peter Hentschell. The job sheet records the following:

20.06.94.

1145 hours	Directed to telephone ESR and ascertain procedure for obtaining 'gunpowder' residue from possible offender's hands or body.
1146 hours	Telephone ESR and speak with Peter Hentschell. A maximum period for recovering gunpowder residue is 3 hours. Anything after 3 hours forget it.
1147 hours	Advise Det Sgt McGregor.

This conversation took place 2 hours and 46 minutes after Detective Inspector Robinson, officer in charge of the case, was asked for a gunpowder residue kit by Van Turnhout, and nearly five hours after the police had arrived. It was fairly obvious to even the most untrained person that the five dead bodies had been executed with a rifle. Almost certainly the rifle would be the one next to Robin's body, and whoever fired that rifle was the killer. Swabs could certainly have been taken from the hands and clothes of Robin and David Bain by 9 a.m. and if any sort of urgency had applied, maybe even 8 a.m. This is not the end of the gunpowder residue test issue, but at this point I shall say again that a serious and significant failure by the police team occurred in not addressing this matter.

It was now lunch time on day one. David was in the CIB offices, about to be questioned very intensively for the rest of the afternoon. He had already made a brief statement but the afternoon would be long and trying for him; good practice for the hours and months to follow, one might say.

At the scene, Weir had finally installed his belated plastic covers, and at 12.05 p.m. Alec Dempster and his assistant were granted access, 3 hours and 50 minutes after attending the police briefing at 8.15 that morning, and having been on the roadside at the scene since about 10 a.m.

I interviewed Mr Dempster in July of 1996. I should point out that Dempster was the linchpin, along with Weir, of the Crown case. He was their key witness, as we shall see. For now I will quote a piece from his evidence-in-chief during the trial, which in all takes up 24 pages of the trial transcript document. His concluding words were: 'From my examination of the bodies the time of death I was not able to provide precisely. The bodies generally had rigor mortis well developed (when I was able to see them) although not completely. I arrived prepared to do core body temperatures but the *delay in being admitted to the scene* was such that I felt there was *no useful advantage* in doing so.' (My emphasis.)

On a '20/20' programme produced in March 1996 Jim Doyle, commenting on behalf of the police, said, 'The advantages of keeping him [Dempster] waiting far outweighed the benefits of allowing him in earlier.' I would love to debate that statement with anyone from the police.

It was about this time, in the early afternoon, that the now famous computer was apparently noticed for the first time. Although the evidence is slightly vague, it seems most likely that Milton Weir came across the computer. The screen was lit up, and on the screen was the following message:

'Sorry, you are the only one who deserved to stay.'

Referring to the house plan (see picture 2), the computer was set up in an alcove off the room marked A, to the right of the front door. The window of this room looks directly towards the front gate. This message and the time that the computer was turned on were to become crucial matters in the police case against David. This evidence holds the key, ultimately, to assessing David's innocence or possible guilt, and is one of the pieces of evidence where the Crown misled the court to sustain their case. More on that later.

Close on the heels of Alec Dempster, the police photographer Trevor Gardiner was also admitted to the house. Photographic evidence is absolutely critical in a case where there are no eye witnesses. To quote Gardiner himself; 'I was and remain extremely bewildered at the delay in Alec Dempster and myself being admitted to the scene.'

It is fair to say, I believe, that at this time the police enquiry had finally commenced, five hours after David's phone call.

In recapitulation then, the sequence of events on the first morning goes like this:

7.09 a.m. 111 call.   David reports the scene.

Approximately 7.33 a.m.   Police make entry.

Approximately 8.15 a.m.   Top level briefing at CIB
                          attended among others by
                          Detective Chief Inspector Peter
                          Robinson, officer in charge of
                          the enquiry; his assistant Jim
                          Doyle; Milton Weir, appointed
                          officer in charge of the scene;
                          and Alec Dempster, police
                          pathologist.

8.30–9.30	Various 'top brass' make cursory tour of the house.
9.45	Milton Weir arrives and takes command at the scene.
10.00	Alec Dempster arrives.
10.19	David is removed by ambulance from the house to the CIB.
10.19–11.40	Weir alone has access to the house.
11.40	Weir and Anderson put down plastic sheeting.
12.05	Dempster followed by photographer admitted to the house to commence examination of the bodies.

I have graphically set this out, as I believe that what took place that morning set the scene for the tragedy of justice that was to occur a year later when David was convicted of murdering the other five members of his family.

Later afternoon and evening

The rest of Monday was spent photographing and examining the bodies in situ, and having them removed to the mortuary for post mortem examinations. Milton Weir correctly appointed an officer to be responsible for each of the deceased, and between approximately 3 p.m. and 7 p.m. that

Monday the five bodies were duly uplifted. Dempster was able to complete four of the post mortems on the Monday night, only Arawa remaining to be done on Tuesday morning.

By now the enquiry was in full swing. Officers were variously appointed to separate tasks: Weir was officer in charge of scene; Dunne, the officer in charge of suspect and area canvas. There was an exhibits officer and photographers. Police armourer Ngamoki from Trentham and finger print expert Jones were brought in. Hentschell and Cropp, scientists from the ESR, were brought in to help with crime scene evidence analysis of blood, clothing and the like.

Milton Weir, as officer in charge of scene, had the biggest task of all. Because the entire house and the caravan were effectively scenes within a scene, he detailed staff to each of the rooms to sift through and gather evidence. He had a draughtsman in to draw a plan of the house and labelled each room by a letter. David's room became known as Scene B, Margaret's room Scene E, Stephen's Scene F and so on. (See diagram in the first picture section.)

A container was parked on the road for the storage of exhibits as they were discovered, and also for the removal of personal effects from the house.

While the massive force of 40 to 50 policemen and experts worked on the case, the residents of Dunedin were in a stunned state of shock. Despite the public image since the murders of the Bain family being a weird bunch of dysfunctional, religiously deviate odd characters, in the five years that they had been living in Dunedin they had become very involved in many facets of life, and the tragedy touched many people in a very personal way. This, along with the atrocity coming so soon upon the heels of the David Gray massacre at Aramoana, was almost more than the residents of conservative Dunedin could handle. Chief Inspector Robinson's demeanour during his daily press conferences took on that of concerned city father reassuring locals that the police had things under control and there really was nothing to worry about. On the one hand his countenance was as though this was just all in a day's work for a cop – 'we have the situation well in control' – but on the other there was the unspoken yet ever-present eerie sense of shock and bewilderment that a community inevitably feels in the aftermath of such an event.

As that first Monday afternoon progressed, the scene investigation got into full swing, and it was at the scene that the police concentrated their efforts. They did make some enquiries in the general neighbourhood but it is evident from the file that their primary concern was the systematic examination of the house itself.

Contrary to normal procedure, Milton Weir took it upon himself to take the dominant role in the examination of Stephen's bedroom. Advice I have received from experienced senior police is to the effect that, as the officer in charge of the scene, he should have concentrated on directing and managing the scene investigation and not been involved at all personally in the search. His own notes, however, and his testimony in the trial refer to him on each of the ensuing days conducting detailed searches of Stephen's room, this despite the fact that he had already appointed detectives to do the same job; he had relinquished his supervisory role to redo what he had already assigned other officers to do.

The following days

As the week unfolded the police began to assemble forensic evidence. It seems that they did little to extend their enquiry beyond the fated house at 65 Every Street. For example, Laniet Bain, one of the victims, had lived in a flat in Dunedin for the past year or so. The police never paid a visit to that flat, nor did they attempt to interview her flatmates or neighbours. The dairy owners directly across the road from the flat have told me that they were amazed not to have seen police personnel making enquiries of them and others in the neighbourhood.

However, forensic evidence was starting to give the police a picture of what they believed happened. David was interviewed throughout the week in a concerned and friendly manner. He went out of his way to assist the police in providing background and any other information they required but, unbeknown to him, the screws were being tightened.

On Tuesday 21 June, the police had established that David's fingerprints, in blood, were on the rifle. In his statements he had denied touching the rifle at all that day, in fact saying that he had not used it since the previous February. By testing the carpet the police found bloody footprints which appeared to have been made by a sock-clad foot going into and out of Laniet's bedroom. These footprints were not visible to the naked eye, but showed up with the use of luminol testing. David denied having been in Laniet's room, and yet he had been wearing white socks with faint traces of blood on the soles when the police arrived. A partial palm print of David's was found on the washing machine. The police told David that this too was a bloody print. He could not explain how it got there. On David's right forehead there was a small bruise which he was unable to explain, and there was a graze to his knee which he could not explain either. When he made the 111 call, he told the operator 'They're all dead.' In his subsequent statement to the police he said he had only seen his mother and father. Another lie, noted down and used in evidence.

On Wednesday, the night before the lens was discovered, Weir had found a pair of white ball gloves covered in blood under the bed in Stephen's room. David confirmed that they were his gloves, but could offer no explanation as to how they got there.

Finally, on the Thursday night, the police, in the person of

Milton Weir, discovered their *coup de grâce*. Despite having searched Stephen's room thoroughly for the past four days, Weir went back on the Thursday evening to continue his search, in the presence of his assistant Jacques Legros. At 8.46 p.m., according to his evidence, Weir located the lens from a pair of spectacles under the toe of an ice skate, about 45 centimetres from where Stephen's body was found. The spectacle frame, slightly damaged, the other lens (separate from the frame) and a spectacle case had been found on a chair in David's bedroom. At last the police had a concrete piece of evidence putting David in the room where apparently a struggle had taken place between the assailant and Stephen. The police deduced that in the course of the struggle, Stephen had dislodged David's glasses, knocking out both lenses in the process. After finally murdering Stephen, David took the glasses frame and one lens and put them on the chair in his room, the police further deduced.

The circumstantial evidence pointed, according to police, to David Bain being the murderer of each member of his family.

On that same Thursday, however, the police obtained another statement, which potentially threw a completely different perspective on the possible events of that Monday morning.

Dean Cottle had presented himself with his solicitor at the offices of the CIB, and volunteered a statement to the police. The gist of what he said was that he had known Laniet Bain for about a year. She was a practising prostitute, and he had lent her his cell phone to assist her to procure her living. She advertised under the name 'Page' in the *Otago Daily Times* using his cell phone number as the contact. Cottle said he hadn't seen her for some time as she had been spending a lot of time lately down at her father's Taieri Beach school house. He had tried to phone her at her mother's and father's places on Friday 17 June, just three days before her death. He didn't make contact on the phone, but coincidentally, that same afternoon about 3 p.m. he ran into her in the street just outside the Guvnor's cafe in downtown Dunedin and they stopped and talked for about ten minutes. Over the course of the previous year, Cottle told the police, Laniet had told him that she had been having sex, incest, with her father and that this had been going on for years. She further told him that she had decided to change her life, to sort out the business with her father, give up prostitution and sort her life out. To that end, Cottle said, she was going home this weekend to tell her family everything and start with a clean slate.

The police, who at this stage had concluded from the forensic evidence they had gathered at the scene that David was the murderer, did not seem interested in making any deductions from Cottle's statement. At the beginning of their enquiry, they had thought that they were investigating a murder/suicide, i.e. that Robin Bain had killed his wife, two daughters and Stephen, and then shot himself. They then, it would seem, decided David was the culprit, but by Thursday afternoon, four days into the enquiry, had not the slightest hint of a motive or reason for the bizarre slayings.

All of a sudden, in came Cottle. It would seem to me that the obvious inference to be drawn from Cottle's statement is that Laniet was intending to tell her mother and father exactly what she had told him she was going to. The father is therefore being exposed for incestuous behaviour over a long period of time. He panics overnight and kills the rest of the family and himself while David is on his paper run. This fits with the police's initial impression of the situation, and provides an explanation as to how somebody could have become so mentally deranged as to commit such a horror.

But, as it transpired, the police decided not to pursue this avenue of enquiry, and the whole matter of Cottle and the issues his statement raised were to become another piece of the jigsaw in the bizarre mystery of the Bain case.

So by the morning of Friday 24 June, just 96 hours after David reported the deaths of his family, the police had decided that they had their man. The funerals were set down for the Saturday. My information is that the police decided that it would be a gross disrespect to the family to have their killer attend the funeral, and were anxious to wrap up the initial part of the affair (which is to say, the arrest) before the funeral service.

They called David into the police station on the Friday morning. He immediately noticed a totally different attitude to him from any shown over the preceding days. David had been interviewed by Detective Sergeant Greg Dunne throughout the week, but on this Friday morning CIB detectives Neil Lowden and Kallum Croudis met with David for the first time and put to him a series of questions. Croudis had only recently been transferred to Dunedin from Whangarei.

David realised before long that he was seriously being considered as a suspect, and having been read his rights for the first time, advising him amongst other things that he had a right to legal advice, he refused to answer any more questions and asked for a lawyer. The police said, 'Who do you want?' to which David replied, 'I don't know any lawyers.' His uncle, Bob Clarke, was waiting at the station, and after some consultation between Clarke, David and the police, Michael Guest was called. He got in to the police station at about lunch time and advised that David would answer no more questions.

At 1.46 p.m. Croudis formally charged and arrested David for the murders of his mother, father, brother and two sisters. David was asked if he had anything to say to which he replied, 'No, I'm not guilty.'

WHO IS THIS DAVID BAIN,

ARRESTED FOR FIVE MURDERS?

David was born 27th March 1972 (coincidentally the same birth date as my eldest son), to Robin Irving Bain and Margaret Arawa Cullen, who had been married a couple of years earlier.

Robin Bain had been brought up in the small rural town of Otaki just north of Wellington and Margaret came from the rural Central Otago township of Alexandra. Robin was one of four children, having two brothers, Michael and Peter, and a sister, Colleen. Margaret was also one of four, but she had three sisters, Valerie, Jan and Andrea.

During the 1960s, Robin, who had trained as a teacher, worked in Papua New Guinea on missionary work for the Presbyterian church. He returned to Dunedin to complete further studies and whilst there met Margaret who was a lecturer at the kindergarten teachers college in Dunedin. Both were trained and qualified school teachers. It seems that Robin and Margaret had a common interest in music but in nearly all other respects were entirely different people, virtual opposites. Robin is described by people who knew him in those days as a quiet, reserved person, wise and circumspect.

He dressed tidily and took quite some pride in his appearance. Margaret on the other hand, even then, displayed many of the traits that were apparent at the time of her death. Friends at the time recall her as being an extrovert, loud in her speech and behaviour. She seemed to display a penchant for speaking her mind, even to the point of deliberately belittling or embarrassing people in her immediate circle.

All of the accounts I have had from people who knew them even in the early days prior to their marriage portray Margaret as the strong and dominant person in the relationship. Margaret was a poor housekeeper, scruffy dresser and did not, even at this stage of her life, seem to take a great deal of pride in her personal appearance and habits.

After getting married, Robin and Margaret lived in 'the old police station' at Jeffery Street in Dunedin. Robin was a teacher at Andersons Bay Primary School. A pastime of Robin's at this time was rabbit shooting, and he owned a rifle for this purpose.

After David's birth in 1972, Robin still had a desire, as one friend of theirs put it, 'to save the world or something' and managed to persuade Margaret to shift back to Papua New Guinea. During their time in Papua New Guinea, they bought the old house at 65 Every Street, the eventual scene of the family's demise. Originally it was a three-year contract to go to Papua New Guinea, but they finished up being there about fifteen years, not returning to New Zealand until Christmas of 1988.

Clearly, the life of a missionary teacher in PNG in those years was not an easy one. During their fifteen years there it seems that Robin pretty much devoted his life to his work, whereas Margaret very much kept to herself and concentrated on bringing up the children, much of the time in fact providing a home education for them. Housekeeping though, was never her forte, and Robin too, it would appear, showed little interest in the state of their domestic surroundings.

One person who got to know them particularly well during the years they spent in Port Moresby was Ross Stevens, who currently works as a reporter for the '60 Minutes' documentary programme. Ross told me that although their home was always a friendly and welcoming one, he felt going there was taking quite some risk to one's state of health because of the lack of normal hygiene standards. 'You needed to wash your cup before having a cup of tea,' I remember him telling me, when I was talking with him about the Bain family early in 1996. At the same time, this aspect aside, he had a great deal of respect for both Robin and Margaret, indeed, Robin became his best friend during those years in Port Moresby.

During the first stage of their life in Papua New Guinea, the Bains lived in outback areas, but Robin acquired the position of Deputy Principal of the Port Moresby Teachers College, and they spent the last five or six years in Port Moresby itself. It seems they were quite a sociable bunch, who mixed with a large circle of friends and extended liberal hospitality in their home to their friends. They were very involved in music and church-related activities, and outside of their work this seemed to take up most of their time.

A general tone of being slightly off beat or eccentric comes through in most people's description of them. Margaret was developing an ever-increasing devotion to her own personal spirituality, which quite definitely saw her withdrawing from mainstream Christian practice. She was into home health care and naturopathic medicine and seemed to view herself as having special healing powers.

I have listened to a tape recording of a radio interview that Robin and Margaret undertook not long before their return to New Zealand in 1988. She is very effervescent and expresses herself in a very interesting way. Her close relationship to the environment and her surroundings comes through very strongly as does a sense of humour and sensitive nature. Robin on the other hand seems very much the prudent, deliberate and conservative type. His views on almost all subjects discussed on this tape come from an entirely different perspective from Margaret's. His manner of speech is pedantic and uninteresting by comparison with his wife's.

The children were very much closeted at home in 'the early years' in particular. They learnt a pidgin English through mixing with the natives, and did not learn to speak English as we know it until they started school. Margaret did much of their teaching at home, and some of the children also had lessons from the New Zealand Correspondence School.

David recalls most of his life as quite idyllic up there. Not much work to do, lots of field trips, and a close association with nature. His account of his years in Papua New Guinea, from the age of one and a half years through to seventeen, certainly supports the general theme of Margaret being very much the dominant figure in the family and Robin devoting most of his time to work and church activities. And Margaret always seemed to get her way. At one stage in David's schooling, when he was about nine or ten, there was a serious dispute between the school headmaster and Robin as to whether David should attend the school or be home taught. It seems from all accounts that Margaret was having none of this. She told the school exactly what she intended to do and that was that, so to speak. Diplomacy, tact and compromise do not appear to have been her strong points.

As the eighties drew to a close, the marriage was beginning to display quite severe cracks. I believe that Margaret eventually had had enough of Papua New Guinea, and told Robin, 'I'm going back to New Zealand to live, with the children, whether you come or not.' He did not want to leave Papua New Guinea, but perhaps out of a sense of responsibility to his family he did agree, and they returned to Dunedin.

Although the relationship between the parents was deteriorating, the decade and half spent in this remote and primitive land had not been without a great deal of pleasure for the growing Bain children. David reports getting his scuba diving licence, learning to sail and skin dive, a lot of these activities with his father at a favourite family beach called Subba Subba. At another inland camping place where the family would go with their church group, the Quakers, David reports, 'We would spend a couple of weeks there, getting burnt, doing plays for each other, making music, playing games of all sorts and experiencing as many new things about the bush as possible. It was also the place I learned to abseil and rock climb.'

About the age of twelve, he also discovered a great interest and some talent in athletics, particularly running. He says about his schooling over those years from age thirteen through sixteen, 'Jumping into grade 6 after four years of correspondence was hard, and I was also recovering from malaria, contracted on an eight-day walk into the interior, but after an initial settling in stage I quickly moved up to getting average to good marks for my work. Maths was my strong point and English my weak one (even though I was an avid reader). I also found I was one of the best athletes in the grade, and was getting first, second or third at almost anything I tried.'

But the deterioration in the state of the marriage was starting to take its toll. Margaret was getting more and more involved in holistic healing, massage, homeopathy, crystal healing, acupuncture, touch for heal and t'ai chi, along with a deep personal spiritualism. It seems Robin did not approve and they began to argue a lot. David ran away from home a couple of times but 'came back the next morning,' he says – 'I realise now that I just needed the time to cool off.'

Port Moresby was a fairly unfriendly place for a white family to live in the late eighties. Most of David's friends had returned home to their native country, and the last few years were not very pleasant. For safety reasons, the children couldn't go anywhere without their parents. 'We were constantly hearing of rapes (two of which were friends of ours), break-ins, violent assaults, etc, which got so bad "state of emergency" periods were enforced one year. Basically it meant that I had little freedom.'

The picture I have drawn from personal contacts with various people who knew the Bains in Papua New Guinea, statements in the police file about Robin and Margaret from friends and associates, and from David's account of life in Papua New Guinea, adds up to a family returning to New Zealand under some strain; the father coming with them reluctantly out of a sense of duty; the mother fairly well entrenched into an alternative lifestyle mode of thinking and behaviour. Clearly they were not getting on well. As to whether they thought that returning to Dunedin would help to improve their relationship, I am unable to say.

When they returned, it was to an old house that had been rented out for many years and was pretty much a derelict shambles. The site of the house was quite lovely however, being a sizeable section in a good location and having stands of large trees. It seems that Robin and Margaret intended to build a new house on the site, but this was never to be, mostly, it would appear, because of a rapid and severe deterioration in the state of their relationship upon returning to Dunedin.

Robin was unable to find meaningful employment, and this was a source of considerable embitterment to him. He did various odd jobs until he eventually got the job as headmaster at the tiny school at Taieri Beach after having been back about three years.

For her part, Margaret went into a decline. Not long after settling into Every Street, she moved out to live in the old caravan parked at the rear of the house. Her diaries demonstrate a confused and distorted mental state. She was very much driven by a powerful oblique spirituality, and a compulsion to discover some sort of peace within herself. At the centre of this search was her husband, who she continually refers to as being 'filled with Belial'. 'Belial', a word of Hebrew extraction meaning 'the Devil' or 'Satan', appears over and over in her diaries, and she seemed to think that it was her mission to rid those about her of this evil spirit, a sort of exorcism. Margaret's diaries over the period from 1990 to 1993 are revealing not so much for what they say but as a clear indication of her state of mind. She was obsessed with God and the Devil. She couldn't in her mind get Robin 'clear' of Belial, so decided she must rid herself of him. She was clearly a woman dreadfully confused and dejected. At the same time she had not lost her dominance or powerful influence over the family, particularly Robin.

After a month or so, she moved back into the house, and relegated Robin to the caravan. On 13 December 1992 she wrote, 'Robin is not of 65 Every Street. I suddenly feel excitement as I contemplate God's solving of that problem. I pray for tranquillity/serenity throughout the process. After months (years) of fear over this I finally feel confident that God will allow him to do no harm. I understand that harm is flexible and depends on circumstances.'

By this time, Robin had acquired the job at Taieri Beach School, about an hour's drive from Every Street. He had developed a pattern of sleeping and living in his battered Commer van while at the school and coming home to stay in the caravan at Every Street on weekends.

Laniet couldn't stand life at home any longer, and at the age of sixteen had moved out to go flatting. Unknown, it would appear, to the rest of the family, she had taken to prostitution and drugs as her way of life.

Arawa had done well since returning to New Zealand. She had plenty of friends, including boyfriends. She was particularly attractive and outgoing, and also was doing well at training college.

Stephen had been involved in a few minor incidents but seemed to be a fairly happy, healthy young teenager getting on with life.

David had the most difficulty in adjusting to life in New Zealand when the family first returned. Perhaps his own description of his life would best explain the four and a half years of freedom he had in New Zealand.

That first year was quite hard for me, and probably for everyone else as well. I found it hard to make friends and related better to the adults than any of the students my own age. I was still recovering from malaria and hadn't reached the 10 stone mark yet (which is what I was before I contracted it) so I was skinny and tall and rather weak still. Because of this and where I had come from, I attracted a lot of teasing, which I wasn't used to in Papua New Guinea. I gradually became withdrawn and quiet. I didn't join any sports groups, clubs, etc that involved too much contact with other people. But I did fight that fear down enough to join the school choir to continue my singing. I didn't do exceptionally great academically, but well enough to carry on to seventh form.

Seventh form was a better year for me. I had settled in better, found a few friends and I started getting more involved in music and sports. I joined the school madrigal choir as well as the full choir and later in the year, the Royal Dunedin Male Choir. In sports, I got involved in running, and competed regularly for the school as well as outside of it. Later I got involved in triathlons. Also, because of the love for sailing I had, and my involvement in scouts in Papua New Guinea, I joined the venturers in Andersons Bay that was also a part of the sea scouts. I had many enjoyable trips and weekends sailing on the harbour, and competing against other groups. The next year I left that group and joined the Cargill Rover crew. Being a member of the scouting movement led to a chance of showing my singing and acting skills in the 1990 Gangshow. I really enjoyed that show and I think it is what led me to the Opera Company in the end. The seventh form was no more successful than my sixth form year academically, and I found that I wasn't enjoying the subjects any more (biology, chemistry, geography, physics and maths). Even though this was the case, my parents pushed me to continue them at university. It wasn't the greatest of years and I failed all the papers I took. But I did do well in my running. I came twentieth in my age group in the National Cross Country Champs in Invercargill.

The next year I left university, went on the dole and started my search for what it was that I was supposed to be/do/become. That first year went by fairly quickly and I can't remember much about it. A couple of major events happened though. In August I was sponsored by the Lions Club to go to Anakiwa to do the Outward Bound Course. Then in September I joined Opera Alive (for the acting and singing). Those two things changed my life a great deal. For a start, Outward Bound forced me to examine who I was and pushed me to the limits, physically, mentally and spiritually so that I could find out what I could do. It helped me to become more confident in my abilities, less self-conscious and critical of my actions, and helped me to gain confidence in communicating with people. When I got back and joined Opera Alive, I was tested yet again by being given a lead role in my first production. So as time went, and I did more shows etc, my self confidence grew, and I became less shy about being my true self in public.

Over the next year and a half (through '93) I stayed on the dole but worked basically full time on shows for the Opera Company and Opera Alive. After about the third show, I realised that this was what I wanted to do in my life. So I started voice training and went to university again, hoping to major in music, drama and a language, with associated papers in classics, English and some extra languages done on the side. All of this, hopefully, leading to work on the operatic stage.

David wrote this account for a psychiatrist a couple of months after his arrest. It is clear from this and from David's interviews with the two psychiatrists after his arrest and from my own investigations with David and people associated with him over this time, that although he understandably had some difficulty in coming to grips with the culture change from life in Papua New Guinea to urban New Zealand in the nineties his life had come together well. In the year before the deaths of his family, he had successfully completed an Outward Bound course, run the Dunedin marathon, competed in triathlons, taken a leading role in the operatic group and established firmly in his mind the direction his life was to take.

In February of 1995, eight months after David's arrest, the police obtained a report from one of David's lecturers at Otago University. This was the only opinion sought from any of the university staff – and one has to wonder why it was not asked for sooner. As well as noting David's maturity and musical ability, the report said in part:

> I have to say that at the time I found it almost impossible to believe that David Bain had committed the murders, and I expressed this view quite freely. There was nothing that I saw in his behaviour that would

have created the slightest suspicion of an unbalanced mind or of murderous intent. On the contrary, he gave every impression of being a mature, self-confident, well motivated, competent and happy person.

Another statement obtained after David's arrest, on 26 September 1994, was from Mason Ramsay, director of intensive care at Dunedin Hospital. The police had asked him for his opinion of David's medical condition at the time he was discovered after making the 111 call, and his report says in conclusion:

> It is of interest that the pulse rate was 75, which is normal. However, if Bain was a trained athlete and normally had a resting pulse in the 50s or even 60, this would represent a 50% increase in pulse rate and would be consistent with a moderate fit . . .
>
> I note the bruise on the forehead was not noticed for some time afterwards and it may have occurred during the time when he fell back and was dragged out by Andrews to the recovery position. No detail was to hand from Andrews as to how he moved and repositioned the patient. The photophobia and headache experienced later would be consistent with a blow to the head. The period of relative inertia where Bain lies for nearly an hour in one position without shifting, would be consistent with a postictal (post-fitting) state. A normally conscious person would find such experience very uncomfortable and indeed very painful and would endeavour to shift their position.

Ramsay's opinion raises serious doubt as to the later suggestions made by the Crown during the trial that David's fitting and convulsing was a 'Hollywood' act designed to mislead the police, and also provides another possibility for the origin of the bruising on David's forehead.

Neither Ramsay nor David's lecturer was called to give evidence at the trial.

The last few weeks before the tragedy saw a few events take place that would turn out to be significant.

David had been taking singing lessons with local identity and singing instructor Mrs Kathleen Dawson. These two had developed a great mutual respect and friendship during the time David had been having lessons with her. On the Thursday night (16 June) before the murders, David had finished his lesson and was heading home. Mrs Dawson lives on a rather steep hillside; one of Dunedin's many. David tripped on the wet steep slope and his spectacles fell off and broke. It was raining quite hard so Mr Dawson took David home. On the following morning David took his spectacles into the optometrist for repair and that is where they were at the time of the murders. As we shall see, the matter of a pair of spectacles and a missing lens will become a key point in the police case against David Bain.

About three weeks before that fateful 20 June, David went to a ball at Larnach Castle, with a girlfriend from the Opera Alive club. In the process of hiring a suit, and as an indication of his confidence and sense of occasion, he purchased a pair of white gloves to wear to complement his ball attire. Apparently, it caused quite a stir at home when David dressed up for the ball, gloves and all, so the family were very aware of his having made the acquisition. After the ball, the gloves were neatly packed in the drawer of his dresser with his best clothes, sitting on top of the other items. As we shall see, David's white ball gloves were also to become a focal point as the case against him unfolded.

For Margaret Bain, I believe, life continued much the same. She hadn't got rid of Robin entirely, but he did not seem to be quite the bother he had been prior to settling in down at Taieri Beach School. Margaret and David were in the process of doing some quite interesting landscape work about the house, but apart from that, the pattern was pretty much one of late nights in front of the TV and late mornings in bed. As the children had got older, Margaret had relented considerably in her efforts to have them follow her spiritual lead.

For Arawa, life appears to have been pretty rosy. The night prior to her death she had been babysitting as she regularly did, and was dropped home by a member of that family at about 11 p.m.

Robin was feeling the pressure in many ways, and this manifested itself in both his behaviour and demeanour. Just a couple of months before his death, after about two years of living in the Commer van at the school, the school house became available and he moved into it. A male friend of Laniet's, Kyle Cunningham, moved into the house too, as Robin's boarder. Cunningham was to be one of only three witnesses called by the defence.

In the period just before the murders, Laniet was spending quite a lot of time at the Taieri Beach house with her father and Cunningham. Despite this, she maintained her residence at the Russell Street flat in the city where most of her possessions remained. The word amongst Laniet's friends was that she intended to sort her life out at this time. She was looking to get off drugs and give up prostitution. In the light of information now available, a significant factor for her in achieving a new, healthier lifestyle was dealing with the issue of the relationship she had with her father. This matter was certainly coming to a head at the time of the murders, and was more than likely the predominant force behind Robin's depression.

At the time of the tragedy, leaving aside the situation in respect to Robin's relationship to his daughter Laniet, life was going pretty well for the Bain family.

David was enjoying significant success and satisfaction in his classical music studies, opera participation and the resulting positive social interaction. Arawa and Stephen were getting on with life, as they had been throughout. Margaret and Robin were still disagreeing about their marriage, but this had been going on for some years and if anything seemed to be less acrimonious, with the prospect of a reasonable outcome quite likely.

The only source of real desperation, it would appear, was that of Laniet's incestuous relationship with her father. For Laniet, ending it would have been the beginning of a new and wholesome life. For Robin, the exposure of his dark secret, hidden for so long, would be the ultimate humiliation and disgrace he could not bear to face.

COTTLE AND APPEALS

On 29 May 1995, at the Dunedin High Court, the jury of seven men and five women found David guilty on all five charges of murder brought against him. Upon hearing the verdict read out, David fainted, and when carried off to the holding cell he is reported to have been fitting and convulsing. On 21 June 1995, a year and a day after the family was slain, David Bain was sentenced in the High Court in Dunedin.

The trial had commenced on 8 May 1995 before Justice Williamson. The jury was sworn. Following the opening address by the Crown, they called 103 witnesses to sustain 'their' case, over the following two and a half weeks. The defence case, led by Dunedin barrister Michael Guest, consisted of David Bain giving evidence and two other witnesses, a forensic psychiatrist, Dr Paul Mullen, and Kyle Cunningham, Laniet's friend, who was boarding at Taieri Beach with Robin Bain at the time of the murders. On 26 May, after a hearing lasting 18 days, the Crown and defence completed their summing up, and on 29 May, after the weekend break, the judge summed up. At 11.45 am the jury retired to consider its verdict. The jurors had lunch from 1 to

2 p.m., returned to the court at 5.23 p.m. with four questions requiring clarification from the judge, had tea from 6 to 7.30, and finally returned their verdict of guilty on all counts at 9 p.m., after a total of about 8 hours of deliberation.

The jury was discharged and excluded from further service for five years, and David was remanded in custody for sentencing on 21 June. He was sentenced to life imprisonment with a minimum parole period of sixteen years. The judge made a couple of other rulings, the most significant being permanent suppression of the contents and subject matter of Dean Cottle's statements. In the process of delivering his judgement, the judge, in imposing a minimum term before parole of sixteen years (the mandatory period is ten years) said:

> In the absence of any evidence of insanity, or of interference with mental functioning, the jury's verdicts in this case lead inevitably to the conclusion that David Bain killed the other members of his family deliberately, *and with a significant degree of cunning and deliberation*. In the case of Stephen, the trademark fatal and final close-range shot to the head was preceded by *considerable violence*, *determination* and *perseverance*. [My emphasis.]

He later added:

> David Cullen Bain, on reviewing all of the facts of your case, and for the reasons I have indicated in the judgement, I conclude that this is a case of an horrendous nature and exceptionality to the degree where I should impose a minimum period of imprisonment of sixteen years.

In issuing the permanent suppression order in relation to

Dean Cottle's statement, the learned judge said in part:

> Permanent orders for suppression are only made in special circumstances. The general rule against suppression reflects the public and open nature of the courts. In this case the defence sought during the trial to lead hearsay evidence from a proposed witness, *who I found to be totally unreliable.* I did not believe him at the time. My conclusions were justified because a few days later he gave an explanation to the court which was totally at variance with his earlier statement. [My emphasis.]

I have quoted these extracts from the judge's rulings, to exemplify the nature of the case brought against David. There is, and could never be, any doubt that for David to be found guilty, it had to be accepted that he acted in a premeditated, cunning and ruthless manner. We shall see, as I examine the evidence heard by the court, that this hypothesis advanced by the prosecution and accepted by the court is so full of holes, littered with half truths and devoid of reasonable logic, that it is difficult to imagine how it was not exposed.

The situation in relation to Dean Cottle, and the judge's subsequent suppression order, would become the worst-kept secret in Dunedin, and would be the primary basis of further hearings by the New Zealand Court of Appeal and the judicial committee of the Privy Council in London.

A close examination of the two matters raised here (the issue of David's premeditation and pre-planning, and the issue of the circumstances surrounding Cottle and the contents of his statement), leads to my primary contention, that the police acted prematurely in arresting David. This caused them to become subjective in the manner in which they dealt with evidential matters, and led to the unexplained mysteries with which this case is riddled.

These two issues, in particular, raise the question of motive. We all generally understand what is meant by motive, but to explain legally it will be of help to utilise the judge's words when he was addressing the jury in his summing up in this case; for as lay people, which the jury of course are, we often confuse intent with motive. As a prelude to his explanation regarding motive, the judge explained that in proving a case of murder three essential elements must be established. They are, he said, 'First, a homicide, which is defined in our law as a killing of one human by another directly or indirectly by any means whatsoever.' Secondly, it must be proved that the homicide was culpable, in other words blameworthy. For the purposes of this trial, the homicide is culpable when it consists of killing by an unlawful act, that is, shooting them dead. There was for example no suggestion that self defence could have justified the killings. The third element, the judge goes on to say to the jury, relates to murderous intent:

> The Crown's case against the accused is based upon the simple intent that the accused meant to cause the death. It hardly needs any explanation from me. You have to decide on all of the evidence whether the killer actually meant to cause death.
>
> It is not necessary in a case such as this for the Crown to prove motive in order to establish the charge of murder. Motive really means the reason or emotion that has prompted a particular act. Intention on the other hand, includes meaning to bring about a particular result or being aware or believing that that result will happen.

The judge went on to give the jury an illustration to assist them in their understanding of the difference between 'intent' and 'motive':

> A person may blow up an aircraft in order to get insur-

ance money for some goods on the aircraft. The motive or object may be to get the insurance money, but the means of doing so include an intention or the inevitable consequence that the crew and passengers in the aircraft will die. That illustrates the difference between motive and intent. What the Crown must prove is intention.

Quite clearly in this case, when the killer fired the gun at point blank range into the victims' heads, he intended to kill them.

What I am intending to illustrate is that it is difficult to accept that a sane person would set out with a premeditated plan to kill his whole family without having a compelling reason or motive to do so. The Crown's case, as summarised by the judge in his sentencing, had to have David planning the murders and attempting to deceive the police by incriminating his father. The reason that David set up this elaborate scheme of ruthless execution has never been determined. The Crown attempted to allude to financial gain as being his motive, but all accounts I have heard, and certainly my readings of the file, indicate that this proposition had little to sustain it, and had little if no impact on the proceedings. So at the end of a year-long investigation and a three-week trial with over a hundred witnesses, the case ended with no clue as to why this atrocity was committed.

I again quote the judge in his summing up to the jury. While recapping the prosecution case, he said (referring to Mr Wright, the Crown prosecutor): 'He said to you that, just as to why it happened it is not possible to ascertain. That these events are so bizarre and abnormal that it is really impossible for the human mind to come up with any logical or reasonable explanation for them.'

I believe that there is a very reasonable, logical and understandable explanation for what happened. I further believe that had the police not arrested David when they did, but (while keeping a close eye on David, perhaps) instead thoroughly investigated the prevailing circumstances surrounding the family at that time, they would have construed the circumstantial evidence used against David in a totally different way, and reached an entirely different conclusion as to what actually happened.

Almost immediately following his conviction, David insisted to Michael Guest his determination to appeal the verdict. He even more adamantly, if that could be possible, maintained his total innocence, and so in December of 1995 Guest took the case to the New Zealand Appeal Court. The prime cause for appeal was that the jury had not been given the opportunity to hear the evidence of Dean Robert Cottle.

It is worthwhile explaining in detail the circumstances surrounding the entire Cottle affair, because not only does it throw new light on the case, it is also extremely revealing as to the manner in which 'justice' is administered in New Zealand and the lengths the police will go to in their pursuit of a conviction.

Dean Robert Cottle was 27 years old at the time of the murders. I have met with Dean, his father and the lady Dean lives in a permanent relationship with in Dunedin. Dean's father owns a substantial vehicle dealership in Dunedin, and although Dean himself worked in vehicle-related occupations, he described himself as unemployed at the time of giving his statement.

At that time he had no prior convictions and I must say that in all my meetings with Cottle himself and with his father, in matters related to the Bain affair, his account of events has always cross-checked perfectly, and carried the ring of credibility.

The essence of Cottle's statement is that he had known Laniet Bain for about ten months, had gone out for dinner with her and got to know her quite well. She had told him that her father had been having sex with her for years, and now she was working as a prostitute. He had seen her outside a coffee bar in Dunedin on the Friday afternoon prior to the murders, and stopped on the footpath to chat with her for five or ten minutes. In that discussion she told Cottle, according to his statement, that:

> She was going to make a new start of everything, that her parents had been questioning her about what she was doing. She said that she was going to tell them everything and make a clean start of things. I thought by this she was going to tell her parents about prostitution. I also presumed that she was going to talk about incest because she said 'everything'.

This statement was taken by Detective Malcolm Inglis (Det 6145) at the Dunedin CIB in the presence of Cottle's own lawyer at the time, Derek Russell. The full statement is reproduced as Appendix 1.

Now how Cottle came to make this statement is quite interesting. He had lent Laniet his cell phone some six months previously to assist her in her prostitution work, and she advertised in fact in the *Otago Daily Times* using Cottle's cell phone number and the work alias of 'Page'. Immediately Cottle became aware of the deaths he contacted his lawyer, Derek Russell, and related these facts to him, asking what he should do. According to Cottle, Russell's advice was that once the police located the cell phone, they would no doubt contact him, and to wait till then. They contacted him on the Wednesday following the murders and he made his statement at lunch time on Thursday 23 June.

It is a very salient point that less than 24 hours would elapse from the time Cottle gave his statement until David was charged with the murders. The only follow-up by the police in the intervening time was that Inglis, the detective who took Cottle's statement, went with him the same afternoon to identify one of the flats that Laniet had lived in before moving into her current residence in Russell Street. Inglis states that during the course of that visit, Cottle told him that he thought Laniet had a list of all her clients in her personal diary. This diary, along with many other items, appears to have disappeared.

The police job sheets surrounding the sequence of events described above are extremely revealing. On Tuesday 21 June, the day after the murders, Inglis was given a note from a Sergeant Binney which said: 'For enquiry with Dean Cottle. He is the subscriber for the cell phone used by Laniet Bain.'

Inglis did not get to see Cottle until two days later. It was not until Monday 27 June, after David's arrest, that Detective Binney applied for a search warrant and fax record to the Telecom Malicious Call Centre in Hamilton regarding subscriber details for:

(03) 479 2929   The Russell Street flat phone number
(025) 344 342   Dean Robert Cottle cell phone number

On Thursday 30 June, the following message was received at the switch board of the Dunedin CIB:

To: Det Sgt Brett Roberts
From: Dunedin CIB
Date: 30th June 1994
Message
Toll records for 25-344342.
1 January 1994 to 20 June 1994.
Believe it or not, Telecom Cellular have no toll records made on this number at all.
Sorry
'? ?'

Quite obviously, even the writer of the message finds this information somewhat bewildering. My own research, and information provided to me in Dunedin, has confirmed that in fact this phone was extensively used by Laniet, to the extent of $400-odd of phone calls per month. There is no record of the police attempting to follow up in any way on this glaring anomaly.

On Tuesday morning, 21 June, the day after the murders, another statement was given to the police by a former flat-mate of Laniet's, Alan James Hunter. He had lived in the Russell Street flat and had seen her as recently as the Friday before her death. He stated that he had got to know her really well. 'I think she found an outlet in me to tell me about her problems. We spoke often,' he said. Although Hunter did not specify an incestuous relationship between Laniet and her father, he very clearly described the father's attitude to Laniet as being weird and strange. He also told the police that Laniet had told him that she had been raped in Papua New Guinea when she was about eleven years old.

Hunter told the police that on the Tuesday morning of the previous week, Robin had called at Russell Street about 8.45 a.m. He described Robin as being 'a strange guy in a very bad mood. He was really agitated.' Robin had called to collect Laniet but she was in the shower and asked Hunter to tell him she would be down later. Hunter told Robin this and, 'He just lost it. He clenched his fists and said, "Tell her I'll wait".'

It was obvious then that by lunch time on the day after the murders, the police knew that Laniet was a prostitute, that her relationship with her father had some strange tension in it, that she was in possession of Dean Cottle's cell phone and that she resided at 56 Russell Street but also spent quite a bit of time at her father's place at Taieri Beach School. Hunter's statement also indicated that she very rarely spent any time at or even visited the family residence in Every Street. The day before David's arrest on Friday 24 June, the police had Cottle's statement alerting them that Laniet might well have been incestuously involved with her father, and even more significantly that she intended *that very weekend* to go home to tell them 'everything', and to try to start a new life. And of course they knew that she did go home, because she was found dead with three bullets in her head, in the spare bed of the Every Street house.

Assuming Cottle's information to be true, one might well think: Laniet has been attempting to resolve the situation between herself and her father in the course of sorting out her personal life. As part of doing this, she has arranged to go home on this Sunday night to have the whole thing out with her mother and/or father. If the father was about to be publicly exposed for the sexual molestation of his daughter since she was a child, one might well think, this would be the type of thing that could cause a man such extreme humiliation, distress and anxiety, resulting in a deranged state of mind, that he would totally flip out, hence providing the explanation for the atrocity the police were confronted with.

Remarkably the police did not pursue this line of enquiry at all. Quite the contrary, in fact. They arrested David the following morning on the basis of some circumstantial forensic evidence that, viewed from a particular perspective, could be construed as linking David with the crimes, but went no further than that.

The Cottle affair did not begin to gain real momentum until a few weeks out from the trial. Michael Guest, David's attorney, had been struggling to come up with any sort of defence. Indeed, as recently as a couple of months before the trial, he had tried to talk David into pleading guilty on the basis of insanity. This despite a forensic psychiatrist's report stating that he could find no evidence of any mental disorder in David. David flatly refused, saying he would not make any sort of mitigating plea whatsoever because he 'didn't do any of it'. Guest subsequently visited renowned Auckland barrister Peter Williams QC, to discuss with him the possibility of a plea of automatism. In lay person's language, this would mean accepting responsibility for the act but attempting to prove that David had been in effect acting as an automaton, a robot without any conscious volition at all. A person is not deemed criminally responsible, for example, if committing an act whilst sleepwalking or in a trance or fit. In this case this was clearly quite ridiculous, as David did the paper run in the midst of the murders if he was the murderer, and David would never have agreed to such a plea anyway.

However, just weeks before the trial was due to begin, Guest was thrown a lifeline. He had employed an assistant to help him in what would be the most serious case he had ever taken on. Ms Jonelle Williams was given the task of examining all of the documentation provided to Guest under discovery. Once again, in lay terms, the Crown (police) are obliged to provide all information in relation to the investigation to the defendant. This includes police job sheets, statements obtained from witnesses, forensic evidence, photos and the like. These are called the 'discovery documents'. According to Guest, Ms Williams came across Cottle's statement just weeks prior to trial time among these documents.

As I have explained already, and bearing in mind that there was no conclusive evidence against David – it was all circumstantial – suddenly the defence had a witness whose statement provided a real and compelling motive for the other prime suspect in the police enquiry: David's father Robin. The defence team was ecstatic, and approached the coming trial with renewed enthusiasm and confidence.

It appears to me however, that the defence team acted in a rather odd way. Here they had, out of the blue, an ace, as though dealt from the bottom of the pack, giving them a hand they could play with confidence. Inexplicably, and I have canvassed the matter with Mike Guest but never obtained a satisfactory answer, instead of the defence approaching Cottle in a pleasant and co-operative way, a subpoena was issued to be served on him requiring him to appear as a witness for the defence.

Here again we have something that would appear to be obvious being overlooked, this time not by the police, but by David's own defence team. The obvious factor I'm referring to is that Cottle's association with a known prostitute could well be a matter to be treated with some delicacy and discretion. It's not as though Cottle was difficult to locate or far away. His address and phone number were contained in the statement and he lived only minutes from the Octagon, where the defence team's offices were located. It would seem to me that considering that Cottle might well have been Guest's only witness – and regardless of the number would most definitely be his prime evidence giver – he would have been approached with kid gloves not, as in fact was the case, by using a private detective to slap a subpoena on him in the street.

I have come to know the private detective in question well during the process of working on this case. Wayne Idour is a former police officer who had worked in the force in Dunedin from 1972 to 1992 as a sergeant, and who now works for himself as a licensed private investigator under the name of Idour and Associates. Both Idour and Cottle agree that there was some confusion about the serving of the subpoena by Idour on Cottle. Cottle accepts readily, and in fact has sworn in affidavit form, that he did not wish to become involved in the trial. His fiancée was unaware of his relationship with Laniet, and the fact that he had lent her his cell phone could easily be construed unfavourably as to his degree of involvement in her prostitution business. It is easy to see that if he could it would be best for him to remain well out of the way. Finally, following some heated conversations with Cottle denying his identity and warning Idour to get off his property, Idour deposited the subpoena at Cottle's front door. Cottle has always maintained that he was not properly served. Regardless of his feelings it seems that the defence expected him to turn up to give evidence during the trial, on 22 May. Cottle claims that following the service (valid or not) of the subpoena he called Detective Inglis at the Dunedin CIB. This is the same detective who took his original statement almost a year earlier.

From this time on Dean Cottle was to become the focal point of some bizarre events, more in keeping with a Hollywood cops and robbers show than with the process of justice in conservative Dunedin, New Zealand.

The facts as we know them at this point are:

- On 23 June (three days after the Bain deaths) Cottle made a statement to Detective Inglis of the Dunedin CIB.
- Nearly a year later, shortly before the trial was due to begin on 8 May 1995, Cottle's statement was found by defence counsel for David Bain among the piles of discovery documents obtained by the defence team from the police.
- The defence team made no personal or direct contact with Cottle, but instead had him served by private investigator Wayne Idour with a subpoena demanding his appearance as a witness for the defence at the Dunedin High Court on 22 May 1995.
- Cottle claims that the service was not effected properly, and so on the date of his due appearance he did not show up.

Cottle maintains that the reason he did not appear was that Detective Inglis, by clear implication, let it be known that the police too were not that keen on Cottle turning up to give evidence. Cottle says that he asked Inglis what would happen if he didn't turn up, and Inglis told him to 'look at the back page of the subpoena'. Cottle says they then had a conversation about what it said on the back page, which was that the maximum penalty for failing to appear was a fine of $500. Cottle further maintains that he had a number of conversations with police personnel subsequent to the alleged service of the subpoena.

In light of these discussions, and bearing in mind his reluctance to become involved, Cottle left Dunedin; 'went on holiday,' as he put it to me, during the week when he was supposed to appear.

The trial took its course, and on 22 May Cottle was due to appear for the defence. He did not show up, and so the defence filed a notice of service sworn by Wayne Idour with the court at 2.15 p.m. Guest applied for a warrant to be issued for Cottle's arrest for failing to appear. The warrant was granted by the judge at 2.15 p.m. the following day, but apparently lay in court until the following morning, Wednesday 24 May.

On the Monday afternoon of Cottle's non-appearance, Guest asked Idour to locate Cottle. He was about to commence presenting the defence case, the linchpin of his defence was nowhere to be found, and he had not even met or spoken with him.

The information I am able to reveal of what took place over the next few days has been gathered from the sworn statements of Cottle and Idour and also from interviews I have conducted with each of them as well as discussions with Michael Guest and Dean Cottle's father.

On the evening of Tuesday 23 May, Wayne Idour established that Cottle had made a toll call to a person in Dunedin at about 7.30 p.m. that day. He immediately notified the senior sergeant on duty at the Dunedin central police station, knowing that the police could have the call traced. He called the police back about 10.45 p.m. that evening and was advised that nothing could be done until the following morning. Remember that at 2.15 p.m. of this same day a warrant had been issued for Cottle's arrest. At 8.40 am the following morning Idour again rang the police, and had his call returned at 9.20 by a Detective Thomson, who said that he could not help him and knew nothing about the request to have the call traced.

At 4.30 that day, Idour called the duty sergeant (Sergeant Stapp) and again requested the trace, which apparently was actioned.

At 5 p.m. Idour spoke with another sergeant, MacDonald, who said that the earlier request had actually been actioned and the call had been traced to an address in Ranfurly.

At 6 p.m. Idour again spoke with MacDonald to see what progress had been made. He was informed that Detective Senior Sergeant Jim Doyle (second in charge of the Bain homicide investigations) had informed him that no such trace enquiry linking the call to a Ranfurly address had come to the police. This was in direct conflict with what Idour had been told by MacDonald just one hour earlier.

Idour also maintains that he had given the police details of the likely vehicle and registration number that Cottle was using, but that this information was never passed on to the Ranfurly police constable.

The gist then of Idour's account of proceedings is that the police were at best ponderous, and more realistically downright obstructive to any effort to locate the elusive Mr Cottle.

Had Idour been aware of what actually was happening (this according to Cottle but tallying perfectly with Idour's comments) he would never have bothered seeking any assistance from the police in the first place. For Cottle alleges in the affidavit he swore for the Court of Appeal, and has confirmed to me, that he was actually in touch with the police from Tuesday afternoon right through the period of that week following the issue of a warrant for his arrest on that

Tuesday afternoon. He maintains that he spoke with the police by phone from Palmerston, about 35 miles north of Dunedin, three or four times that week, and gained the clear impression that not only was it not necessary that he attend, but 'that they did not want me to give evidence in this matter, and therefore I followed that clear impression and did not bother to contact the defence'.

In the meantime, David Bain had given lengthy testimony and been intensely cross-examined by the Crown. The defence's other two witnesses, both of little consequence, gave their evidence, and the case for the defence was over without the jury ever being aware even of the existence of Dean Cottle, let alone what he had to say.

I should point out that the defence had attempted to have Cottle's statement admitted as evidence, but the judge would not agree, mainly because Cottle was not available to be cross-examined.

So Thursday 25 May, the trial of David Bain was over, except for the summing up of the Crown prosecutor Bill Wright, defence counsel Michael Guest and Judge Williamson. The jury were completely oblivious of Dean Cottle and the saga that had been unfolding, as all of the discussions regarding him and his evidence had been in chambers rather than in the public court. On Friday morning Bill Wright delivered what was considered to be a powerful, persuasive, brilliantly orated three-hour summation to the jury of the Crown case.

At the same time Dean Cottle again rang Detective Inglis to ask whether the police were looking for him. Cottle says that he asked what he should do, and Inglis told him not to come to the police station but to ring back in twenty minutes. Cottle says that when he rang back Inglis advised him to make a voluntary appearance at the Dunedin High Court and to tell the court, which he said would probably be a couple of justices of the peace, that his brother Craig had just told him that the police were searching for him. Cottle believed he was going in solely to tidy up the matter of the fine for not having answered the subpoena.

Unbeknown to Cottle, that same day, no doubt as a safeguard in case the defence did manage to get Cottle to present his evidence, the Crown and Detective Inglis were busy sorting out a rebuttal.

Malcolm Inglis swore an affidavit at Dunedin on 26 May 1995 (that is, the day of the summing up by Bill Wright) in which the primary theme is that he alleged Cottle to be 'showing signs of being a manic depressive'. He based his expertise to make this judgement on the premise that his own brother had suffered from this illness for 25 years, and says that he saw his brother on a regular basis 'and have learnt over those times to recognise symptoms when he is swinging into a manic state'. He also says, 'The statement he [Cottle] made was partly true but also may have been extended on as part of his imagination and to please the police.'

The final sentence of his affidavit says, 'It is my belief that he is in need of psychiatric assistance but is not mentally unstable.'

I am unable to say categorically whether this statement was seen by the judge, but I can say that there is no record that it was. Regardless, it is a remarkable example of the determination of the Crown to leave no stone unturned to win the case. For the record, Dean Cottle has no record of ever having any type of mental or psychotic illness, and nor does any member of his family. Cottle argues that if Inglis spent 25 years with a psychotic brother it might well be Inglis himself who has a problem.

Back to Friday 26 May 1995, and Bill Wright was just finishing his summing up about noon, when an unshaven, casually dressed, relatively unkempt-looking Dean Cottle presented himself at the High Court, expecting to be treated with quite some degree of civility by the police. But to his surprise, on making himself known Cottle was arrested and locked up in the Great King Street police station before being handcuffed and taken back to the High Court holding cells. Cottle asked for a legal advisor but was refused. At 2 p.m., Mike Guest was ready to begin his summing up of the defence case when he was notified that Cottle was being held in the court cells. He immediately sought permission from the judge to brief Cottle and have the trial re-opened so that Cottle could take the witness stand, give evidence and be cross-examined. Naturally, Cottle at this time was in a state of total confusion, with no idea what was going to happen next. He was persistently refused the opportunity of legal advice, and was marched into the High Court and onto the witness stand. The jury were absented by Judge Williamson, but Cottle was faced with the full High Court barrage of reporters, four barristers and a judge. He felt threatened and uncertain, and was dressed in old holiday clothes. Entirely ill prepared, one might say. For all he knew, taking it to the extreme, and bearing in mind he had been arrested without explanation and was standing before a High Court judge in a homicide trial, he might have been about to be accused of some complicity in the actual proceedings! It is easy to imagine his feeling of vulnerability.

The judge for his part had acceded to Guest's request to have the trial re-opened for Cottle to appear, but not for him to give evidence. He allowed both sides to put questions to Cottle but only on matters relating to his reliability, memory and general character. The judge also put questions to Cottle on the same issues. Now, Cottle is the first to admit that he would have appeared very dodgy during this voir dire, as it is called. Not having any idea as to what was going on, he acted dumb, prevaricated in responses and generally was as evasive and unco-operative as could be imagined.

I have already quoted the judge's findings on the situation, in essence that he did not believe Cottle, based on his own judgement and I quote, 'his appearance, his demeanour, his background and his general conduct'.

Cottle, after finally arriving, still never came before the jury to give his evidence but was ordered by the judge to return to court at 2 p.m. the following Monday, when he was fined $200.00 for failing to appear.

You could see this as a tremendous victory for the police, an abject disaster for the defence and serious blow for the common bloke as to the process by which justice takes its course. But it was not over for Dean Robert Cottle. He may well have been basking in relief on the Monday evening, when despite all that had taken place his only loss was $200 and the judge had suppressed release of his name and evidence.

I have treated the Cottle episode up until the end of the trial in quite some depth, because of its significance as to whether David Bain received a fair go at the hands of the police and our justice system. What subsequently happened to Cottle is no less significant, but not in relation to the David Bain case, so I shall but outline briefly his plight.

Over the ensuing months, commencing immediately after the trial, he was continually in trouble with the law. Naughty boy, one might say. In fact, no. I have met with various counsel who have worked for Cottle over this time, and seen the records of what took place. In my opinion he was harassed by members of the Dunedin police force. He was charged with numerous and continual offences, arrested unceremoniously, followed around town by police vehicles, had his house broken into and alleges his phone was tapped. He ran up a legal bill of some $20,000.00 defending himself on the charges, all but one of which was either dropped by the police at the last moment, or thrown out of court by the judge. The one count that went to proceedings saw Cottle convicted but subsequently exonerated by the Appeal Court. He has been unable to work because one of his arms was severely damaged when he was, according to him, quite brutally arrested, and has been unable to pay the legal fees run up in defending himself against this tirade.

He made a complaint to the Police Complaints Authority, an institution which appears hopelessly inadequate to ensure that the police and/or individuals within the police are held accountable. Cottle's complaint, as is normal procedure with the authority, was referred to the Dunedin police for the Dunedin police to report on and file the report back to the authority. The policeman responsible for undertaking this task was none other than one of the officers who had made the alleged brutal arrest on Cottle and was himself the subject of the most serious matter in the complaint!

In the end, after a year's deliberation, the authority reported back to Cottle, finding that no serious matters were upheld against the police. Later Cottle was awarded $500, towards the cost of appealing the matter which had been thrown out by the Appeal Court.

If this harassment took place, why? The only answer can be that the police, in the sure knowledge that if Guest were to appeal David's conviction then the Cottle episode would probably be his main platform, decided to discredit and frighten Cottle as much as possible. Should he ever be required by the defence in the future he might either be too intimidated to co-operate with them, or at least if he did, a big fat file to be used for cross-examination purposes, throwing his character into contention and raising the spectre of Detective Inglis' affidavit claiming Cottle to be psychotic, would be available to the police.

What other reason could there be? Cottle cannot think of one and neither can I.

For my part, and after having exhaustive meetings with all concerned in this affair, I have great sympathy for Cottle and in general terms believe him. This is not to suggest that he is a persecuted angel, far from it. But if there is a 'set a thief to catch a thief' mentality in our law enforcement authorities, then we might as well let the Mafia take over. Cottle was very frank with me throughout our meetings, and although I noticed a tendency for him to react with spontaneous outbursts, he is far from psychotic in my view. Unfortunately, as far as it has to do with the issues related to the Bain affair, I doubt that justice will ever be done for Dean Cottle either.

So as July 1995 began, David Bain was serving the first of his minimum term of sixteen years in Paparua Prison in Christchurch. Mike Guest was busy preparing a submission to appeal David's convictions in the New Zealand Court of Appeal, Dean Cottle was according to him the subject of police harassment, and the police were presumably getting on with their job safe in the knowledge that justice had been served.

Appeals

Mike Guest did get the Bain case to the New Zealand Appeal Court in December 1995, and he did primarily base the appeal on the fact that Cottle's evidence should have been heard by the jury. I do not propose to go into the legal arguments surrounding hearsay, reliability and the like, partly because I am not qualified to do so, and partly because the logic and law used in the process of decision-making by the judges was a matter for them. Suffice it to say that although it was, according to Michael Guest, a pretty close call, the Appeal Court refused David's appeal for a retrial. One interesting point to come out of the appeal, however, was the following statement made by the Crown in submissions to the Appeal Court judges. In part it said, 'Had the jury heard Dean Cottle's evidence it may well have tipped the scales.'

This makes it all the more easy to see why what had previously happened to Cottle did in fact happen.

David spent his second Christmas in prison, by now extremely depressed, disillusioned and at times suicidal.

There was no more legal recourse for him except the Privy Council in London. He had no family support whatsoever, and the few friends who had stuck by him were predominantly students, without the financial resources for such an undertaking. He was an extremely disturbed young man that Christmas of 1995, questioning everything that had been the foundation of his life, his Christian upbringing and faith in human beings.

How could my father murder his family, my family? How could my remaining extended family leave me so desolately in the lurch? Why me, why didn't he kill me too, to spare me this ordeal? Did I go mad and do it and deserve to be here? Oh Mother, Mother, please console me; where are you? The police, they were so nice to me when it first happened. Why can't they see I'm telling them the truth? And God, the God I've been brought up to believe in, are you really there?

What do I have left?

What's the use of going on?

Oh, God, please help me, I'm going insane.

MOMENT OF TRUTH

Although Christmas 1995 brought David an overwhelming sense of loss, loneliness and despair, resulting in desperate and regular near suicidal depression, the New Year of 1996 threw him the lifeline he so desperately needed.

It did not come in the form of any officialdom, authority or legal avenues of hope, but in the form of his friends. The epic saga of the ordeal of David Bain should never be recalled without acknowledging the friends who have stood by him. They have displayed all of the virtues that really good people have, that a friend in need deserves. Selflessness in a most difficult time. Courage in the face of officialdom and establishment ignorance. Perseverance when all seemed lost. Loyalty despite the odds. And above all, perhaps that most telling of all motivators in human endeavour, faith. Not for one moment did Kathleen Dawson or her husband John, Heather Hall, Lindsay Robertson, Catherine Spencer, Patti Styles and Rebecca Greet, who made up the group of people closest to David at the time, doubt his innocence.

Kathleen Dawson was David's singing teacher and has been a local identity in music circles all her life. She did not personally know Robin Bain, but many of her friends and associates in the music and opera world did. She did know Margaret quite well, though, and opines very definitely that despite various off-beat spiritual beliefs Margaret had her life quite well in control.

John Dawson is a now retired lecturer in German, and although he did not get to know David well, he did see David regularly when he came for music lessons.

Heather Hall had known David for about eighteen months through Opera Alive. She says that she was no more than 'just friendly' with David during that time. However, following his arrest she began to visit him and has done so ever since.

The others were friends or associates of David's who were certain that a mistake had been made when he was arrested. Rebecca Greet, only fourteen at the time, was a close friend of Stephen Bain, and through him had got to know David quite well. She has never wavered in her conviction that David is innocent.

This committed group of people met with Michael Guest in Dunedin one Sunday morning in January 1996 and decided that somehow they wanted David's case to be taken to the last port of call, the Privy Council in London. As I write, it is one year ago exactly that I read the *Herald* account of their intentions to 'start a fund raising campaign for David'. Since my involvement the group loosely known as 'the friends of David Bain' has expanded to include others who feel the same way. But this hard-core bunch still meet every month, for although they have not actually been able to physically or legally do very much, their support in spirit and resolve is undaunted. How lucky David is to have these people now, and how much he will appreciate them when his ordeal is over.

Having become officially involved as part of the 'defence team', I was spending a lot of time reading and studying the file that Guest had supplied to me, which included the trial transcripts, the Appeal Court documents, 2500-odd pages of discovery documents from the police, the depositions statements, and much of the defence file itself. Not being a lawyer, and never having been involved in a criminal case, this was new and intriguing stuff for me.

Part of my agreement with Guest was that I should remain anonymous until I decided otherwise. When I first committed myself to this cause, it was entirely out of compassion for David's plight and circumstances. Coming face to face with a guy convicted of having brutally slain his entire family was an intimidating experience for me at first. I made extensive notes following my first and second meetings with David on 25 and 26 January 1996. At the same time I met Mike Guest for the first time too and extensively recorded my impressions and notes of the matters discussed.

In relation to Mike, I wrote at the time: 'Had little to ask me, wanted to talk about himself. Told me he was insolvent about the time of the '87 sharemarket crash. Had been a district court judge in Southland but had to resign as a result. Had been very confident doing deals, living the high life, etc. Did a deal with TV3 following his appointment as Bain's solicitor to do a programme on "the defence", for $7,500. Used this money to take his wife and kids to Fiji for holiday, which cost about $12,000, "but what the hell, I'm earning good money again as a Barrister now". He elaborated somewhat on his personal life also.'

I concluded my notes writing, 'Who is on trial here? Talks a helluva lot. Self assertive, positive, listens well too. Very talkative, very "sales like" in his approach to me.'

I actually made fifteen pages of notes recording my first two meetings with David, and will not cover it all, but I think it is salient here for me to record some of my first impressions.

Guest and I were taken by prison staff to meet David, in what I recorded as a 'messy room', at 6 p.m. on 25 January

1996. We sat down on some old chairs about two metres apart. I noted: 'Good handshake, looked me in the eyes, quite a forthright guy (did not expect that). Guest seemed reluctant to leave us alone. I insisted – said he would give us 10–15 minutes. This turned into about 1 1/2 hours! with myself and the country's most notorious multiple murderer all alone.'

I go on to record:

> I liked him. I like things he likes e.g. cooking – reading – he's a good thinker and not afraid to express bold views.
> Impression – nice guy; intelligent; speaks with resonant voice; good looking in his own way; tall, gangly, about 6'3"; he impressed me.

I noted that 'we really covered his life!'

When I asked him what he felt about the police he said, 'Nothing really, I suppose they were just doing their job. Except for one (I can't remember his name) who tried to hit me hard. He offered $10,000 to my cellmate after I was arrested to try to get a confession out of me.'

On his arrest and trial I recorded him as saying, 'I wasn't too worried because I am innocent and thought that justice would be done.'

On prison life, he said, 'It's really tough. There's no one here I can relate to in a meaningful way.' But he acknowledged it has been good for him in one way, though: it has taught him to stand up for himself and be more assertive.

On Michael Guest: 'I get on with him well – well, I've had to, my life is in his hands. The only time I got angry with him was when he first told me he was bringing all the evidence about the incest and prostitution and that he needed to bring it out in the trial. I didn't want that about my family made public.'

On the prison wardens: 'I told them when I first got here

that I could co-operate if they were fair with me – I didn't resent them, they have a job to do and we've got on well since then.'

David talked to me about his life in Papua New Guinea, his music, how his father wanted him to be a vet and so his first year at university was wasted as he hated those subjects and failed them all. How he'd run the Dunedin marathon last year 'but only did 3 hours 30 minutes which wasn't too good'. How he had been really depressed and suicidal since the appeal had been turned down, but had decided, 'Life's what you make it, so I'm trying to make the best of things while I'm in here,' so he started studying again, and worked in the prison kitchen long hours every day to keep himself busy.

He told me how it was his dad who encouraged him to buy the rifle and who also taught him how to use it. 'Dad had always had rifles and loved the outdoors, shooting, hunting and tramping.'

About the argument he could hear after going to bed the night before the killings, he was adamant that 'it was pretty heated because Dad never raised his voice, but he did that night'. He couldn't actually hear what it was about, but could hear the angry voices.

Likes a range of music, from Beethoven and Mozart to Gilbert and Sullivan and modern bands. Reads most nights from about 8 till 11, mostly fiction thrillers as an escape form.

Smokes: 'Yeah I do now, we all do here!'

Later that same night I recorded, 'David Bain, a murderer – No way.'

In short, those were my recorded impressions of 'the person' David Bain, and 'the person' Michael Guest.

The day following that first meeting, Guest drafted our tri-lateral agreement. He signed for his part, and made arrangements for David and myself to sign. My notes made that day in the Ansett Golden Wing lounge at 2.30 p.m. record:

9.30 a.m.	Finalised arranged for my involvement with M.G. and D.B.
10.30 a.m.	Await typed agreement to be faxed through from M.G.'s office. Drop Mike at the airport.
12.00	Meet D.B. at Paparua.

David told me he was just 'overwhelmed' by my involvement and Mike was pleased to know that he could now fire into the Privy Council matter safe in the knowledge that the funding was in place.

My second meeting with David was much more open and trusting. We actually discussed details of the case, and his own recollections and opinions. I explained to him that it seemed to me that the whole affair was riddled with controversy and, if nothing else, I hoped that my involvement would lead to a discovery of the truth, and justice for him.

In trying to explain to me his recollections of what he did and saw that terrible morning, David used a useful analogy. He described it as being like waking up the morning after a party when you've over-indulged with alcohol and not remembering much. As the day goes by, and perhaps your memory is prompted by talking to others, it all starts coming back to you. Except that for him, it has not come back properly, only flashes here and there, like still photos with no links between them.

He has, according to his account to me that day, perfect recollection up to finding and realising his mother was dead. He has virtually no recall of the rest of that morning. I find that quite understandable, but the police claimed it to be 'a convenient lack of memory'.

The date for the application seeking special leave to appeal before the Privy Council was set for 29 April. In the intervening weeks I read and studied the huge file of papers, statements, opinions and records provided to me by Guest's office.

The actual origin of the Privy Council jurisdiction dates back to the time of the Norman Conquest, and the premise that: 'The King is the fountain of all justice throughout his Dominions, and exercises jurisdiction in his council, which acts in an advisory capacity to the Crown.'

It is interesting to note some points contained in an explanatory document prepared by the Registrar of The Privy Council, particularly in relation to 'Leave to appeal', which was what Guest was applying for:

> An appeal is not admitted unless either leave to appeal has been granted by the court appealed from, or, in the absence of such leave, special leave to appeal has been granted by the board.'
>
> It is unusual for the court appealed from to have power to grant leave in criminal cases and the Judicial committee will not grant special leave in such cases unless the petition raises questions of great and general importance or there has been some grave violation of the principles of natural justice. [My emphasis.]

Guest and his wife Barbara flew to London separately from me, but we met and had dinner together the night before the hearing. Guest appeared pretty pleased with his work on the appeal, and had a fairly confident outlook. His brother Steven (a law lecturer living in London who had assisted Guest in preparing the appeal documents) and another friend of Guest's attended the hearing at the Privy Council chambers in Downing Street, London with us.

The police had sent a Crown prosecutor, Mr Pike, and an assistant to present their side of the case, and we all gathered in a waiting room outside the courtroom itself. It was a sunny and quite warm London day, but the nervous tension generated waiting our turn, distracted our thoughts from the weather in no uncertain terms.

Being escorted in there was a humbling feeling. On the one hand was the feeling of pomp and splendour, of excitement and expectation, awe and wonder at being involved in something so filled with history and protocol, and on the other hand the sobering knowledge that the events of the following hour would likely determine the outcome of young David's life.

Both sides had made written submissions to the Lords which they had studied over the previous days, and so the three esteemed and learned gentlemen were now ready for us, about 2 p.m. on 29 April 1996.

Michael Guest as the applicant was first to present his case. He was required to articulate David's plea to the Lords, who sat stony faced, listening intently. Occasionally one of them would interject for clarification on a point. Guest spoke very well, as I would have expected. He explained that there was absolutely no categorical proof that David had pulled the trigger even once on that fateful day. It was only circumstantial evidence upon which he had been tried, and each piece of the evidence was simply explained by David's account of events as to his being the 'finder of the scene', rather than the perpetrator. Further to that, in all of their enquiries, Guest pointed out, the police had not come up with even a sliver of evidence as to any possible motive for David. And yet, here, in Cottle's evidence, suppressed by the judge, was an unexplored but obvious answer to an overwhelming compelling motive for David's father. He pointed out that the same Mr Pike standing beside him on behalf of the Crown, had said in the New Zealand Appeal Court that had the jury heard Cottle's evidence, 'it may well have tipped the scales.' His plea was based on the contention that a miscarriage of justice occurred because the jury was prevented from hearing the evidence of Dean Cottle.

After Guest had spoken for 25 minutes or so, it was the Crown's turn. It was interesting to witness the contrasting style and approach. Pike, in a far more tradesmanlike and slightly condescending tone, totally ignored any explanation to the Lords in regard to the matter of Cottle, and concentrated (as the police have continued to do since) on what they refer to as 'the overwhelming mountain of evidence against David'.

He told the Lords that David's bloody palm print was found on the washing machine (which is not true). He told them that David's bloody fingerprints were on the rifle. (He failed to add that they were in a 'pick-up' position, and not in a place where a person would hold the rifle to fire it.) He told them it was David's rifle and David's ammunition, but failed to add that twenty spent cartridge shells fired by David's rifle were found in the father's caravan. David's bloody gloves were found in Stephen's bedroom where a frightful struggle had taken place, he went on to say. He failed to say that there was no evidence that David had been the wearer of those gloves. And so it went on.

After asking a few questions of the two protagonists the Lords retired. After maybe fifteen minutes, we were called back into the courtroom, where their decision was announced. They do not issue a judgement, nor do they give any explanation of the reasons for their decision. And so their judgement was passed: 'Special leave to appeal is refused.' The key to any legal redress for David Bain is finally thrown away.

Television New Zealand news were waiting outside in Downing Street, and I gave my first interview since becoming involved in January. Now the country was made aware of the identity of the 'Auckland businessman' who had funded the appeal. I was not mentally prepared to address the camera at that moment and stuttered my way through a few comments. I would have much preferred to regather myself overnight, and make a more in-depth statement the following day.

That evening I rang Christchurch prison to let David know of the result before any press releases came out. He was naturally very disappointed but as always took the news fairly stoically.

Guest and his wife took the opportunity while in Europe to take an extended holiday, and so I arrived back in New Zealand well before they did. I had a decision to make now, and it was a far-reaching one with serious personal ramifications. In a nutshell I had to decide whether or not I would continue to fight for David's release, or fade away and put the whole episode down to experience. The next few weeks was a time of careful deliberation and soul-searching, an even closer analysis of the evidence against David and, as a consequence of having become known publicly as David's sponsor, a continuous need to handle the media speculation as to my involvement, which seemed to focus more on my motives than on David's plight.

POST PRIVY COUNCIL

It was now well into the cold depths of winter in New Zealand, particularly in Dunedin and Christchurch. I decided that I needed to have another meeting with David himself and also with his supporters in Dunedin as, now that the legal avenues were exhausted and my concerns were being publicly aired, they too felt the need to be a part of the process.

So on 1 June I made yet another trip to the South Island and met with David in prison at Christchurch; our first meeting since the Privy Council appeal was turned down. In notes made the day after that meeting, I recorded my impressions of our meeting in the following words:

> David Bain – convicted of five murders. What really happened that day, and why? Bain has had a trial, an appeal to the New Zealand Appeal Court and an appeal to the Privy Council, each of which has been unsuccessful. Is it possible that the justice system has failed him so miserably! Throughout the entire proceedings he has consistently and steadfastly maintained his innocence, and furthermore, his account of events

has remained consistent even under the most extreme of conditions (i.e. with two different forensic psychiatrists, with his defence lawyer, friends, under oath in the trial and to me personally), despite the severest of grillings.

David was disappointed and upset at the result of the Privy Council appeal. He was nervous and unsettled, unsure what to do next. His friends wanted to continue the battle but did not know where to start. Others wanted to write a book. Various media were chasing him for his story.

I told him that I believed in his innocence and was prepared to continue the battle, but on certain conditions, the predominant one being that his cause needed to be promoted with a united front, a single spokesperson and a single-minded goal – being to obtain his pardon and release.

I offered to undertake this role with his agreement and co-operation. I told him that the only course of events that would cause me to drop the case would be if I were to find out that he was deliberately misleading me or lying to me, by either omission or commission. We got down to a very emotional 'from the heart' discussion about the whole affair. In fact later David described our meeting of that day as the single most valuable discussion he had had with anyone since that fateful day of 20 June 1994. I told him that I considered he needed to face up to the events of that day, as difficult as it might be. I told him it was my belief that when his father set out on this rampage of death he intended initially to kill David as well, and that I could easily understand his loss of memory bearing in mind the horror he was confronted with that morning. I advised that we should set up some sessions with the psychiatrist to assist him in dealing with the psychological effects that the events of that day had had on him. He began to cry, to sob desolately, and explained that the thought of reliving that day was so terrifying that he did not want to think about it.

'I have blocked what I saw that day from my mind. I try to remember my family as they were in happier times. I wasn't allowed to go to the funerals. I have never been able to grieve. It will be so painful to go over it all again,' he sobbed.

I too was now pretty emotional. I explained that sooner or later, for his own peace of mind, he would need to face up to the reality of it all. He understood and, despite his fear, agreed to 'give it a go'.

I told him that although on the one hand I saw myself as friend and benefactor, almost a foster father figure, now that I would also be 'in charge of the case', so to speak, we would need to address the case itself dispassionately and clinically, and despite the difficulty for him, I needed his help. He understood. This was a long and emotional discussion, bullet pointed here for directness.

- We now had an emotionally charged scene. We are living his life together. We are examining the very fabric of his existence and fate. His entire credibility is at issue. This is no longer court room theatrics, diplomatic manoeuvring, what should be said, when it should be said.
- We are at the coalface of human existence. His very sanity relies upon what I am going to do for him, how I view him. His entire personage, if you like, is on the line.
- We then canvassed again his memories of that day.

It was so critical for me to analyse that meeting, to be objective in my conclusions, to put aside my feelings, because I was well aware that my next step, if there was to be one, would take me into uncharted waters. I believed then, as I still do, that of all the people who gave evidence in the trial that led to his conviction he is one who 'told the whole truth and nothing but the truth'. And so, believing this, I made my decision, that I would see this through for David, for justice, for truth and for myself, because it would have haunted me for the rest of my days had I walked away at that point.

I had a fresh agreement drawn up establishing the 'professional' relationship between myself and David. David had not heard from Michael Guest since the Privy Council, and in any event there really was not much more Guest could do. In fact David wrote to me on June 12th to give me the name of the person in charge of the prison psychological services, and mentioned in that letter that he hadn't heard from Guest. In essence, our agreement confirmed David's wish to have me act on his behalf with all decisions entirely at my discretion. He afforded me his full power of attorney, including the right to appoint legal counsel to work on the case at my discretion. We also agreed that, in his best interests, he would not talk to any media without first agreeing with me what, if anything, he would say. As I said to him at the time, as much as anything else what he had said or not said to the police and others in the days following the tragic events had led to his downfall, and we should learn from that.

Now David and I had an intimate and recorded understanding of where we stood with each other; I resolved to a 100% application to the fight for justice on his behalf and he committed himself to absolute co-operation with me whatever that may entail.

It was over the next few months that the action really began, and it was in many ways precipitated by a meeting I had a few days later, in Dunedin. Having made the decision to take up the cudgel, so to speak, I took a few quiet days to ponder my course of action. I decided that before any major publicity, which with the media interest in what I was doing seemed inevitable, I should make myself known to the authorities and attempt to clarify my concerns in a conciliatory way.

I was in Dunedin with the intention of meeting with some of the key people, including Dean Cottle and other associates of the Bain family, but felt a little uneasy at breaking this ground. So I rang the Dunedin police headquarters and asked to speak with the regional commander. As it happened he was out of the country at the time, but his deputy, Mr Athol Soper, took my call and agreed to see me the same day.

We had a very cordial meeting and I laid my cards on the table. I told him that my involvement was due solely to a belief that the jury had not had all of the information laid before it, that there appeared to me to be some serious anomalies resulting from my study of the police file, and that my only aim was to satisfy myself that justice had really been achieved. I requested certain information and also the opportunity of an informal meeting with senior staff involved in the enquiry to give them the opportunity of satisfying my concerns. In general conversation regarding the case Mr Soper said to me, 'I can understand your concerns because when David was charged it caused considerable polarisation within the staff here.' I could not get him to elaborate, but the implication was very clear. Bear in mind, too, that Soper himself was one of the senior police staff to have visited the house early that first morning while David was still lying on the floor in his bedroom.

That same afternoon I also phoned pathologist Alec Dempster and, despite some considerable reluctance on his part, managed to get a meeting with him in his office at Dunedin Hospital. This was a very revealing meeting. Dempster, like Soper, was extremely personable at first. I expressed some of my concerns regarding his findings and sought explanations from him. He had the court exhibit photograph file sitting prominently on his shelves, and so we were quickly able to get directly to the point. It became very clear, very quickly that Mr Dempster was defensive and unsettled by my questions.

'How do you feel about being kept waiting on the street for so long?' I asked him. Reluctantly he answered that it was 'unfortunate' and he didn't have any explanation for it.

'Did you consider measuring Robin's arm length at the time of the autopsy?'

'No, it's not something we do, but if I ever get another situation involving possible suicide and a rifle I certainly will be sure to,' he said.

'Isn't it obvious that the father's head has been moved?'

'Yes, well it does look a bit like that, we did have some theory on it but I don't recall exactly what it was.'

The meeting was about fifteen minutes old by this time, and Dempster's body language clearly indicated a degree of discomfort. I could see that little progress was likely, so in the interests of courtesy and civility I made a pleasant exit.

The very day after these meetings a message was conveyed to Michael Guest from the Dunedin police, informing him that 'the police intend destroying all of the evidence' relating to the Bain case. Clearly, coming the day after my visits to the Dunedin police and Alec Dempster, I considered this unlikely to be coincidental. Michael Guest responded immediately by fax to the Dunedin central police station, protesting vehemently, and reminding them that 'there have been previous cases which have caused public concern about the destruction of police "evidence".'

In my naivety, I was horrified. For the first time, the realisation struck me that justice is not what we think it is, but rather a game of win or lose. My competitive instinct was aroused, one might say. In addition to that, it was sheeted home to me in an alarming manner that the system, the bureaucracy, the establishment can effectively do this sort of thing without individuals fearing personal reprisal. I had just met with two extremely personable and no doubt sincere gentlemen and yet 'the Police' as a body had an entirely different reaction. The battle was on.

I telephoned the Ombudsman's office, to get advice on what avenues were open to David, and received an extreme-

1. The author.

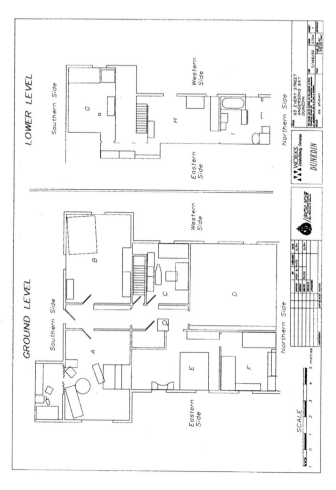

2. Plan of the house.

A: Front lounge.
B: David's bedroom.
C: Study where Laniet was sleeping.
D: Main living room.

E: Margaret's bedroom.
F: Stephen's bedroom.
G: Arawa's bedroom.
H: Kitchen.
I: Bathroom/laundry.

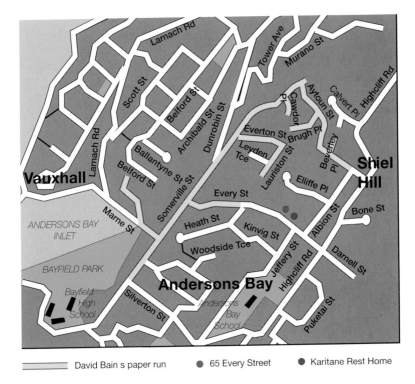

David Bain s paper run	● 65 Every Street ● Karitane Rest Home

3. Street plan showing David's paper run.

4. The back door at 65 Every Street. Note the plastic sheeting in the entrance way.

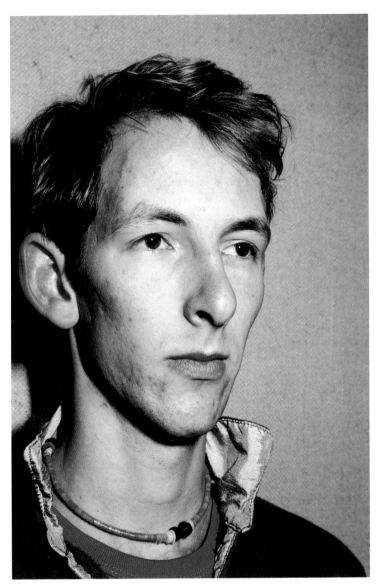

5. David Bain. The small bruise above his right eye was alleged to be the result of the struggle with Stephen.

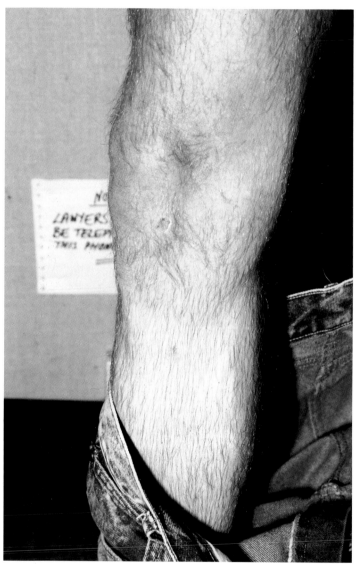

6. This small scrape on David's knee was also allegedly the result of the struggle with Stephen.

7. David's bedroom. The glasses frame and one lens are visible on the chair at lower right. David's walkman is on the bed, and the new shoes he wore to do his paper run are on the floor. David was lying on the floor at the foot of the bed when the police made entry.

8. David's bedroom. The trigger lock, with the key in it, and several bullets are in front of the wardrobe.

ly prompt response. That same afternoon I drafted a letter (authorised by my power of attorney for David) under the provisions of the Official Information Act and the Privacy Act, demanding access to anything and everything held by the police in relation to David's conviction. I faxed a copy of this letter to the Commissioner of Police in Wellington, the Regional Commander of Police in Dunedin and the Minister of Justice. I received an acknowledgement from the Minister's office in the form of a short note from his senior private secretary, and the Ombudsman's office was also very co-operative. On 8 July I received a lengthy response from Mr Soper of the Dunedin police, quoting various sections of various acts sustaining the police attitude that 'the police are justified in declining to take this matter further'.

Momentum was gathering rapidly by now. I had discovered through my analysis of photos, police documents and trial testimony the strong possibility of what appeared to me to be incorrect evidence given to the court by the police.

I felt a real need for fresh, enthusiastic legal assistance. I contacted renowned Auckland QC Peter Williams, and we had two or three meetings during which he listened to my concerns. He didn't really have the time to devote to the case that I felt was required, though, and so he remained on board in an advisory role, but never actually got into the file itself in any depth.

I had faith that so long as I persisted things would fall into place, and an unexpected development in the form of a call from Trish Carter, producer of 'Holmes', set this in motion. I was still very tentative in my dealings with the media at that time, and so I had quite a few informal preliminary discussions with Trish to establish what it was we were setting out to achieve. Unbeknown to me, 'Holmes' had made an application through its solicitors to the Appeal Court to have the suppression order on Cottle's evidence overturned. Hence they had a double interest in the whole affair, hoping to secure the first major publicity on my involvement, but also to access Cottle himself in the event that their appeal was successful. I had already established quite a reasonable liaison with Cottle and his father, and so there was a mutual benefit in the 'Holmes' people working together with me.

After a lot of work and many meetings, 'Holmes' reporter Jacqui Maher conducted an in-depth interview with me, and I appeared live with Paul Holmes on 11 July. This was the first attempt that I had made to explain publicly why I was involved and to proclaim my belief in David's innocence. Generally speaking, the response was excellent and I received many unsolicited calls and letters of support from all over the country. Many of the media, however, were suspicious about my motives, and understandably so – I had no legal background and no previous connection with the Bain family.

The first real breakthrough in the case came a few weeks later when five judges of the Appeal Court upheld the appeal, lodged by Holmes, to have Cottle's evidence released for the first time. At last the public had an opportunity to absorb the information so long suppressed, which provided a reasonable explanation for what had taken place at Every Street more than two years earlier. For David it was distressing to have the family's dirty washing aired in public, but at the same time it forced him to face up to and come to grips with the pressures that existed within the family at that time and which had led to its demise.

A further interesting development was that at the same time as all of this was taking place, *Mindhunter*, a new book written by high profile ex-FBI 'criminal profile' expert John Douglas, was hitting the bookshelves of New Zealand, and Douglas himself was here to promote the book. I was able to make contact with him, and in fact part of our discussion was recorded by '60 Minutes' for a profile they were doing on Douglas, bringing the issues I was dealing with even further into public scrutiny. As a result of this never-ending turmoil of publicity, quite a number of people were volunteering information to me, some of which was vital to the cause.

The desperate need for new legal counsel could no longer be ignored. Through contacts in Dunedin, I had Mr Colin Withnall QC, prominent and respected barrister of Dunedin, recommended to me. I first made contact with Colin Withnall on a Sunday in Dunedin, when he came to visit me in my room at the Southern Cross Hotel. As a result of the arrangements made at that meeting, the following day I notified Michael Guest that I was formally appointing new legal counsel for David. He was initially very co-operative. Stephen O'Driscoll arranged to meet me at Colin's behest, and Stephen was formally appointed as David's lawyer. Stephen, Michael Guest and myself met to ensure that there should be no misunderstanding, and that same afternoon Stephen instructed Colin Withnall to carry out the task of completing a review of the case against David Bain. (A barrister has to have instructions from a solicitor to act; a member of the public cannot directly engage a barrister. Hence the need for O'Driscoll's appointment.)

That night, in a further 'Holmes' programme on the Bain affair, I had Paul Holmes announce the new appointments. This was a deliberate and calculated decision on my part, because although I could easily imagine that Michael Guest would be aggrieved at such a public announcement, I wanted to ensure that the people of New Zealand knew David's circumstances were being treated very seriously. This also provided a clear guide as to who anyone with information to volunteer on the case should approach. The *Otago Daily Times* carried a front page story the following morning, with a photo showing Stephen O'Driscoll and myself studying a file document.

Guest was upset at the boldness of the way I had replaced him as David's lawyer, but I make no apologies. In fact, it was to assist in bringing an immediate response. After responding publicly by casting some aspersions on my motivation, and asserting that he was still David's lawyer, Guest retracted in a letter to myself and O'Driscoll, and offered his ongoing assistance which he has, I am pleased to say, provided.

Amidst a furore of publicity, of claim and counter-claim between the police and myself and my team, the scene was now set. The stand-off would continue over the ensuing months, fuelled even further by a documentary done by the '20/20' team on TV3. The producer of this programme was Mike Turner, a Dunedin TV3 news reporter, and it was presented by Melanie Reid. We worked together over nearly three months to produce this hour-long documentary. Just before this programme screened, TV3 also screened the two-hour 'Inside New Zealand' programme on defence lawyer Mike Guest, focusing on the Bain case. The *Otago Daily Times* had stories running almost daily, and many of these were carried by other newspapers throughout the country. The week before the parliamentary elections on 12 October 1996, my revelation that David could not have been home when the computer was turned on (obviously whoever turned it on was the murderer) and that the police knew, or should have known this, was the lead item on the TV3 prime time evening news.

In the months leading to the close of 1996, the David Bain story was taking a very prominent place in New Zealand's media.

NEEDLE IN A HAYSTACK

It is well established in this case that no reasonable motive has ever been proposed for David Bain to have planned and executed this crime, and I have explained that the Crown does not need to prove motive in order to sustain a homicide conviction.

Perhaps the same set of rules should apply to the series of mishaps, mistakes and misdeeds that my examination of the investigation and prosecution of David Bain has revealed.

Perhaps the motive was just 'that justice is a game, to be won or lost'.

Perhaps there are more sinister connotations, or perhaps a set of freakish circumstances conspired entirely by coincidence, leaving David as the unfortunate victim.

Whatever the reason, I have resisted the temptation to examine why things went so wrong, and restricted my analysis to what actually went wrong. I am about to unveil the facts surrounding some of the perplexing matters that have become evident from my analysis.

It is necessary to remember when considering this case exactly what the allegation against David was. This was not, and by its very nature could not have been, a crime of passion committed indiscriminately on the spur of the moment. He had to fully intend doing what he did, and then do it, as the judge said, with a considerable degree of stealth, cunning, planning and deception, not to mention a single-minded and ruthless perseverance.

In committing the crime, according to the Crown, David had to intersperse the paper round between the fourth and fifth deaths; he had to leave four dead people – and not just any people, his mum, two sisters and brother – in their bedrooms while he trotted about the neighbourhood with his dog delivering papers; he had to have planned to set up his own father as the murderer; he had to fake a distressed 111 call on the telephone; he had to feign shock, distress, fitting and convulsing to the ambulance and police staff; and then, when subjected to the most intense scrutiny, hold himself together and hang on to his story.

This then is the supposed coolness and brutality of the man convicted.

There is one piece of evidence brought against David which I believe to be absolutely vital to the whole Crown case. I am referring to the left glasses lens alleged to have been located by the police under the toe of an ice skate boot in Stephen's bedroom. The frame and other lens, also dislodged from the frame, were allegedly on a chair in David's bedroom at the time the police arrived at the scene. The ultimate allegation was that in the fight which allegedly took place between Stephen and David, David's spectacles were dislodged, and this left lens fell out and finished up under the ice skate boot. The police had, then, they argued, a direct link to David in the act of committing one of the murders.

The story of this lens is worthy of a book in itself. The pair of spectacles was the subject of one of the four questions raised by the jury after five hours of deliberation. Two of the others were simply clarifications and the fourth also, like this one, addressed a most serious matter raised during the trial, and will be the subject of the following chapter. It is clear that the jury too considered the matter of the glasses lens to be a serious issue. In fact I believe that it was the primary evidential matter upon which they determined David's guilt.

In order to examine this matter, it is necessary to go back to the beginning. On the Thursday evening before the murders, David had tripped and fallen when leaving the premises of his music teacher, Kathleen Dawson. His glasses were damaged in the fall, and so on Friday he dropped them in to optometrists Stewart and Caithness of George Street, Dunedin for repair. David is short sighted, but is able to do most things without his glasses.

There are a number of statements on the police file confirming that over the weekend David was not wearing glasses. One is dated October 11th, and is a statement made by Helen Saunders, David's girlfriend at the time, who was with David on the Friday night and the Sunday immediately prior to the murders; on each occasion, she states, 'he did not have any glasses as his were broken'. Another is a statement made on 28 June by Wallace Chapman, a well-known local music identity who was the musical director for a Shakespearian production that David was involved in at the time. On the Friday evening prior to the murders, Chapman had set up a recording session with David and some other singers. He also states that David had broken his glasses. The third is made by a Nigel Jenkins, and it was made on 25 June – as with the other two statements, *after* David's arrest. Jenkins' full statement is:

> On Friday night at 9 p.m., David Bain came around to my address with his friends, I don't know their names.
>
> He was to sing with Wallace Chapman; I have a small recording studio and they were going to record their singing.
>
> He seemed to be in a really good mood that night, he

was quite outgoing.

I have a recording of the singing they did. Four of us went for a cup of coffee after.

There was myself, David, Wallace and the fourth I don't know.

We talked generally about music, local performances and different styles.

We went to The Grazory in Moray Place. The person I don't know dropped me and Wallace off at home and left.

He did mention that he had broken his glasses and didn't have them, and that made it quite a strain.

He did try on the guy who was driving the car's glasses, but they were no good.

He did say he didn't have a spare pair.

So on the police file I have located three independent statements, in addition to the Dawsons confirming that David broke his glasses at their house on the previous Thursday, verifying that David was not wearing glasses over the weekend and also that he said he did not have a spare pair, which seems to make sense as, if he did, surely he would have been wearing them!

On the Monday morning of 20 June, the police made entry to the Bain house as a result of David's call for help at about 7.30 a.m. Constable Van Turnhout was directed to stay with David and commenced that duty just after 8 a.m. At about 9.30 a.m., while David was still lying semi-comatose on the floor of his bedroom, Van Turnhout records that David opened his eyes and tried to sit up. He said, 'I want my glasses. I can't see.'

Van Turnhout goes on to record: 'Beside me and to my right as I faced David was a chair. Sitting on that chair which was at the entrance to the room was a pair of glasses. They appeared broken and *there were no lenses in them*. There was also a small brown glass case sitting beside the glasses. There were other objects on the chair. The frame of the glasses appeared to be a metal frame *and there were no lenses in them.*' (My emphasis.)

Photo 7 shows the chair with the frame and one lens tucked in between the arms. I believe that had there been only one lens with the frames on the chair then Van Turnhout would have recorded exactly that – seeing spectacles with one lens is like looking at a clock with no hands.

Remember Van Turnhout is the constable who asked Inspector Robinson at 9.00 as to the whereabouts of the gun powder residue kit. His notebook recording the events that took place during the two hours and twenty minutes that he was with David in David's bedroom is detailed to the point of having little drawings and making exact counts of various items. I believe, meticulous as Van Turnhout was, that had he seen only one lens with the frames, he would have recorded that. The inference to be drawn from his statement as it is worded is that he saw either no lens, or two, both being dislocated from the frame. In the scene shown in photo 7, it would have been impossible for him to see the frame but not the lens so we can only rely on what he wrote at this time. Remember that the photo was not taken until sometime later that day, after the period during which Weir had sole access to the house.

Exhibit 176 produced in the trial was a right lens and Exhibit 175 was a metal-rimmed frame. These, according to the police, were seized as exhibits from the chair in David's bedroom on the third day of the enquiry, 22 June, at 11.55 a.m. On the following day, David's own repaired glasses were collected from the optometrists by his uncle.

From the Monday afternoon through until David's arrest the police investigation centred on a microscopic examination of Stephen's bedroom, primarily because Stephen had clearly been involved in a struggle with his assailant to some degree or another. They obviously expected that the assailant might well have lost some personal items or sustained telling injury during the struggle, which would lead to his identification.

Detective Sergeant Weir, as the officer in charge of the scene, was responsible for directing and monitoring the scene examination and the resultant careful collection of exhibits. As previously stated, it would be normal and proper procedure for the officer in charge of the scene to restrict himself to directing proceedings, particularly in such a large-scale murder scene as this one. Weir, though, so clearly believed that Stephen's bedroom definitely held the key to solving the crime that he personally carried out much of the detailed examination of the room. Notwithstanding his personal efforts, he also detailed two detectives to be responsible for the scene examination of Stephen's room, as he did for each of the other rooms. Weir states in his evidence: 'After I had made the various orders for the total scene examination, on the Monday afternoon, I continued then to maintain an overall supervisory role of the entire scene, but I carried out a detailed examination of Scene F (Stephen's bedroom)'. This was at 3 p.m. on the first day of the enquiry. From a close examination of Weir's log book I have established that Weir spent about two hours that very afternoon, and a considerable time on each of the next three days, in Stephen's bedroom sifting through the labyrinth of junk, clothing and bedding.

In each of the scenes the police used little black arrow stickers to identify the blood stains and splatters. As can be seen in photo 12, these arrows are all over Stephen's room, and were the result of a very systematic process of examination and a great deal of care. This process was going on all day through Monday afternoon, Tuesday, Wednesday and Thursday. In addition to the inspector's minute examination, the police photographer using both a zoom lens video camera and a normal camera photographed over and over the scene as the examination was in process. Although only a hundred or so photos were produced to the court as exhibits, over two thousand were taken at the scene, and although only a twelve-minute edited version was seen by the jury, a total video footage of three to four hours was taken. My point is that by Thursday evening, the police in the form of Weir himself, other detectives and the photographer, had conducted a microscopic examination of Stephen's room for three and a half days.

By Wednesday 22 June, the police were pretty much leaning away from their initial appraisal of the situation as being a murder/suicide. They had David's fingerprints on the gun, some footprints in the bedroom and hallway they considered to be his, and by this time had also found David's blood-stained gloves in Stephen's bedroom.

The laborious search continued. On the evening of Thursday 23 June, Detective Sergeant Weir went back to Stephen's room again. At 8.46 that evening, Weir himself discovered the left lens from a pair of spectacles under the toe of an ice skate boot about 45 centimetres (18 inches) from where Stephen's body had been lying.

At this stage Weir was recording his efforts by dictaphone rather than in his notebook, and the discovery is recorded as follows:

Side of the bunk – seized as an exhibit is a black ice skate. There is a very small amount of blood on the front metal blade of the ice skate. This is the right foot, seized and labelled as SF 579.

2046 hours Underneath the ice skating boot is a lens from a pair of optical glasses. Appears to be the left lens and could possibly correspond with a missing lens from a set of glasses recovered from David's room. Seized and secured as exhibit SF 580.

David was arrested and charged the following morning.

From the Monday morning until his arrest on Friday 24 June, David had been interrogated regularly and had provided four written statements. The police were aware that he wore glasses but was without them at that time. The statements were exhaustive, some taken over a period of four to five hours. At no time in any of those statements was David ever questioned about the whereabouts of his own glasses or about the broken glasses on the chair in his bedroom. Bearing in mind the intensity of this enquiry and the obvious anomaly of a spectacles frame 'with no lenses in them' and apparently only one lens sitting beside them on a chair in his own room, surely the fate of those glasses and the location of the 'missing' lens would have been paramount in the minds of those conducting this 'copybook' enquiry. David was questioned and willingly answered questions on every aspect of his movements, and on any and every matter that needed clarification about his family, their habits, their clothes and whereabouts. How can it be that he was not questioned about the broken glasses found on the chair in his room where he was lying when the police arrived?

During the final interrogation before his arrest, when David realised he was about to be charged and requested a solicitor, the police put some questions in writing to him. By that time Guest had arrived and advised David to refuse to answer any further questions. One of those questions was a request to David to explain how it was that a lens from the broken glasses in his room was found in Stephen's bedroom. This is the one and only time that the police attempted to seek an explanation from David about the broken spectacles.

I first became suspicious about the lens found in Stephen's bedroom when studying the file and realising that it was Weir himself who found the lens and that the discovery was made at 8.46 in the evening, on the fourth day of the investigation, in a location inches from the body in clear view to

the naked eye. I decided to look further into the circumstances surrounding the issue of the glasses and the lens
because it did not seem possible to me that this lens could
have been where it was and not been noticed over the preceding *four days*.

I went to the trial documents to read Weir's evidence in
relation to the lens, and my curiosity was even further
aroused. I looked at the photos submitted as evidence and
referred to by Weir in his testimony and became ever more
suspicious. It was at about this time that Colin Withnall QC
became involved, for the purpose of conducting a review of
the file, and it was wonderful for me to at last have someone
else to bounce my ideas off. Colin's experience, meticulous
methodology and expertise have been invaluable to me. He
was intrigued by my concerns in regard to the glasses lens,
and so as a team we set out to get to the bottom of things.

It is necessary to refer to photos 60, 61, 62 and 99 from the
exhibit photos in the trial, portions of which are reproduced
in the second picture section. Photos 60 and 61 showed
Stephen's body in its death situation. The area just behind
Stephen's lower rear is a racquet, and to the rear of that can
be seen the black ice skate boot. The toe of the boot is at the
lower end of the photo almost butting up to a grey squarish
carry case. To the fore of the area where the ice skate boot
and the bag meet is an orange-coloured poster which if
viewed from the angle of the bottom right of the photo in
photo 60 can be seen to show a person's face.

In Weir's trial testimony in regards to the finding of the
lens he says: 'While examining this floor area I came across a
particular item – near an ice skate which is just visible in
photo 97 it is here (indicates where) the middle left hand of
the photo, I located what appeared to be a lens from a pair of
glasses. Looking at photo 62 it is a blown up, *what is meant
to be a blown up portion of photo 61,* you can just make out the
edge of the spectacle lens just in front of the ice skating boot.

When I say in front, that is the top of the boot as you look at it in the photo on the left hand side of the boot. [Witness leaves jury box and points out the lens to the judge and jury.] The photo 62 was taken on Monday as Stephen's body is still there and the lens is on the underneath side of the skate. *On the Thursday, the lens as seen in photo 62 that is the position I found it in when I found it on Thursday.*' (My emphasis.)

Guest was able to ascertain from Weir that the lens was only partially under the ice skate boot, that he discovered the lens at 8.46 pm on the Thursday night, and Weir agreed with him that prior to the struggle the ice skate boot would have been in the position it is seen in.

Following cross-examination, the judge intervened and the following discussion took place.

Judge: 'Could you put your pen on where that lens is again?'

Weir: 'Right here, your Honour. I actually spoke to the police photographer this morning. I believe one of the photo books may have a better quality photo of the remainder. It is there. I was looking in the wrong place.' As if a 'better quality photo' would have been ignored on such a vital piece of evidence.

When Colin Withnall and I examined the court exhibit photos, which are photo prints adhered to a piece of white paper and then slipped into a plastic sleeve, Colin removed the paper so that he could scan the photos on his computer. It turned out that the photo 62, which Weir says 'is meant to be a blown-up . . . of photo 61', was in fact a photocopy of a digital enlargement, and not a print. It is the only picture in the book of evidential photographs that is not a print.

The next point that became obvious is that photo 61 did not in fact contain the area in question in photo 62. Photo 61 stops on the left side just before the end of the skate, whereas photo 62 includes the skate and the suitcase. On further comparison, photo 60, which does contain the area in question, did not indicate any of the reflections that photo 62 (the so-called enlargement of photo 61) did, which it was alleged depicted the lens.

Photograph 12 illustrates the work done by the police in placing little black arrows everywhere that they detected blood staining. It is evident from this photo that these arrows are in the area within inches of where the lens was found by detective Sergeant Weir at 8.46 on the Thursday evening. Now to police photo number 99, referred to earlier, which is a photo taken after the larger items around the lens have been removed, showing the lens itself in isolated splendour.

Colin and myself were extremely perplexed by this entire matter. David for his part maintained in his evidence that he had not had anything to do with this pair of spectacles, and had no idea whatsoever as to how they came to be in his room as they allegedly were on that Monday morning. Furthermore, he stated, they were his mother's old glasses, and although one of the lenses was a help to his sight, the other was of a totally unsuitable strength because his mother had astigmatism in one eye, and so the glasses were of no use to him anyway. This is supported in my view by the fact that he had not used any spectacles from the time his were damaged on the preceding Thursday evening. Moreover, it seemed a ridiculous proposition that David would go about his daily life for three days without spectacles and then seek out his mother's glasses to commit these shootings at point blank range in the dark. It seemed even more ludicrous, when considering the police theory that David was the killer, that the spectacles were dislodged in the struggle with Stephen, that somehow with minimal damage to the frame both lenses were dislocated from the frame, and then David took the frame and one lens and placed them neatly on a chair in his own bedroom, leaving the other lens where it was.

Adding even more controversy to the entire matter is that neither the frame nor either lens had any evidence of having been associated with the bloody struggle or being handled.

There was no blood, hair, strand of cloth, fingerprint or anything similar to support the police theory that they were broken in the struggle with Stephen or handled by David.

To recapitulate at this point:

1. David's spectacles were broken and in the optometrist's for repair at the time of the murders.

2. David did not wear glasses for the three days prior to the discovery of the murders.

3. At 9.30 a.m. David asked Constable Van Turnhout, who was minding him in his bedroom, for his glasses.

4. Van Turnhout recorded that a pair of metal-framed spectacles were on the chair in David's room 'with no lenses in them'.

5. On Monday afternoon and throughout Tuesday, Wednesday and Thursday a detailed and thorough examination of Stephen Bain's bedroom was conducted, including marking every spot of blood, zoom lens photography and video recorded photography, overseen and participated in by the officer in charge of the scene, Senior Detective Weir.

6. At 8.46 p.m. on the Thursday evening, Weir himself discovered a lens from the said pair of spectacles in David's room, in a position only inches from where Stephen's body was found; a position which had been in full view of the camera and the naked eye for the past three and a half days of the examination.

7. During the period leading up to David's arrest the police asked no questions of David to establish any information regarding the status of the broken spectacles found in his room.

8. There is no forensic evidence to link the lens or frames to the 'bloody struggle' purported to have taken place, or to David having worn or handled them.

9. The one photo purported by Weir to depict the lens,

photo 62, is referred to by him in his testimony as being 'A blown-up, what is meant to be a blown-up . . . of photo 61'.

10. The area purporting to depict the lens in photo 62 is not even in photo 61.

11. Photo 62 is the only evidential photo in the exhibits which is not a print.

12. Weir in his evidence when asked by the judge to point the lens out again (presumably because he could not recognise it the first time) points it out and then says 'It is here, I was looking in the wrong place.'

13. The police enquiry team made no effort whatsoever during the four days prior to David's arrest to acquire any information about the broken spectacles found in David's bedroom.

The significance of the final point, it seems to me, is that during the time in question the place was swarming with experts including ESR scientists, police armourers and fingerprint analysts. The rifle, the washing machine, blood stains from everywhere were being lifted for testing: every conceivable object was under scrutiny. And yet at 9.30 a.m., less than two hours into the enquiry, we have a suspect who is without his glasses, a broken pair of glasses with only one lens beside them on the chair in his room, another lens in full view in the most conscientiously scrutinised area of the house and nothing whatsoever was said or done during the period prior to his arrest to ascertain the facts. The inescapable question is simply, 'Why not?'

After discovering the left lens in Stephen's bedroom and arresting David, the police then began to research the origin of and other matters related to the various pairs of spectacles – Margaret Bain's, which were found in her bedroom, David's which were in for repair, and the broken pair found on the chair. This could have, and in my opinion should have, been done immediately on the Monday. Adding to my contention that David was prematurely arrested, imagine the difference in the police positioning had they already known on the Friday morning that these glasses were previously David's mother's and of no use to him, and that he had not been wearing glasses for the previous three days.

The Crown called five optometrists as witnesses, attesting to the history of the various spectacles worn by David, his father and his mother. One gave actual evidence as an expert; the other four had their evidence read to the jury by agreement between the defence and the Crown. This evidence in itself, all collected after David's arrest, amounted to little, except that it left the jury with the impression that the broken spectacles might well have been David's old glasses, and not his mother's as he claimed; the jury had to choose whether to believe David or the Crown.

The actual question the jury came back to the judge with after five hours of deliberation was: 'The glasses found in David's/Stephen's room. Whose were they according to the optometrist?', and the judge read the following excerpt from the optometrist's testimony:

> The prescription of the two lenses that fit this frame is similar to the prescription supplied to the accused in October 1992. It is similar but not identical; it is consistent with being an earlier prescription. When I first saw these lenses that is what I concluded.

The judge then, in balance, read David's testimony about the glasses which in short denied that he knew anything about the glasses, how they got broken or were found where they were, and claimed them to be his mother's old spectacles.

As a disclaimer to the optometrist's conclusion above, based on my own research, I should point out that David's lens prescription in 1992 was for clear lenses to be put into his existing Martin Wells glasses, whereas the broken glasses were an older frame, Saxon Brand, with tinted lenses and his mother had always worn glasses with tinted lenses. The actual prescription details are as follows:

Broken Spectacles:
Rt Lens: Exhibit 176:   -2.25/-1.00 x 85
Left Lens: Exhibit 172:   -3.40/.5 x 180

David's Glasses:
Rt Lens: -3.00/-.25 x 110
Left Lens: -2.75/-0.50 x 50

My own research supports David's contention that he would not have been able to see out of one of these lenses at all, and the other would have provided only partly improved vision. Further to this, in the deposition statement made by the optometrist witness, he said the prescription details of the lens found in Stephen's room, i.e. Exhibit 172 above, were: -3.00/.50 x 180, whereas in the trial he described it as -3.50 dioptres plus 0.5 at axis 90 to correct astigmatism.

So now, added to the list previously stated, we have the clear confusion created in the jurors' minds as to the possible ownership of the broken glasses, with their only real way of answering being to decide on David's credibility as contrasted to that of the evidence called by the Crown.

As well as the contrasting relative strengths of the lenses in the two spectacles, it seems odd that David (if the broken glasses were an old pair of his), would change from tinted to clear lenses in his new glasses.

Had the defence bothered to have an independent expert analyse the photo evidence and lenses and prescriptions, and put forward the contrasting point of view to support what David said in his evidence, I believe that this whole matter would have been satisfactorily accounted for in David's favour. I make that statement based on independent advice I have received from an optometrist and the file notes on the various glasses prescriptions. As with all other highly contentious expert opinion proffered by the prosecution in David's trial, none was brought in balance by the defence, but that is another story.

The two matters that concern me now are that the lens, exhibit 172, found in Stephen's bedroom, is the subject of extremely dubious evidence; and the suggestion that these were David's old glasses or that he was wearing them is just that, no more than a suggestion – another cog in the wheel of circumstantial evidence against David with nothing whatsoever to support it. The fact is that David did not wear them anywhere he went on the Friday, Saturday or Sunday, and this fact, despite being attested to by the statements in the police file of Saunders, Jenkins and Wallace that I quoted earlier, *was never heard by the jury*. Had they heard those statements, I am sure that they would have concluded, as I have, that if David did not wear any glasses on those three days it seems likely that he did not wear any on that fateful Monday morning.

In contrast to establishing the origin of the broken spectacles, which I am powerless now to do, on the point of the photographs evidencing the finding of exhibit 172 in Stephen's room I could do something.

I took the relevant photographs (numbers 60, 61, 62 and 99), along with the police video, to the photographic section at the Auckland University Audio Visual Centre for analysis. Their report makes the following points:

1. The area indicated by Weir in his testimony does not present to them a spectacle lens.
2. From the position the lens is shown in as being found in photo 99, it is not where it is described as being by Weir

as pointed out in photo 62. See photograph 14 in the second picture section.

3. The area pointed to by Weir in photo 62 (between the toe of the skate boot and the small suitcase) contains some crumpled white paper and a perforated piece of plastic. Reflections that may be construed as a lens in that area are in fact accounted for by the shadows and reflections caused by the paper and the plastic, and that is all that is to be seen.

Conclusions:

1. The lens is not where Weir said under oath that it was.
2. The appearance in photo 62 of what is meant to be a lens according to Weir is in fact a specular effect created by the paper and plastic.

This report, coupled with the lack of evidence to support the theory that the frames and lenses were dislodged in the struggle, or that they were even handled or worn by David, throws grave doubt on the authenticity of this evidence.

I believe, without any shadow of a doubt, that had the jury been privy to the facts as laid out in this chapter, they would have dismissed the evidence of the glasses, the key piece of evidence that placed David in the midst of the struggle. Further, the credibility of the Crown testimony would have been so severely damaged, that their case, based on supposition and proposition as it was, would have been dismissed. The jury, in the process of making their decision on the judge's instructions that 'If you are left with any doubt as to the guilt of the accused, you must find him innocent', would in fact likely have done just that on this issue alone.

THE PHANTOM MURDERER

At 12.05 p.m. on Monday 20 June, almost exactly five hours after David had called 111, the police enquiry really got under way. All that had actually been done up to that point was to have David removed from the scene (10.19 a.m.) and taken to the CIB for medical examination and questioning, and to have plastic sheeting laid on the floor to protect it from foot traffic contamination, at 11.40 a.m.

During that afternoon, two facts, in fact the only two certainties about the events of that morning, emerged: that David had undertaken his daily paper delivery run that morning, and that there was a message typed on the family computer in an alcove near the father's body which had undoubtably been written by the murderer. The message read: 'Sorry, you are the only one who deserved to stay.'

It was plainly either Robin Bain's suicide message, written to David, or a cunning ploy by the actual murderer, attempting to advance the appearance that the father was in fact the murderer who then turned the rifle upon himself. Clearly, then, if the writer of the message could be ascertained, it was very likely that the police would have their man.

Subsequent investigations led me to the view that this part

of the enquiry was handled in a dreadfully sloppy manner by the police, as was the issue of the spectacles, and they then used the fudged and inaccurate results arrived at to their advantage in the trial.

In essence it came down to this. The police were able to ascertain the time that the computer was turned on, and there was also some very specific testimony regarding the time David finished his paper run. Obviously, for the police to sustain a case against David, they needed to have him at home when the computer was turned on, otherwise he might well have become known as the 'Phantom Murderer'.

It is not only the sequence of events in regard to this all-important timing evidence, but also the attention to detail in compiling the facts and the manner in which they were manipulated that are the key issues.

First let me track what actually happened. Milton Weir discovered the message on the computer at about noon on the first day of the enquiry. That afternoon was very hectic, with various body inspections, photographic work, and arranging to have the bodies removed to the Dunedin morgue. Weir's log book records at 5.45 p.m. that day: 'Last Victim removed from premises'. Below that, as a footnote to the afternoon's work, is a further note: 'Obtain services of computer expert regarding obtaining time etc. input Philips P3105 disc drive.'

The task of following up on the computer analysis was assigned to Detective Kevin Anderson, and he arranged for Martin Cox, a computer adviser from Otago University, to carry out the process of attempting to ascertain the time that the computer was turned on.

There is no need to go into detail here as to what Mr Cox did to arrive at his conclusions, but his statement ends: 'In conclusion we can say that the word processor was started 31 hours and 32 minutes before we saved the message, and that time was recorded by the constable (Anderson). So by subtracting that time from the time the message was saved we can establish the time that the word processor was started.'

This statement was taken by the Dunedin police at 10.20 a.m. on Wednesday 22 June, the day following his appraisal. In a job sheet from later on the same day, the police concluded the following:

1. Message saved by Martin Cox at 1416 hours on 21 June 1994. This time recorded by Detective Anderson.
2. Cox estimated the computer was turned on at 65 Every Street 31 hours 32 minutes prior.
3. This calculates out to 0644 hours on June 20 1994.
4. Message therefore put on computer anytime after 0644 and before the time it was discovered by Detective Sergeant Weir on June 20th.

In other words the conclusion arrived at was that the computer was 'turned on' at 6.44 a.m. on the Monday morning of the murders but because the message had not been saved, the actual time that the message was typed in could not be determined. The critical factor however, was that whoever turned the computer on certainly wrote the message as well.

Another method one might suspect would have assisted in determining who wrote the message would be to fingerprint the computer, particularly the keys and various switches that would by necessity have been used to access the necessary file and type the message. The first record I can find of this being attempted was on Saturday 25 June – the day following David's arrest, and more importantly, some days after the computer had been used by Martin Cox to ascertain the time it was turned on. Presumably it would have been impossible for Cox to do what he did without touching much of what could have been tested for prints, thereby eliminating what may have been vital evidence.

The police lifted one print from the computer from beside

the on/off switch. It did not match the prints of any member of the Bain family, according to the fingerprint expert. This information was not in the hands of investigators until after David's arrest. To this day it is not known who this print belongs to. Tongue in cheek, I have wondered if it might be Martin Cox's print?

Furthermore, clearly, the keys used to type in the message must have been pressed by the writer. Although I understand an attempt was made to get prints from the keys themselves I wonder whether the best technology was sought. My understanding is that highly specialised methods not available in New Zealand could have gone much further to get this answer.

The obvious question, once the police had drawn the conclusion that the computer was switched on at 6.44 a.m., was: where was David at 6.44 a.m.?

According to his own statements, he delivered the final paper on Every Street about 350 metres down the hill from his home at about 6.40 a.m. *according to his watch*. This is a very steep hill and, with a tired dog and having just done an extensive newspaper round, he says he then walked casually up the hill.

David's paper round covers quite some distance. He delivered 135 papers each morning, and it is in an area of steep hilly terrain. Every Street itself is a very steep incline and David's round finishes at 26 Every Street, which is just before the intersection of Heath Street and Every Street.

Depending upon the effort put in, and bearing in mind that he had a fattish unfit dog with him, that he had been delivering papers for nearly an hour and that the climb from Heath Street to home was very steep, the time taken to travel the 300 or so metres from that point to home could be anything from three minutes to six minutes, or even more.

Independent testimony was at hand, though; almost next door to the Bain residence is the Karitane Rest Home, and many of the staff there commence their daily shift at 6.45 a.m., a striking coincidence bearing in mind that the computer was supposed to have been activated at 6.44.

The police conducted extensive enquiries at the rest home from about lunch time on the first day of the enquiry. There is a list of many people spoken to on that day, most of whom knew nothing of the Bain family and had nothing to report as to the events of that morning.

Another instance of the inconclusive nature of the police work can be found on the job sheet recording these interviews. A Tania Pratt stated that she started work at 6.45, came to work with Linda Burck in her *white* car, and came along *Highcliff* Road to work.

Linda Burck, on the other hand, said that she also began work at 6.45. That she drove *up* Every Street to work (that is, the opposite direction from Highcliff). Then she said she drove a *red* Nissan Sport. These two statements were given on the same day, the first at 12.45 and the second at 1.25 p.m. One wonders whether the investigators even read them, as there is nothing on the file to suggest that the clear contradictions here, about the colour of the car and the direction from which they came, were ever clarified.

However, one person was found that day who did have some vital information. Her name was Tania Lesley Clark, and her first statement was taken at 1 p.m. on 20 June, the day of the murders. She stated that day:

> I used to live at the bottom of the street [Every]. I have been working here for six years. I didn't know the family but saw them coming and going on a number of occasions.
>
> This morning I drove to work. I drive a Mitsubishi Tredia, coloured white.
>
> I *arrived at work at 6.45*. On my way to work I saw a male Caucasian, aged about 50 years, medium build,

light coloured clothing, average height. I've never seen this man before, he looked like he was carrying a torch or something in his hand. I also saw the paper boy, he had a dog with him. The older man was walking across from Every to Sommerville. I got the feeling he was walking down towards Bayfield.

The paper boy was crossing the mouth of Heath Street heading up Every Street.

The following day Jim Doyle, second in command of 'Operation Every', issued the following directive:

Would you please arrange for T.L. *Clark* to be seen and full details obtained from her regarding the following:
Male Caucasian aged 50 years
Attempt should be made to identify and have this person interviewed.
The exact time the paper boy was seen.
Description of clothing worn by the paper boy.
Description of paper boy.

Constable Van Turnhout interviewed Tania Clark the following day, at 2 p.m. The interview is recorded as follows:

NZ POLICE
JOB SHEET
OFFENCE: OPERATION EVERY
DATE/TIME
21.06.94
1400 hrs
Karitane Rest Home, Every Street (454 2281)

Tania CLARK
[...]
OCC Nurse Aid/Care Giver

Q   What time exactly did you arrive at work yesterday, 20 June 1994?

A   Definitely 6.40. I made myself a cup of tea. We don't start until 6.45.

Q   Where exactly did you see the paper boy?

A   Crossing Heath Street, coming this way. He had a cream and tan dog. Average sized dog.

Q   What was he wearing?

A   I think it was a hooded sweatshirt.

Q   Do you know the colour?

A   Black I think or dark navy.

Q   Long sleeved?

A   Yes definitely.

Q   You saw another person also. Where was he when you saw him?

A   He was at the bottom of Every Street walking over to Somerville Street.

Q   So he would have passed the paper boy if he had walked down the hill.

A   They were on the same side. If he had walked down from the top he would have passed him.

Q   Did you know Mr Bain by sight?

A   No not him I don't think, no.

Q   Could the elderly man have been Mr Bain?

A   I don't know, that was at 6.40.

Q   Can you describe him?

A   A cream tan jersey, a torch or something in his hand. In his 50s, average height, medium build.

Q   Did you notice if the paper boy wore glasses or not?

A   I only saw the back of him. I didn't see his face.

Q   Did he appear as he always does. Was there

anything unusual?

A   No.

Q   Is that the place you would normally see him?

A   Yes, usually around that area, yes.

Q   So he wasn't late or early?

A   No, he's usually around that area as I come up the hill.

Sourced 10094

Name: T E VAN TURNHOUT Checked by

Rank: Constable

Reg No: 8041   Rank:

Date: 23 June 1994   Date:

My comments are these:

- This woman had been working at the Karitane Rest Home for six years, driving up Every Street nearly every day.
- In her first interview of the previous day, she stated categorically that she arrived at work at 6.45 a.m., whereas in this second statement she changed this to categorically being 6.40.
- In all other regards her second statement is identical to the first statement.
- There is no record whatsoever on the police file of the police attempting in any way to find and interview the 50-year-old male Caucasian seen at the bottom of Every Street by Tania Clark.
- David, according to Clark, was doing his paper run in exactly the normal way he did it as she had seen him over the prior six years.

Only one other person from the Karitane Rest Home was able to furnish the police with relevant information. Her name is Denise May Laney.

As will be noticed from her statement, she too was working at the Karitane Rest Home on Monday 20 June 1994, she too started work at 6.45 a.m., and she too had been working there for six years. Although Laney was working on Monday 20 June, and the shift goes from 6.45 a.m. to 3.15 p.m., there is no record of her having been seen by the police that day when they called at the rest home and recorded statements from seemingly all of the staff there.

The only record of Laney being seen by the police is when the following statement was taken, on Monday 27 June at 1.52 p.m., a full week later, and three days after David had been arrested. Laney's full statement given that day is:

> 1.52 p.m.
> Karitane Rest Home
> 27.6.94
> DENISE MAY LANEY STATES
> That is my full name. I am an enrolled nurse at Karitane Rest Home, Every Street, Dunedin. [. . .] I have been working at the rest home for about six years.
>
> I am speaking to Constable Low regarding the homicide enquiry at 65 Every Street, Dunedin.
>
> On Monday 20 June 1994 I was working at the rest home and I was supposed to start work at 6.45 am but I was a bit late. [My emphasis.]
>
> As I drove to work I came up Every Street from Somerville Street, Dunedin.
>
> I drove past 65 Every Street, Dunedin. As I did so I noticed a person going past the partially opened gate at 65 Every Street, Dunedin.
>
> As I saw this person I thought I must be running late as I normally see him down by Heath Street, Dunedin.
>
> I looked at the clock in my car and it read 6.50 am. I know the clock is 4 to 5 minutes fast as it was about

6.45 am as I drove past him.

think he had a lighter coloured top on and the bottom was darker. I couldn't see if he had shorts or trousers on as he was nearly in the gate.

I didn't see the dog with him.

I have seen him before and he has had his dog with him. I can't remember what he normally wears.

I've read this statement; it is true and correct.

D M LANEY

Statement taken and signature witnessed by:

S L LOW

Constable D625

2.10 pm

Clock read 2.16 pm on car

S. LOW watch 2.11 pm

My comments are:

1. She had six years' experience of driving up Every Street to come to work so is likely to be familiar with her surroundings.
2. She is very explicit about being late for work.
3. She is very explicit about seeing David entering his front gate.
4. She is very explicit in stating: 'I looked at my car clock and it read 6.50.' but that it was 4 to 5 minutes fast; therefore the time was about 6.45 or possibly even 6.46.

When it came time for the trial a year later, Tania Clark's evidence and that of Denise Laney was submitted to the court in the following statements sworn for the depositions hearing, by consent and agreement of the defence and prosecution. That is, neither person was called to give evidence, their statements being accepted by both sides.

Also on the file, though, is a full statement taken from

Clark, on Tuesday 22 June, when the police were working on the premise that the computer had been switched on at 6.44.

The full depositions statements of Clark and Laney as read to the court in the trial of David Bain are:

IN THE MATTER of the Summary Proceedings Act 1957 Sections 160A and 173A
TANIA LESLEY CLARK STATES
My full name is Tania Lesley CLARK.

I am a caregiver at the Karitane Home and Hospital.

I live in Dunedin.

On Monday the 20th of June I was working a morning shift.

The standard hours for a morning shift is 6.45 am to 3.15 pm.

My alarm clock is set for 5.50 am.

On 20 June 1994, I lay in bed for about 5 minutes and got up at 5.55 am.

By the time I had showered and had breakfast I guess I would have left home at 6.25 am.

It would have been no later than that because I was concerned about icy roads.

It normally takes me 15 minutes to drive to work or a little longer when it is icy such as on this morning.

I drive to work by myself in my Mitsubishi Tredia coloured white, registration number MC9120.

I am fairly certain that I arrived at work at 6.40 am. I was the first one here and I had time to have a cup of coffee.

As I cornered at the intersection from Somerville Street up onto Every Street I noticed a man crossing from Every Street onto Somerville Street.

He was about 50 years old, Caucasian, no hat, grey hair, he was about 5 ft 8 inch–5 ft 11 inch.

Further up Every Street at the intersection with

Heath Street I saw the paper boy.

He was crossing the mouth of Heath Street walking up Every Street.

I normally see the paperboy. He has always got the dog with him, as he did on this occasion.

PHO (WITNESS TO REFER TO AERIAL PHOTO)

He was dressed in a black or navy blue sweatshirt with a hood.

The hood was on.

The garment was quite short down to the waist; it could have been a jacket or a sweatshirt; it had long arms.

It was not a Parka/oilskin type.

He had dark coloured long trousers.

I'm not sure what footwear he was wearing.

I'm not certain if he had a newspaper bag on.

If he did it would have been worn on the right shoulder.

I did not see his face.

He was walking and had his dog with him.

The dog is a medium sized fat dog of mixed breed.

I think it was tan and cream; it was walking beside him.

I was travelling between 30–40 kmph when I passed him.

I used to live at 12 Every Street 6 weeks ago prior to moving to Fairfield.

I used to walk up Every Street to work and know of the place where the shootings took place.

I did not know the residents at the address but had seen them on a number of occasions.

I would not know if the old man I saw at the bottom of Every Street was Mr Bain as I did not know him.

The times I had seen people at 65 Every Street were while I was walking to work.

I had seen the mother Mrs Bain a couple of times in the garden and some younger people at the address whom I do not know.

This statement is true to the best of my knowledge and belief. It has been made by me knowing that it may be admitted as evidence at a preliminary hearing and that I could be prosecuted for making a statement known by me to be false and intended by me to mislead.

IN THE MATTER of the Summary Proceedings Act 1957 Sections 160A and 173A
DENISE MAY LANEY STATES
That is my full name.

I am an enrolled nurse at Karitane Rest Home, Every Street, Dunedin.

I live in Dunedin.

I have been working at the rest home for about six years.

On Monday 20 June 1994 I was working at the rest home and I was supposed to start work at 6.45 a.m. but I was a bit late.

As I drove to work I came up Every Street from Sommerville Street, Dunedin.

I drove past 65 Every Street, Dunedin.

As I did so I noticed a person going past the partially opened gate at 65 Every Street, Dunedin.
As I saw this person I thought I must be running late as I normally see him down by Heath Street, Dunedin.

I looked at the clock in my car and it read 6.50 am.

I know the clock is 4 to 5 minutes fast as it was about 6.45 am as I drove past him.

I think he had a lighter coloured top on and the bottom was darker.

I couldn't see if he had shorts or trousers on as he was nearly in the gate.

I didn't see the dog with him.

I have seen him before and he has had his dog with him.

I can't remember what he normally wears.

This statement is true to the best of my knowledge and belief. It has been made by me knowing that it may be admitted as evidence at a preliminary hearing and that I could be prosecuted for making a statement known by me to be false and intended by me to mislead.

My comments are:

1. Clearly the statement of Denise Laney, if correct, means that David could not have been the person who switched on the computer if he was outside the house at 6.45 when the computer was turned on at 6.44.

2. It seems more than curious that Clark was seen on the Monday, Tuesday and Wednesday, yet despite the fact that Laney was also at work, certainly on the Monday, there is no record of her being spoken to by the police until the following Monday.

3. Clark's original statement on the Monday that she got to work at 6.45 has been altered in her subsequent statements to 6.40, but is prefaced by the words 'fairly certain' in her final statement.

4. In the first statement taken from Laney, Detective Low compared Laney's car clock with her own watch and confirmed, according to her watch, that Laney's car clock was indeed five minutes fast, but only as it related to the time on Low's watch.

5. It is noticeable that Clark's final depositions statement is a considerable elaboration on her earlier statements, whereas Laney's is word for word identical with the statement she first gave to Low on Monday 27 June.

6. Clark's description of David's attire was incorrect on two

counts. He did not have a hood on, and he was wearing shorts, not long trousers.

In the light of all of this I have to ask myself, and have done so many times, the following question:

'If the Crown prosecutor had known *prior* to David being arrested, that there was a clear, explicit undisputed statement contradicting the theory that David had turned on the computer and written the message, what would his advice to the police have been?'

But this is not even the entire story – it gets considerably murkier yet.

It will be recalled that the time of 6.44 a.m. as being the time the computer was switched on was calculated by saving the message at a prescribed time as recorded by Detective Anderson and then deducting the time the computer had been running from that time. The actual calculation was:

Computer running time:	7 hrs 32 mins.
plus one day	i.e. 31 hrs 32 mins.
Time when saved according to Detective Anderson:	1416 hrs 21/6/94.
Therefore time computer turned on:	0644 hrs 20/6/94.

Now on 28 June, four days after David's arrest, and seven days since the above conclusion was reached, somebody thought to check Detective Anderson's wrist watch. This despite the fact that at 3 p.m. the previous Tuesday, 21 June, computer expert Martin Cox had sent this message to the Dunedin CIB:

TELEPHONE MESSAGE
TIME: 1510 hrs
DATE: 21.06.94

111 CALL: YES/NO
FROM: Martin COX   PHH 479 8531 PHW
ADDRESS:
MESSAGE:
Message on screen typed 31 hours and 32 minutes
before COX saved that file.
Approx 7.00 am.
Check real time on watch: Detective ANDERSON's.

A B ROBERTS
Detective sergeant 4700
21 June 1994
COMMENTS – REFERRAL/OFFENDER
DETAILS
For Detective Sergeant WEIR.
Associated 10360

Clearly Cox recognised the importance of the accuracy of
Detective Anderson's work.

This check was done by Detective C.J. ROBINSON, and
New Zealand police job sheet recording this exercise is:

NZ POLICE
JOB SHEET
OFFENCE: OPERATION EVERY
DATE/TIME
28.06.94 Time check comparison with Detective Kevin
ANDERSON's wrist watch and Telecom 111 call cen-
tre.
Phoned 111. Telecom logged my call at 1025.
Time recorded on Detective ANDERSON's wrist-
watch 1027 (approximately). Minutes on his watch not
indicated.
Time difference approximately two minutes.
Sourced from 10359

Name:	C J ROBINSON		Checked by
Rank:	Detective		
Reg No:	7172	Rank:	
Date:	29 June 1994	Date:	

Cox had requested this accuracy test of Anderson's watch to be done on 21 June, but it was not recorded as being done until a week later, on 28 June, four days after David's arrest.

I wonder what went through the minds of those responsible for the arrest of David Bain when this information was conveyed to them. If any consideration was given to the thought that they may have made a mistake, it was obviously short lived. By 29 June, after Anderson's watch had been found to be running two minutes fast, the police had evidence that rather than having been turned on at 6.44 a.m. the computer had in fact been started at 6.42 a.m. All of the evidence the police had in their possession at that point, four days after David had been arrested, told them clearly that David *could not have been home to turn the computer on*.

Let me quote from the trial transcript. Remember, Anderson was the detective who recorded the time that the computer was turned off according to his watch as 2.16 p.m., 21 June 1994, and we know that subsequently his watch was shown to be running two minutes fast.

Anderson's evidence in regard to this is:

> Approx 2.10 pm (on Tuesday 21/6) I entered the house with Mr Cox. Mr Cox examined the computer in the alcove. The message was still on the computer screen and the computer was in its original condition from the time we first arrived at the scene. It had not been switched off at all. At approximately 2.16 pm Mr Cox carried out a number of functions and he will tell you about that.

Bearing in mind that the time of 2.16 p.m. was possibly the most critical piece of evidence in the whole trial, to have it prefaced by the word 'approximately' should have been like a bombshell to Mr Guest. The recorded cross-examination of Anderson runs for about two and a half pages in the trial transcript. Those pages do not record even one question from Mr Guest in relation to anything to do with Cox, the computer, or the time.

Cox himself is the only person who gave evidence that the computer was turned on at 6.44 a.m., and I quote from his testimony: 'I had saved the message at sixteen minutes past two on Tuesday 21 June 1994'. Mr Cox was not cross-examined at all.

Readers may well be asking themselves, 'If all of this is true, how did Bain come to be convicted? And what if anything did Guest, Bain's lawyer, do to expose it?' The answers are simple.

The jury did not hear the truth, and as far as Guest is concerned, 'very little' is the short answer. A proper reading of the file would have alerted the defence to the fact that Anderson's watch was two minutes fast and then surely he would have asked a question which would have forced Cox to alter his evidence stating that the computer was turned on at 6.44 a.m.

This clearly misleading evidence given to the jury, if exposed, would have thrown the credibility of the entire Crown case into considerable disrepute, to the extent that I would venture that it alone might well have been enough for them to have dismissed the case against David as a concoction of theories based on incorrect information.

In July of 1996 I had a report undertaken by a former CIB superintendent, addressing the manner in which the police conducted their enquiry from the time of David's 111 call until the time of his arrest. This man's credentials are impeccable: when he retired after 30 years' service in the New

Zealand police, he held the highest ranking position in the New Zealand CIB of Detective Superintendent. He is the holder of a post graduate diploma in Business and Industrial Relations.

He identified ten major deficiencies in the manner in which the enquiry was conducted during the said period, and noted that each of the deficiencies 'had the potential to disadvantage David Bain'.

In relation to the issue of time, he states in his report:

'The non establishment of a 'time base' in this enquiry is a *serious deficiency.*'

Immediately it became apparent that time was a critical issue in this case (on the first day) a calibrated, accurate timepiece should have been set up as the 'time base' against which all other time-related matters would be judged. For example, although Laney's car clock was cross-checked with Low's watch, we do not know whether or not Low's watch was accurate. We do know that Anderson's watch was inaccurate.

In addition, the police should clearly have made enquiries with staff at the rest home as to the *sequence* in which various people arrived at work as an additional check on their information. This could have verified, for example, just how late Laney was that morning, or just how early, if she was early at all, Clark was. There is no record of this being done.

A further indication of the poor performance of the police in the matter of timing is the fact that Anderson's watch, apart from not being checked for accuracy, should never have been used anyway – it does not even (according to Robinson's job sheet of 28 June) indicate the minutes.

As I mentioned in the last chapter, the jury asked four questions of the judge after deliberating for five hours. One related to the ownership of the broken spectacles. One was a request to hear the 111 tape of David's call again. The third was a clarification as to whether any police had closed Mrs Bain's eyes. And the fourth was: 'Could we hear the evidence of Denise Laney again.'

Clearly the jury were troubled by Denise Laney's clear, explicit and logical statement, stating she saw David at his front gate at or after 6.45 when the police were alleging the computer was turned on at 6.44. Obviously, the times were close enough for them to think that maybe one of those times was a minute or so incorrect, and the Crown suggested this in presenting its case.

It seems to me that, had the jury known that the computer was in fact turned on at 6.42, they could not have sustained a guilty verdict.

I am not trained in law, and so I am not qualified to comment on whether or not the people responsible for misleading the jury as to this most critical piece of evidence, *which they knew to be false*, and therefore fudged by the use of the word 'approximately', committed an act of perjury. I do know, as we all do, that when taking the oath, police along with other members of our society, swear 'to tell the *whole* truth and nothing but the truth'.

The people responsible for bringing the evidence about the time of 2.16 (and the deduced time of 6.44 a.m.) before the court knew very well that it was false and, more importantly, critical and misleading. Even from Clark's evidence of seeing David at 6.40, it was impossible for David to have turned the computer on at 6.42 that morning.

I feel great pity for the jurors who sat to pronounce verdict on David Bain. I am sure they were perplexed as to why this perfectly normal young man committed this atrocity. They had to base their judgement on the evidence presented to them, not their feelings or emotions. And the evidence was palpably false and misleading.

As to the defence's failure to pick up this vital point or challenge Anderson's evidence, I can offer no explanation. It seems, though, that if he or his assistants did see the job sheet on the file recording Anderson's watch as being fast, then they failed to understand its significance.

Considerable publicity surrounded my efforts to obtain the computer for Colin Withnall QC in late 1996. We eventually did get access to it in Wellington, and Colin's analysis of the computer and the police records have led him to the conclusion that the computer was switched on between 6.40.07 a.m. and 6.42.05 a.m. on Monday 20 June 1994, during which time it was not possible for David to have been at home.

NOTHING FITS

THE EVIDENCE AGAINST DAVID BAIN

'obfuscate' (Latin ob, intensive, and fuscare, blacken):
to obscure or darken; to perplex or bewilder

Up to this point, I have attempted to acquaint the reader with the overall background leading to David's arrest and conviction. You have read in the prologue an account of the events as the police allege they took place. I have detailed the most significant train of events in the police enquiry over the four days leading ultimately to David's arrest on Friday 24 June. I have recounted in quite some depth the 'modus operandi' of the police in their efforts upon having decided to proceed with a prosecution, including the 'Cottle affair', the broken glasses/lens evidence of Detective Sergeant Milton Weir and handling of timing evidence, all so critical in this case. You have read something of the life of David Bain, the 22-year-old university student, active in Dunedin's flourishing musical and dramatic societies, marathon runner, Outward Bound graduate, caring and loving towards his family and friends and generally a stable and well-liked bloke with quite exceptional singing ability getting along well in his social life. You have heard too of the serious and long-running conflict in the lives of David's parents, and how his sister Laniet turned to prostitution, more than likely as a result of the terrible hold her father had exercised over her since a young age.

You have had a glimpse of Michael Guest, David's defence lawyer cum TV star. You have read quotes from the judge (the whole transcript is Appendix 2), describing the Crown case and the defence case, and you have read his sentencing judgement describing David as having 'killed the other members of his family deliberately, and with a significant degree of *cunning and premeditation*. In the case of Stephen, the trademark fatal and final close range shot to the head was proceeded by *considerable violence, determination and persever-ance*,' he said. (My emphasis.)

In the light of all of this, it is probably perplexing as to just how my view can be so diametrically opposed to the verdict of the jury and the judgement of his honour Justice Williamson.

The answer, I believe, is a matter of perspective. If David is guilty, then the judge's summation is precise and accurate. However, if the jury brought down their guilty verdict because the evidence laid before them was misleading and incomplete, then an entirely different perspective emerges.

Notwithstanding all the criticism I have levelled at the police and the prosecutors of this case, it must be said that grave concerns also arise in regard to the adequacy of David's defence. As I have previously stated, in the months immediately preceding the trial, Guest was looking for David to enter pleas of mental impairment, such as insanity or automatism. It was only at the last minute, figuratively speaking, that any real efforts were made to mount a serious defence on David's behalf.

The Crown called expert witnesses on the following matters:

- A pathologist on the likely means of death, on the possibility of Robin Bain having committed suicide and on
  the possibility of Robin Bain having been involved in the
  murders.
- An ophthalmologist on the issue of the glasses and lens
  so critical in this case.
- Fingerprint expert from the New Zealand police.
- Two scientists from ESR on blood grouping, blood testing and other matters.
- A washing machine repair man, on the state of the Bain
  washing machine, and its operational functions.
- A DNA report from an Australian expert.
- The police armourer, who gave expert opinion on various
  aspects of the rifle and ejection of shells.

No experts to rebut any of this evidence were called by the
defence.

Guest contested under cross-examination part of the testimony of nearly every one of these witnesses, and in some
cases (the police armourer, for example) the evidence was
debunked altogether. As to the defence's own case, apart
from David who gave evidence and was subjected to intense
cross-examination, Guest called only two witnesses. One was
a psychiatrist who essentially said that loss of memory from
severe shock (post traumatic amnesia) can result either from
being involved in an incident or from viewing or coming
across it. It would seem that this was hardly of great benefit
to David. The Crown prosecutors were able to jump on this
as opening the door to their own theories.

Ironically, it seems to me that it is not that Guest didn't
understand what was required; it was mainly that he was
largely unprepared due to a lack of detailed analysis and

inadequate manpower, finance and expertise resources. He, in explanation to me, blamed lack of funding under legal aid provisions, but I do not accept this answer. My understanding is that, with proper planning and preparation, in serious criminal cases the defence is entitled under legal aid funding to call expert for expert, regardless of the expense.

So David was disadvantaged in three serious ways even before the case began:

Firstly, a bungled incompetent police enquiry, the results of which were then utilised to their advantage by the prosecution.

Secondly, an inadequate defence.

And thirdly, a general public atmosphere before the trial even began (created by such things as the house being burnt down and media headlines such as 'Paper boy delivers death to family') that David was indeed guilty.

In effect, twelve good and honest citizens, unaware of the obfuscatory nature of the testimony they were presented, spent fifteen long days listening to a hundred witnesses saying, 'He did it,' and David saying, 'I didn't.'

Before examining in detail the evidence against David that they did hear, let me present David's account of what he did that day.

David told the police that he went to bed on the Sunday evening soon after 8.30 p.m., having watched a video with his mother and father, Stephen and Laniet. Arawa was out babysitting, and did not come home until after he had gone to sleep. He read for a short while, and went to sleep just after nine. Later he recalled hearing loud voices from the lounge, possibly an argument.

His alarm went off at 5.30 a.m. the following morning, as always, and after dozing for ten minutes or so ('that is my normal routine') he dressed in his running gear, put on his walkman, grabbed his yellow *Otago Daily Times* delivery bag and along with his dog Casey set off about 5.45 a.m. to do his paper round. He said that he delivered the last paper just before the intersection of Heath Street and Every Street at 6.40 *according to his watch*. He told them, roughly speaking, that at that point he was 'two or three minutes from home'.

When he came into the house he went straight to his bedroom and, without turning on the light, kicked off his running shoes, hung the paper delivery bag on the door and put his walkman on the bed. He then went downstairs, turning on the light at the top of the stairs, and washed his hands of the printer's ink from the newspapers (which anyone who has delivered papers will relate to). The laundry and bathroom are essentially the same room. He then took off the red sweatshirt that he had worn to do the paper run, put it in the washing machine and sorted out the pile of clothes in the cane laundry basket into 'blacks and whites', put in the laundry powder, and turned on the machine. It came to be an accepted fact that David did the laundry in this house every morning as a matter of course, and had done for some years; this is actually referred to in his mother's diary. He went back to his bedroom and, after reaching behind the door to pull the light cord, noticed his wardrobe door open and a pile of bullets, along with the trigger guard lock, lying on the floor in front of it.

He had noticed upon returning home that a light was on in his mother's bedroom, further down the hallway on the opposite side. He ran to her room, wondering what was going on, and once he got close to her realised she was dead. He says he thought her eyes were open. He says he then ran into the lounge looking for his father, and finding him dead too grabbed the phone in the hall, dialled 111, reported what he had found, crawled into his room and remained there talking on the phone until the police made entry to the house. The Telecom printout shows he was on the phone for 26 minutes.

When the police found him, he was wearing white socks,

black shorts and a tee-shirt, which he says are the clothes, along with the red sweatshirt in the wash, that he wore on his paper run. As we know, he was attended by ambulance staff while lying on the floor of his bedroom, and watched over by Constable Van Turnhout until approximately 10.20 a.m., nearly three hours, before he was taken by ambulance to the Dunedin CIB.

Immediately upon arrival he was attended by the police doctor, Dr Pryde, who after explaining to David that the results could be used in evidence against him and that he could call on legal advice if he wanted to, commenced a medical examination of David. This included taking swabs from his hands, genitals and other relevant areas, and recording his general condition. Pryde noted that David had a slight graze to the inside of his right knee, and a small bruise on his right forehead and below his right eye.

On that Monday afternoon he was then formally questioned for about three hours and signed a written statement.

On Tuesday, he made a further statement, written and signed, and then spoke with the detective again on Tuesday evening.

On Friday, he was brought in by his uncle, Bob Clarke, with whom he had been staying since Monday. After being read his rights for the first time, he began to give another formal statement. Then, when he realised that he was no longer being treated as a witness trying to help the police to 'sort things out', but was about to be charged, David asked for a lawyer.

'Who do you want?' said Detective K.D. Croudis.

'I don't know,' replied David.

'We will provide you a list,' responded the detective.

Then Doyle entered the interrogation room with Bob Clarke, and it was agreed that Michael Guest would be contacted.

It is tempting to record the full transcripts of the statements made by David, as they are very revealing. However they take up some 45 pages, and so a precis of the salient points is more appropriate.

The single most relevant point to emerge from these statements as far as I can determine, *is that David did not make one self-serving statement at any time throughout the entire week.* He could have told the police almost anything he liked, as those who might have been able to contradict him – the other members of the household – were of course dead.

At all times, and this at least is acknowledged by those involved, David was completely co-operative. He sought no legal assistance until it became blatantly clear that he was about to be charged and was clearly being treated in a hostile manner. Even then, this cold-blooded calculating killer did not even know the name of a lawyer, and had to rely upon his uncle, who David thought of as his custodian, but who in fact testified against him in the trial (along with Mrs Clarke, his aunt), to advise that he should call Mike Guest.

So what was it about David's demeanour and his statements that led the police to consider him to be the killer?

The transcript of the twenty seconds that David spent talking to the St Johns Ambulance centre reveals the following:

St Johns: St Johns Ambulance. Can I help you?
Caller: Help, they're all dead.
St Johns: What's the matter?
Caller: They're all dead. I came home and they're all dead.
St Johns: Whereabouts are you?
Caller: Every Street, 65 Every Street. They're all dead.

Then it records his name and phone number, and the St Johns person says they'll be there shortly.

In the space of a few seconds, David repeated four times that his whole family is dead. 'I came home and they're all dead.'

However, when he gave his first statement to the police on Monday afternoon, he maintained that after finding his mother dead, he ran directly to the lounge, found his father dead too and dialled 111. He said that he did not go to any other rooms or see the dead bodies of his brother and sisters.

The police notched up contradiction number one, although I cannot understand how it could be construed as being self-serving.

Under further questioning, bearing in mind that by the time the police questioned David on Tuesday they had begun to gather evidence from the house, it seemed David was telling even more lies.

They had established by the use of luminol (a substance that fluoresces with, amongst many other things, blood, in the dark) that a person wearing stockinged feet had been into Stephen's and Laniet's rooms. The size of the footprints apparently matched David's; and the white socks he had been wearing had a faint amount of blood on the soles.

David was telling the police that he saw only his mother and father, but they could prove he went to other rooms too. Lie number two.

They also had his bloody fingerprints on the gun, which he says he did not touch. Lie number three.

As noted earlier, the rifle had a lock on the trigger so that it could not be used without the key. David told the police in his first interview that the key used to open this was in fact the spare key, which he kept in a pottery container on his dresser. The normal key, along with other keys and a few trinkets, was attached to a string necklace that he normally wore around his neck. He said it was his habit to put this on his bedside table when he went to bed each night and then put it on again each morning. David then told the police that 'as far as I knew, no one else knew of the existence of the spare key'.

The police never mentioned the keys to David again. But

it seems obvious that they thought that the missing necklace (it was not on David or on his bedside table), with the key he would normally use, held the secret to resolving the situation. In a self-congratulatory article in the *Otago Daily Times* following David's conviction, Jim Doyle and Milton Weir gave a run-down of their copybook enquiry which the *Otago Daily Times* printed under the headline banner: 'THE UNDOING OF DAVID BAIN'.

One excerpt from this report quotes Weir as saying:

'We had our ordinary meeting with the investigation team that [Wednesday] night and then quite late the same night Peter Robinson (OCI) called a meeting of the three or four senior officers. It was then we made a conscious decision to look at David Bain as a suspect, not a witness.'

Weir found David's blood-soaked gloves under Stephen's bed that same day and late the following night (Thursday) the spectacle lens was located.

'We were absolutely rapt,' said Weir in the newspaper report. 'But we were also looking for the keys to the rifle trigger lock. I expected to find them in Stephen's room because of the fight. I was disappointed they weren't there, it would have seemed the logical place.'

Perhaps the perspective taken on the issue of these keys, more than anything else, highlights what I call 'The Springbok forward mentality' of the police in this enquiry. By that, I am referring to the fact that David had told the police that the spare key was used to open the trigger lock. He had told them that his necklace was missing. He had told them that he didn't think his father was aware of the existence of the spare key. As it turned out, David's necklace, with the other key on it, was located on the Friday afternoon that David was arrested, in Robin Bain's old van. This prompted David to recall that he must have removed it at the mid-winter swim the previous Sunday and placed it in the van for safekeeping.

David had also stated that he had put the washing machine on immediately upon returning from his paper round, and in doing so had sorted the clothes into 'blacks and whites'. For those unfamiliar with 'doing the washing', clearly this means washing things like tracksuits, sweatshirts, socks and under-clothes separately from more delicate items such as white shirts, ladies' blouses and the like. His statement to this effect was verified in fact by items that were in the wash compared with to those that remained in the basket.

As previously mentioned, the interpretation of David's account of that morning's events, along with the slight con-tradictions in some of his statements, is determined by the perspective one takes. The police jumped quickly to the con-clusion that it was an indication of duplicity and deceit, which caused them to view everything related to David with suspicion.

I would pose the following queries in relation to that analy-sis.

How is it possible to reconcile the calculated deceit of a person capable of the slaughter of his family and the coolness of mind and coldness of heart to intersperse proceedings by doing a paper round and then setting up the scene to 'frame' his father, with the same person just hours later making the following statements:

'No one else knew where the keys to the trigger lock were.' Why didn't he rather say, 'Yes of course Dad and Stephen knew where I kept the spare keys; they used the rifle from time to time too.'

'I came home and did the washing.' Surely, doing the wash-ing after committing bloody crimes is the last thing one would admit to if one was attempting to escape attention. What makes this notion even more preposterous is that he sorted the washing into 'black and white'; he did not wash the shorts, socks and tee-shirt he was wearing, and he told the police himself entirely voluntarily that he put the wash on. Why mention doing the washing at all, or even further why not say, 'I came home and the washing machine was going'?

On the matter of denying having seen his brother and two sisters or having been in their rooms, this too, when viewed with common sense, is simply and easily understood. Imagine please, yourself, at 22 years of age, after having been absent from your home for an hour, in the still dark of the early morning, finding the bloody body of your mother shot dead in her bed. I hazard to argue that you would display absolutely no rational thought pattern or behaviour. Instantaneous, subconscious, instinctive bodily and mental functions would take over. In no particular order or degree of importance, they would include extreme shock, extreme disbelief, self preservation, disorientation, terror, fear. Who could possibly say what they would do, or remember in fact what they actually did? A not too unlikely scenario, I would suggest, is that you would stumble panic-stricken and incoherent from room to room to check on other members of the family. You would probably grab them, shake them, cuddle them, talk to them. You would be very likely to faint at some point, upon coming across each one, more gruesome and bloody than the last.

Around this old house with its steep, narrow stairs, untidy and littered with boxes and furniture, you would trip, fall, stumble and bang your way. It's dark. You're terrified. A little graze on the knee (David wore shorts to do the paper run, remember) and an almost undetectable bump to his right forehead and eye, are hardly out of keeping with this. (David in fact told the doctor at his medical examination, and subsequently the police in a later statement, that he could not account for these injuries, but he knew for sure they weren't there when he went on his run. He told them this at the same time as he was being so honest as to say that he put on the washing and his father didn't know where the gun keys were.) If he were attempting to evade attention, why not say he had tripped while delivering the papers and bumped his head and knee then?

Eventually having found his mother, Arawa, Laniet and Stephen he stumbled across his father, with the rifle – his rifle – lying near or perhaps upon his father's prostrate body. Can anybody even start to imagine what his state of mind must have been? Once again, absolutely intuitive and instinctive emotions and reactions would be in control. Maybe, having found his father with the rifle, relief that the killing is over and the killer is dead – a reaction to the primary instinct of self-preservation. Perhaps an instinctive grab of the gun, pushing it away from his dead father, then grab Dad and hold him, shake him. Deep in every child is the feeling that Dad is indestructible; Dad will fix it; Dad will save the day. Not Dad too! Help – I need help. That would be the next instinct, beyond doubt. It would not be surprising to run, to the neighbours perhaps, at this stage. The raging fear, the unspeakable horror and resulting total traumatic state, I believe, make it impossible for any of us to assess exactly what we would do, or what he would likely have done.

David rang 111. He screamed and burbled uncontrollably into the phone – the 111 operator thought he was out of it on drugs or alcohol. His first words to St Johns, 'Help, they're all dead.' Who? Next words, 'They're all dead. I came home and they're all dead.'

Later that day, and during the week, David was to maintain two things that were to be powerful influences in the police assessment of his behaviour. One, that he saw only his mother and father, and two, that he did not touch the rifle.

I need to digress here a little, because another factor comes into play. It will be recalled that David had been seen by Denise Laney as she headed for work at the nearby rest home at the front gate of his home at 6.45 or 6.46 a.m., but he did not make the 111 call until 7.09 a.m., 24 minutes later. What

David said he could recall doing (going to his room, taking off his shoes, paper delivery bag and walkman, going to the laundry to wash his hands of printer's ink and putting on a wash in the washing machine, coming back to his room then finding his mother and father dead) would only account for about ten minutes, according to the police. There is a 'missing' fifteen minutes or so.

I believe the synopsis above describing what he or anyone would have been likely to do, including fainting, falling and stumbling panic-stricken from room to room, easily explains this time lapse. But as I have said, it is a matter of perspective, and the police put sinister connotations on the missing fifteen minutes. Not a lack of memory, they say, but a convenient lack of memory so as not to tell the truth which (they say) was in fact that he was attending to cleaning up, killing his father and writing the message on the computer during this time.

On Monday night, the first night of the enquiry, the police established the bloody sock prints in Stephen's and Laniet's bedroom. They also had his positive prints on the rifle by the Tuesday. It should be explained that these fingerprints are in a position on the gun in which it would be highly unlikely to hold and fire a rifle. It would lead to an extreme degree of awkwardness and difficulty, and due to the fingertip-like nature of the touch, the grip would be so light as to not even have control of the rifle. Such prints are far more likely to be placed there by somebody picking up the rifle from the wrong end, the barrel end. Despite this, there they were and, even more compelling for the police, apparently the hand that put them there had blood on it and imparted the blood onto the rifle; not the other way round. This certainly provided for very emotive language in the courtroom: 'David's bloody fingerprints were found on the rifle.'

So the police now had David being in a room where he said he hadn't been, not being able to explain fifteen minutes of time, and having left his fingerprints in blood on the murder weapon, which he said he hadn't touched.

The 'mountain of evidence' was beginning to build.

On the Wednesday, David's white gloves, covered in blood, were found by Detective Sergeant Milton Weir in Stephen's bedroom. The smidgen of blood on David's black shorts was also determined to have come from Stephen. David's partial palm print was 'found on the washing machine', too; hardly surprisingly, since David had never denied touching the washing machine and was the person in the household who regularly did the washing. The police put to David on the Friday of his arrest that this was a bloody palm print. During the trial they conceded that they had no proof that it was blood at all; it was just a partial palm print.

Then, perhaps the *coup de grâce*, at 8.46 p.m. on Thursday 23 June, the indefatigable Detective Sergeant discovered the lens from the glasses in Stephen's bedroom.

On Friday 24 June David was arrested, and the police then had the job of making sure that the balance of the 'mountain of evidence' supported their case against the accused. As we shall see, they did an excellent job of selecting the evidence to support the crime.

Let's look then, at the Crown case against David Bain. Again, no more learned appraisal could be utilised than Judge Williamson's summing up, when he listed the main points of evidence against David. He lists the twelve main points of the Crown case, and prefaces the list with the statement: 'It [the Crown] points particularly to the combination of the following facts'.

1. *Judge*: The rifle and ammunition were David's and the key to the trigger lock was in an unusual place where he had hidden it.

Answer: The fact that the rifle and ammunition were David's does not advance the case against David if other people had access to it. It was in David's wardrobe where in fact Robin Bain also kept some of his clothes. The key was in a trinket box on David's desk in his room; hardly an unusual place. There were twenty spent cartridge shells in Robin's caravan, proved to have been fired by this rifle, a strong indication that Robin had access to it. Except that David said he thought Robin didn't know where the key was, there was no reason that he shouldn't have known.

2. *Judge*: His bloodied fingerprints were found on the murder weapon.

Answer: These were not in a firing-hold position, but rather in a pick-up place and could very likely have been put there by David in finding Robin dead with the gun lying beside or upon him, as previously explained. Further, David could easily have got blood on his fingers in the process of finding the dead bodies, including his father's. Incidentally, the file does not reveal whose blood it was that David implanted on the gun where his fingerprints were detected.

3. *Judge*: His blood-stained gloves were found in Stephen's bedroom.

Answer: There was no evidence whatsoever that David was the wearer of these gloves that day or any other. They were readily available to any other person who looked in David's drawer. Nothing links David to the gloves except that they were his. This is another absurdity in the Crown case. If David was trying to frame Robin, as the police suggest, and was so cold-blooded and calculating, why would he leave his own gloves in Stephen's room? Bearing in mind that he was supposed to have killed Stephen prior to doing his paper run, why didn't he wash them and dispose of them, burn them or at least remove them from the scene?

4. *Judge*: David had fresh injuries to his forehead and knee.

There was no explanation for them and the nature of them indicates that it was he who had the fight with Stephen.

Answer: I have already covered these injuries. I invite the reader to look at the photos. They do not appear to be the sort of injuries one would sustain in a fight, much more likely in a fall or crash into a wall or door.

5. *Judge*: The glasses (with a missing lens) and fitting his general glass prescription were found on a chair near where he was in his room when the police arrived, and, significantly, the left side of the frame was damaged and the missing lens was found in Stephen's room quite near his body.

Answer: I have dealt with the matter of this lens already. Nothing on this lens in the way of blood, hairs, prints, tissues or fibres links it in any way with David or the struggle. Moreover, Weir's testimony in the light of the expert analysis I have presented in this book throws into grave doubt the whole manner of how the lens came to be where it was said to be, if in fact it was ever there. The glasses did not fit David's general prescription, and one visit to an appropriate optometrist would have confirmed that. The judge said the frame was 'significantly damaged on the left side'. Remember, the very minor bruise to David's forehead was on the right side of his head. Again, as with the gloves, why on earth would David take one lens, which was also dislodged from the glasses frame, and the frame, and put them neatly on the chair in his room if he was attempting to deceive the police? The entire evidence in relation to these glasses and the left lens (exhibit 172) is fraught with doubt.

6. *Judge*: Blood-stained clothing, including the green jersey with matching fibres to those found under Stephen's fingernails, was washed by him and his 'Gondoliers' sweatshirt with blood on the shoulder had been sponged.

Answer: Nothing in the above statement is fact.

a) There was no proof that any blood-stained clothing was washed by David.

b) The fibres under Stephen's fingernails were not proved to have come from the green jersey in the wash. In fact, the detective who recorded the finding of some fibres under Stephen's fingernails noted them as 'black' fibres. The ESR evidence said that the fibres were consistent with having come from the green jersey. The evidence went no further than that.

c) The 'Gondoliers' sweatshirt belonged to David and was not washed but was on the floor in the wash house. It was the opinion of the ESR scientists that it may have been sponged. There is not one scrap of evidence that David ever touched the green jersey or the Gondoliers sweatshirt on that day. The jersey was produced as an exhibit. The Crown asked David to put it on before the jury, and it was patently far too small for him in all dimensions.

7. *Judge*: Blood found on the top of the washing machine powder container, porcelain basin and various light switches must have come from his 'touch'.

Answer: Why 'must it have come from David'? No evidence whatsoever was called to even suggest that. The only way that conclusion could be reached is if one assumes that he was the murderer, then he must have put it there. In fact, according to the blood chart produced by the Crown in the trial, this blood was not even proved to be human blood.

8. *Judge*: Droplets of blood were found on his socks as well as blood which had caused the luminol-observed part sock prints in other parts of the house.

Answer: This is indeed an incredible statement. There were two spots of blood on the soles of his socks. The Crown tried to suggest they were droplets of blood! How do you get drops of blood on the soles of your socks? By lying face down on the floor with your feet upturned in the air so that the blood falls from above onto the socks? Police records and the photos clearly indicate that blood spots and smears were all over the floor of Stephen's room. When David went in there in his socks he would have been bound to get blood on the soles of them. They would have been spots or smears from the blood on the floor that he would have walked on.

As to luminol, it reacts with many things other than blood, including bleach and detergent. Even if David's stockinged prints were in other parts of the house (and this was never proved) surely that is to be expected if, as he states, he found the members of the family dead.

But there is a more illuminating aspect to the blood on David's socks, which was not put before the jury. The running shoes that David used that day were quite new, and can be seen in photo 7 in front of the chest of drawers. The police alleged that David got the blood spots and smears on his socks when he killed and struggled with Stephen. He is then supposed to have put on his running shoes and done his paper round. The police fitted all this together for two reasons: one, that it would be quieter creeping around the house in his socks than his running shoes while murdering everyone before his paper run; and two, because there was no blood found on any of his shoes. However, despite having been thoroughly tested, no blood was found on the inside of David's running shoes. It seems to me to be highly unlikely that fresh blood would not leave some telltale sign on the inside of a newish pair of shoes when they had been worn to run in while delivering papers for about an hour. This lends credence to David's version, that he came home, took his shoes off and got the blood on his socks in the process of finding the other members of his slain family. It debunks in fact the entire Crown case of what David is supposed to have done because, on the one hand, the Crown cannot theorise that he killed them all after he returned from his paper run because of evidence to do with the washing machine timing, and, on the other hand, the absence of blood on the inside of the running shoes lead to the conclusion that he did not have the blood on his socks before he did his paper run. So if he didn't commit the murders before his paper run and couldn't commit them afterwards, when is it that he is supposed to have done them?

9. *Judge*: The computer had been switched on at 6.44, and that you would conclude on all of the evidence that this time was just after David returned home from the paper run, that is, if you accept evidence, including his own, that he was at the nearby corner at 6.40 and that it would take 2–3 minutes to reach 65 Every Street.

Answer: I have already dealt with the issue of timing in detail. It is relevant at this point to reiterate that the computer was not switched on at 6.44. Had the police told the truth or, conversely, had Guest done his homework, the court would have heard that the computer was turned on at some time between 6.40 and 6.42 when, on all of the evidence, including David's, Tania Clarke's and Denise Laney's, it was impossible for David to have been home. Further, when David said that it would have taken 'two or three minutes to get home', he was not speaking literally or definitively; rather he was meaning 'it's just a few minutes away'. Even allowing for a literal interpretation, however, he could still not have been inside the house at 6.42.

10. *Judge*: David's partial recovery of memory may have enabled him to suggest explanations for some of the blood on him, but it does not explain other vital items such as the fingerprints, the clothing or the glasses. *It confirms however, the Crown says, that David confidently denies matters that he cannot remember although they happened.* (My emphasis.)

Answer: Had the court known the true facts, this statement could not have been made. Following upon the police arrival on the scene at about 7.30 a.m., and the ensuing attendance of ambulance officers, the ambulance officer's report clearly states that David was unconscious for about three minutes. This report, although on the file of discovery documents given to me by Guest, was never put before the court. Anyone who has ever lapsed into unconsciousness for whatever reason knows that a partial or entire lapse in memory, particularly in the short to medium term, is very often an inevitable consequence.

I recall an interesting example, going back to my own football playing days. In 1974, the All Blacks played the Barbarians at Twickenham. As often has happened, the festival nature that the term 'Barbarians' depicts was eliminated from the game when British authorities selected a full-scale 'British Isles' XV. The game took on an All Blacks vs Lions intensity, and was played in real test match style. Grant Batty, my good friend and All Black wing three quarters at the time (who incidentally set up a magnificent try for Bryan Williams during the match), sustained a heavy knock to the head during the game. Towards the end of the match, with the score at 14-14, the ball came to Batty in an ideal attacking situation, and he casually kicked it into touch. The game ended, and when we got into the dressing room, Batts was the only guy in our camp happily cracking the tops of celebratory bottles of beer. Being such an intense competitor, I couldn't follow what was going on, and when I asked him, he thought I was bonkers. Batts had no recollection that the Baa Baa's had scored a late try to bring the score from 14-10 to 14-14, and thought we had won the game – hence his kicking the ball out and his celebrations. He was shocked, and it was some time later, after having events recounted to him and seeing the TV replay, that he was able to recall the try scored by the Baa Baa's. It's lucky it didn't happen in Dunedin; it might have been considered a crime!

It seems to me entirely logical and understandable that David remembers finding his dead mother, because at that stage he was still in his normal state. The last thing he remembers is knowing that his father was dead and ringing 111. If the resulting trauma, and the subsequent unconsciousness he suffered, caused him to be unable to remember the sequence of events in between, is that not entirely understandable?

Although this issue is not actually a matter of evidence it played a significant part in the trial, because it, the 'missing fifteen minutes' that is, and the minor contradictions in David's memory, were sinisterly represented by the Crown as throwing David's entire testimony into discredit. I refer to my earlier account of what David would have been likely to do when he found the scene of bloody mayhem, and would like to recount some other experiences to put this whole matter of David's so-called 'convenient' partial recovery of memory into perspective.

I am sure that many readers will relate through their own personal experiences in life to the Batty story above and to other similar events. There are two or three of my own that I feel are very relevant.

About ten years ago my wife and I were on holiday in Russell, Bay of Islands with another couple, very close friends of ours, who had a young daughter being cared for in their absence by a Karitane nurse. In the early hours of the morning in our motel, I took a call from the police, advising that this little girl had died, of cot death. You can imagine the awful job I had to wake the parents and tell them the news. After I had broken the news to them, we packed up, hopped in the car, and drove back to Auckland, the mother sobbing and crying uncontrollably all the way down. My wife accompanied the couple on the two aeroplane flights to return to their home in the South Island, where they arrived late in the afternoon. To this day, the mother of the little girl has absolutely no recollection whatsoever of the drive from Russell to Auckland, being at Auckland airport or of either of the flights. She has the odd flash of being at an airport or getting on a plane, but cannot in any way recount what happened that day. Her husband, on the other hand, during the drive from Russell to Auckland chatted away as though we were on a Sunday drive. How differently people are affected by shock.

Another example relates to my own father, who as a seventeen-year-old was home with his elder sister on Christmas Eve while the family were out shopping. His sister had a heart attack and he found her dying in the bath. Apparently he got her out of the bath and called for help. But again he has no recall whatsoever of what he did after finding her in the bath and, even further, cannot remember the events of that evening or even Christmas Day. He too was suffering from severe shock and trauma, resulting in memory loss.

Another very close friend of mine had a son, to whom I was godfather, born with a terminal illness. He finally died when he was seventeen years old. Despite having known for fifteen years that this lad would probably die before he was fifteen, when it finally happened his mother too was affected by the event to the extent that she has no recollection whatsoever of what she said or did, who she saw, or where she went, from the time he died until his funeral. Had she been interviewed at the funeral, or had my father been interviewed on Boxing Day many years ago, their account of what they thought they had done would have been riddled with contradictions and inconsistencies, and yet they were not confronted with anything like the horror that lay before David.

In fact, an interesting corroboration to this premise comes from the police file of the Bain case itself. Recalling that four police officers were first on the scene, and that two of them went through the house, one of them said in his statement: 'We went downstairs. Sergeant Stapp said that he and I went

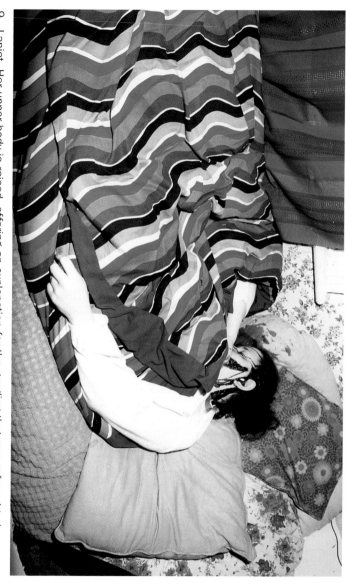

9. Laniet. Her upper body is raised, offering an explanation for the gurgling that was referred to by Alec Dempster.

10.The computer on which the message was left.

11. Stephen's room; part of police photograph 60. The missing glasses lens is alleged to have been found in the area between the orange poster, the grey suitcase and the tip of the ice skate boot.

12. Stephen's room. The police have placed black arrows pointing to all the splashes of blood.

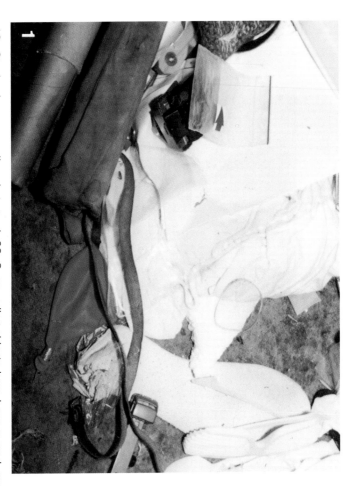

13. Stephen's room; police photograph 99. Surrounding objects have been moved, and the lens is clearly visible, but in a significantly removed position from where Weir said he found it. The curved edge of the paper under the plastic near the centre of the photo accounts for what Weir pointed out as being the lens.

14. Police photograph 99, with a section of photograph 61 overlaid. This clearly indicates the disparity between where the lens was said to be and where it actually was.

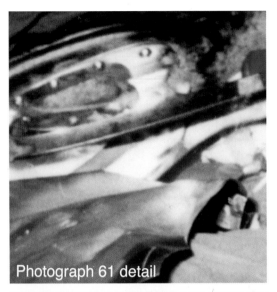

Photograph 61 detail

Photograph 62 detail

15. Highly magnified details of police photographs 61 and 62. What appears to be a lens at the toe of the ice skate is actually just a reflection caused by the plastic and paper. Note that photo 62 was said to be a 'blow-up' of photo 61, but 61 does not contain much of what is in photo 62.

Photograph 60 detail

16. Highly magnified detail of police photograph 60 (see photograph 11 in this section). It does not indicate anything that could be the lens.

into the bathroom and laundry, but I cannot remember being there. *If he said I did, though, I must have.*'

This was a trained police officer giving a statement within days of the event. But for the Crown, so desperate to paint a picture of the lying cold-blooded murderer, David is supposed to have perfect recollection.

11. *Judge:* If David heard Laniet making gurgling noises, then she must have been alive at that time and consequently he was by her bed before the last fatal shot was fired. Other comments of his such as that his mother's eyes were open when he went in, and to his aunt that they were 'dying, dying everywhere' tend to confirm that he remembers in part being there before the deaths.

Answer: Remembering that the judge refers to this list of the main evidential points against David as 'facts', the only facts in the above statement are what David said. Neither of the judge's conclusions are facts.

Firstly, on the eyes being open and the gurgling, we are relying on a memory that was severely distorted for the reasons previously explained. As far as the open eyes are concerned, I do not know whether her eyes could have been open in death and closed in due course or not. For all we know, David on finding her may have tried to open her eyes to see if she was dead or not. As I have said, and I reiterate, any of his recollections in regard to this period of time should not carry any weight.

The same applies to the gurgling, of course, although there is more to this. The background to the gurgling starts with Alec Dempster, the pathologist, and the evidence he gave in relation to the post mortem examination he had done on Laniet Bain. Laniet was shot three times in the head. One of the shots was through her cheek and would have damaged the base of the brain area, but also according to Mr Dempster would have caused considerable blood and mucus to run down her airways into her lungs. Mr Dempster considered that this shot would not have been immediately fatal, but either of the subsequent shots would have been. He said:

'The ingestion of blood into the lungs is partly ingestion of blood into the lungs and partly due to blood being formed in the lungs but I would have anticipated that Laniet would have been making audible gurgling or similar noises as this material accumulated in the airways.'

I believe that this evidence can be interpreted in the following way: the upper torso of Laniet is quite elevated (see photo 9) and this would have caused blood and mucus to run down into her lungs, more so than if she was lying down flat. It seems obvious to me from Dempster's statement that, although in part the airways became congested due to her breathing (ingestion) while still alive, the congestion was also a result of fluid being formed in the lungs. Had he wanted to say that the gurgling noises would have occurred only while she was still breathing (that is, while she was still alive) then that is what he would have said. Even after she was dead, 'as the blood and mucus formed in the lungs and air passages', it would necessarily have been replacing air and could easily have caused what Dempster referred to in his evidence as 'audible gurgling or similar noises as this material accumulated in the airways'.

The Crown jumped on David's statement during his testimony when, unprompted, he said, 'I can't remember walking anywhere but the next thing I remember is being in Laniet's room and I could hear her gurgling.' Maybe Dempster's evidence prompted his memory to think he had heard Laniet, or maybe it reminded him that in fact he had. Either way, it does not mean that he was in there prior to her death and as the Crown alleged must therefore have ultimately killed her. It was powerfully emotional stuff from Crown prosecutor Bill Wright, but does not stand up to scrutiny as proving a damn thing. Guest vehemently argued against Wright's submission in his closing address.

And again, if David was clever enough to falsify his entire story for over a day on the witness stand, under the severest of scrutiny, why would he have admitted this? He said it only because he was straining to tell the truth as best he could remember it.

12. *Judge*: Not only does the expert pathologist say it is unlikely Robin Bain shot himself because of the angle of the gunshot wound, but Robin Bain, the Crown says, could not have killed the others because:

a) No one else's blood was found on him;

b) There was no blood at all of any type on his socks or shoes;

c) His fingerprints were not on the rifle, although if he had shot himself he would have been the last person to have gripped it firmly;

d) No gunpowder traces were on his hands;

e) If he had been the wearer of blood-stained clothing and was intent on suicide why would he have bothered to change his clothes and to be *in completely blood-free clothes when he shot himself*? (My emphasis.)

I will deal with these last points later, as they relate to Robin Bain's possible actions rather than the evidence against David.

I cannot help but feel that when the judge prefaced his list of the prosecution points 1–12 above, the word 'fact' was rather an inappropriate choice to use the word in describing them.

Of the first eleven points listed by the judge, it can be seen that only two of them are solely fact; one is an outright false-hood (and the police knew that it was); the balance are either a combination of fact and assumption or total assumption. When it comes to the crunch, what, really, once the theorising and tenuous assumptions are put aside, remains of the 'mountain of evidence' against David?

I believe that the jury were pretty much right on the mark in the two areas that they sought clarification on from the judge – the glasses lens and the timing issue. All of the other so-called pieces of evidence are easily attributable to David the finder as opposed to the perpetrator, and do not link him to the actual acts of execution. The timing issue, right from when Guest told me about it on the first night we met, struck me as having a strange eeriness about it that seems too much to be coincidental, and seemingly this played on the jurors' minds also.

The difficult point to overcome is that David is known to have arrived home at about 6.45, and the computer is alleged to have been turned on at 6.44. It is rather like, if I may use an example, a spouse who sees his or her partner leaving a motel room with a person of the opposite sex: it doesn't matter how good the explanation, or how much rationalisation is applied, the mental picture as to what may have been going on will be fixed in the mind of the unfortunate discoverer of this event forever. So too in the minds of the jurors considering this timing evidence. On the one hand, we have clear-cut definitive and reliable evidence putting David outside of his property at 6.45 or 6.46 and the computer allegedly turned on at 6.44. The Crown surmised, according to the judge's summary of their case:

> Counsel [prosecution] contended that the accused went and did the paper run because that was part of an essential element of the whole plan and that the accused must then, on return from the paper run, have gone to the alcove in the lounge and switched on the computer at 6.44 am. Counsel said that you would be satisfied about that time because of all of the evidence about the paper run being carried out a lot earlier that

day and because the accused himself had said that at 6.40 am exactly he was at the corner of Heath and Every Street and it would have taken two or three minutes at a moderate walk to go from there to Every Street. So the argument Mr Wright put to you was that the evidence would confirm that it was the accused who switched this computer on at this significant time.

I know that I have already devoted an entire chapter to the issue of *timing*, but I cannot let it pass, in discussing the case against David, that the judge's words to the jury about the prosecution case are so affirmative, and yet are based on untruths and tenuous assumptions. We now know, and Guest should have exposed it in the trial, that the police and the prosecution team were well aware that the time the computer was turned on was not 6.44, but at the very latest 6.42, and possibly as early as 6.40.

Learning this now would be like the spouse in my example above, having divorced the partner seen at the motel, finding out that the meeting was for a genuine reason with a long-lost relation! I must emphasise that I am not questioning the judge here; he was recounting to the jury the case for the Crown as previously put to them by Bill Wright the Crown prosecutor.

I am though, intending to emphasise that these words came from the mouth of the judge himself and they make David's 'master plan' sound so very neat and tidy. This is ridiculous when other factors are taken into account. Robin Bain's alarm clock was set for 6.32 a.m., as it usually was on a Monday morning so that he could prepare for work before driving back to his school, 45-odd kilometres away. David, 'as part of his essential plan', it is proposed, decided to get home fifteen minutes after his father woke, during which time Robin could well have discovered the dead bodies of the family in the home! The essential plan then requires David to have run directly into the computer room, switched on the computer, and hidden in the alcove. Again, this involves a number of improbabilities and assumptions.

Firstly, that his father is not already up and about. Secondly, David would have had printer's ink all over his hands from delivering the papers, and none was found on the computer or elsewhere so one must assume that he washed his hands first somewhere. Thirdly, that Denise Laney was wrong in her evidence when she said she was 'late for work', which started at 6.45. Fourthly, that Robin Bain is going to come so close to the alcove where David is hiding, without hearing the whirr of the computer or detecting the light emitting from the screen, and put himself in such a position that David can put the rifle to his head and shoot him. Remember, pathologist Alec Dempster's conclusion, because of the soot around the entry wound, was that this was a contact wound.

You will also recall that the judge says that 'the accused himself said that at 6.40 am he was at Heath Street, and it would have taken two to three minutes at a moderate walk to get home'. But what David actually said was: 'I told an officer it takes two to three minutes to get home, that is an approximation, I can't tell you exactly how long it takes.' The judge also said that David did his paper run earlier than usual, but that is in direct conflict with both Laney's and Clark's evidence. Incidentally, two police staff walked this street; in both instances the time taken was more than three minutes.

In summary, the one-minute time difference between 6.44 (when the computer was supposedly turned on) and 6.45 (when David returned to the house), is small enough that the accused is obviously at or near the house at the time the computer was turned on; the conclusion that follows is that he 'must' then have done it. But as we now know, it wasn't 6.44 at all but some time between 6.40.7 seconds and 6.42.5 seconds, when David could not have been home to turn it on.

The second question the jury asked was in relation to the glasses. Great emphasis was placed upon the glasses, because they were a link with the so-called struggle between the assailant, David, and Stephen. Like the computer message, the lens was proffered as a direct link between David and an action. The jury asked the question because, clearly, they were unsure about the origin of the particular spectacles.

Referring to the motel analogy again, had the spouse known that the person seen with the partner was a relation, and that the meeting had a genuine basis, no argument would ever have occurred, let alone a divorce. Likewise, had the jury known the truth surrounding the time the computer was switched on, and the origin of the glasses, along with the fact that the lens was not where it was said to be, both of these critical pieces of evidence, recounted so graphically by the judge, would have been thrown out I believe by the jury altogether. The case against David would have crumpled.

Even more bewildering, though, if that be possible, are the matters raised in the twelfth of the judge's points. These include the Crown proposition that there was no evidence to link Robin Bain with the murders, and that Alec Dempster considered it highly unlikely that Robin Bain could have committed suicide. This was a means of making David guilty by implication, the conclusion being that if Robin didn't kill himself or the others, then it must have been David. Throughout the case there was no contention by either side that a person from outside the family was responsible for the shootings. The choice was between David and Robin.

Let's look first at the proposition that nothing linked Robin to the murders of other members of his family.

Detective Mark Lodge was assigned to be in charge of the deceased body of Robin Bain. The police investigation apparently disregarded Lodge's findings; a grave omission. His job sheets in relation to his work with the body of Robin

Bain at the scene, and also at the mortuary, are very detailed, including drawings and diagrams.

He noted the following matters of interest:

1. Smear of blood on heel of thumb inside left hand.
2. Smear of blood on left little finger.
3. No blood on right hand.
4. What appears to be contact gunshot wound to left side of forehead.
5. Minor abrasion of back of right hand surrounded by a circular bruise.
6. Tiny abrasion on knuckles of second right finger.
7. Splash of blood on nail of second right finger.
8. Abrasion on upper portion of left first finger.
9. Very small abrasion on base knuckle of left hand.
10. Left and right foot from heel to tip of big toe 27 cms.
11. Clothing worn on upper body of Robin Bain:
    – dark blue hooded sweatshirt
    – brown woollen jersey under sweatshirt
    – striped shirt under jersey.
    – white tee-shirt under shirt
    – green woollen hat inside hood of sweatshirt.

In his testimony during the trial, as well as referring to some but not all of the above, he mentioned the following:

12. A moustache; otherwise clean-shaven.
13. Spots of blood on the blue tracksuit pants about the thigh and knee regions.
14. Smears of blood on the tracksuit pants on the lower left leg.
15. Having secured Robin's clothing at the morgue on the Monday night I made a closer inspection the following day and noted: 'on the sweatshirt there was blood staining on the back of the hood, and heavy staining on the

top of the hood and also on the right shoulder'.

Remarkably, having made these statements in his testimony, Mark Lodge was asked no questions, not cross-examined at all, by Michael Guest. The next Crown witness was Cox, the computer expert, and he was asked no questions either!

The incredible fact is that *none of the blood itemised by Lodge on Robin Bain's hands or clothing was tested by the police for blood grouping*. In fact, the judge's twelfth point finished with the comment, 'why would he have bothered to change his clothes and to be in completely blood-free clothes when he shot himself?'

If any of the blood spots, smears or 'heavy staining' referred to by Mark Lodge had been analysed and found to have belonged to any other deceased members of the family, then again, the case against David would have collapsed. More importantly, had the police tested the copious amount of blood on Robin and detected that it belonged to other deceased family members, *they would never have arrested David in the first place*. This goes to the heart of my contention that David was arrested prematurely, and that following his arrest, the investigators in charge were interested only in discovering and making available evidence that matched their theory that David was guilty.

The smudges of blood on the bottom of the left leg were the subject of a memo issued by Jim Doyle a few days after David was arrested. It said: 'Have the ESR scientists examine these smears to see whether David could have put them there while rearranging his father's leg to enhance the appearance of suicide.' Not surprisingly, he does not seem to have received a response.

In Dempster's post mortem report on Robin Bain, he said: 'There were *recent* minor injuries involving both hands.' (My emphasis.)

He then went on to list the six injuries that Mark Lodge

had noted.

David, it will be recalled was deemed to have been involved in the struggle with Stephen because of the bruise on his forehead and graze to his knee, yet Robin had *six recent* injuries to his hands.

It is immediately evident that item 12(a), that there was nobody else's blood on him, is extremely misleading, as none of the copious blood on him was ever tested for blood grouping. Likewise, 12(e), that he was in completely blood-free clothes, is downright untrue, as you can see in the photographs of the clothes Robin was found in. In relation to point (b), that there was no blood on Robin Bain's shoes or socks, it is interesting to note the evidence in relation to the footprints alleged to have been made by David in his blood-stained socks. According to Lodge's evidence, Robin's feet measured 27 cm from heel to toe. Weir, in his evidence relating to the footprints that showed up under the luminol test, said that one measured 24 cm, and another 28 cm. In the washing done by David that morning were two pairs of socks. It is not clear from the file whose or what type they are, but let's say Robin was the perpetrator, and he moved around the house in his socks to be silent as the police allege David did, and took them off subsequently. It seems quite reasonable, if one wished to speculate to the extent that the police did, that Robin may have made the luminol-detected footprints in his socks and then left them in the machine for David to inadvertently wash them.

The matter of fingerprints on the rifle, item (c), is again an example of the presumptuous nature of the Crown case.

When the rifle was first examined, a fingerprint was noted as being beside the trigger guard, as well as David's prints at the other, barrel, end of the rifle. There is no mention of what result was obtained from this print. Presumably, it did not give a clearly identifiable print, but, in a file so riddled with anomalies, it is hard to be sure. The testimony of the police fingerprint expert, Mr Kim Jones, is also of interest, as his comments about the leaving of fingerprints are directly relevant to point (c).

This exchange between Michael Guest and Kim Jones is from page 211 of the trial transcripts:

Guest: 'In relation to other fingerprints in the house you didn't find anything of evidential value?'

Answer: 'No.'

Guest: 'Fingerprints don't pop up that easily on every article that someone may have touched?'

Answer: 'That is correct, sir.'

The remaining point referred to by the judge is (d): 'No gunpowder traces were found on his hands.'

This is a disgraceful submission by the Crown, who used the sloppiness and incompetence of the police investigation to their own advantage. The Crown made a play of the fact that there was no gunpowder residue on the hands of Robin Bain, yet none was found on David Bain either.

This matter of gunpowder residue is another important area where the police investigatory team failed miserably. It is one of the major deficiencies identified in the report I have had done by a former CIB superintendent. I have obtained copies of scientific forensic manuals relating to gunpowder residue, as well as having the CIB superintendent's report form and discussing the subject with independent pathologists. The main points are as follows.

When a rifle is fired, sooty and gaseous particles are emitted from the firing mechanism area, and also from the end of the barrel. In this case, for example, Dempster was able to ascertain that the shot which killed Robin Bain was a 'contact' wound (that is, the barrel was touching Robin's skin at the time the shot was fired) because of the sooty deposit on the skin immediately around the entry hole.

At the other end of the rifle, the stock end, gases emitted from the breech will generally deposit themselves about the front area of the firer and his or her firing hand and arm. The critical factor, as far as the forensic value of this gaseous residue is concerned, is that it is shed or dissipates from the surface on which it is deposited in a relatively short time, and little value is gained in conducting tests for its presence beyond that time. It is simplest to quote from a scientific forensic manual titled 'Firearms Evidence', written by ESR scientists John Buckleton and Keven Walsh on this subject, under the heading 'PERSISTENCE of firearm discharge residue: (FDR)':

> Immediately after the shooting, relatively large numbers of FDR particles are located on the exposed surfaces of the hands and forward facing surfaces of the body and clothing of the shooter. However, particles are shed from these surfaces within a very short time as a result of post shooting activity and/or environmental effects.
>
> Within two hours, the quantity of primer related particles detected on the hands of a shooter is reduced to only a few and sometimes none. *Even in the case of suicides, where the deceased is in a protected environment and has remained untouched, very low numbers of primer related particles are detected when sampling has occurred several hours after the incident.* Movement of the deceased accelerates this loss. [My emphasis.]

Now, let me retrace the process that the 'copybook' enquiry followed, as far as this issue is concerned. By 7.45 a.m. on 20 June, the police knew that they had two likely suspects, and the firearm which was very likely the murder weapon was lying beside one of the suspects.

Pathologist Alec Dempster was called to a briefing at the CIB at 8.15 a.m. The first inexplicable point is that either he or a homicide detective did not (or if they did, nothing was done to action it) issue a request for an immediate protection or swabbing of the relevant areas of the body and clothing of Robin and David so that appropriate tests could have been carried out to establish the presence of FDR. Had this been done, any residue detected on either Robin or David would immediately have solved the crime, and saved us all this enduring and bizarre mystery.

It will be recalled that Peter Robinson, head of the enquiry, visited the scene at 8.50 a.m. As he was leaving, at about 9.00 a.m., Constable Von Turnhout asked him directly, if a firearms residue kit had been arranged. The only recorded response to his query to Robinson is that he was told to watch over David, and note everything that he said or did.

At 11.46 a.m. the CIB issued a directive for a call to be made to the ESR. requesting the procedure relating to FDR testing. The police officer who made the call recorded on this job sheet that he spoke to Peter Hentschell, of the ESR, who said: 'A maximum period for recovering gunpowder residue is 3 hours. Anything after [that,] forget it.'

At about 11.30 a.m. – more than four and a half hours after the last shot had been fired – Dr Pryde, the police doctor, examined David at the CIB. As part of that examination, he took swabs to be tested for FDR. Those tests proved negative.

Finally, Robin Bain's body was taken to the mortuary at about 3.00 p.m. that afternoon. In the process of the later post mortem examination, swabs were taken from him to be tested, and these also proved negative. In court the Crown prosecutors calmly claimed, 'No gunpowder traces were on his [Robin's] hands', with no reference at all to the fact that testing was carried out some five hours too late, or that none was found on David either.

The police also failed to test fire the murder rifle itself to establish the extent to which FDR was emitted. This is relevant in that the quantity of discharge varies from weapon to weapon. Had tests found, for example, that this particular weapon emitted a substantial discharge, the failure of the enquiry to address this matter at the earliest possible time (about 8.00 a.m.) would be even more disgraceful. An opportunity to gather vital evidence would clearly have been wasted – whether it was evidence showing that Robin had definitely fired the rifle, or an absence of FDR on David indicating that he was unlikely to have fired it. Similar abrogation of responsibility in other professions at the highest level would likely bring censure or dismissal. On the other hand if this particular rifle was very clean-firing, and did not discharge any traceable particles at all, it would be highly misleading to say later in the trial that a major point in the case against David was that no FDR was found on Robin.

The final major point of evidence against David was the pathologist's assertion that 'it is unlikely Robin Bain committed suicide because of the angle of the gun shot wound.'

One can readily understand that in order for the Crown case against David to be credible, any possibility or likelihood of Robin shooting himself needed to be dispelled. Alec Dempster was the primary proponent of the theory that Robin Bain could not have committed suicide. It is worth noting that the Crown advised the defence only a week or so prior to trial that this evidence would form part of the pathologist's testimony. In fact it was only in those last couple of weeks before the trial that, at the request of the police, Dempster conducted experiments for the first time to substantiate this theory.

The shot that killed Robin had entered his head in the left temple, at an angle of about 45° across and towards the back of his head, which means that if someone were holding the rifle they would of necessity be in front of Robin and slightly to his left, but clearly within his range of vision. (See the diagams from Dempster's post mortem report, below.) If Robin's head were directly upright at the time, the barrel of

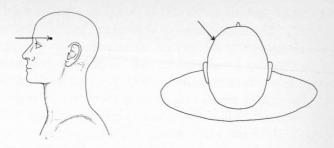

the rifle was held parallel to the floor.

One can easily recognise from this that if David killed his father, he had to be standing almost directly in front of and on Robin's left-hand side, with the rifle barrel touching his head. The implausibility of this scenario led the police to come up with the even more unlikely 'David hiding behind the curtain' theory. Photo 22 illustrates the position of Robin's body, the rifle and the curtains behind which David was supposed to be hiding.

Alec Dempster is not a member of the police force. He is a highly qualified man, working out of Otago University and the Dunedin Hospital. In his testimony he confirmed that he holds degrees Bachelor of Medicine, Bachelor of Surgery, Bachelor of Medical Science, and that he is also a specialist pathologist. His testimony and subsequent cross-examination by Guest is long and involved. This tense dialogue was Guest's most determined effort at cross-examining a witness. A summary of the essential matters to arise reveals, once again, a startling disregard for proper and detailed police work.

I am certain that at the time of Dempster's scene examination of the body, and later that day when he performed the post mortem, the general consensus of opinion in all of the discussions to which he was privy was that they were dealing with four murders and a suicide and I am sure that he concurred with that opinion. I am sure, from a study of the file and the testimony, from my uneasy meeting with Dempster, and from discussions with other pathologists, that, if at the time Dempster performed his examinations he had been aware or even given consideration to the notion that he might be required to testify in a High Court in a multiple murder trial, he would have given far more attention to the overall picture. This is in no way a criticism of him or his work at the time. I believe that the police attitude at that early stage involved a considerable degree of complacency, in that they believed it to be an open-and-shut case of murder/suicide, and that many of the subsequent deficiencies in the investigation were as a result of that complacency.

I note from Dempster's testimony the following points:

He did not measure the length of Robin Bain's arms, and yet he went to considerable trouble in his evidence to suggest that a man of Robin's stature would have had some difficulty in reaching the trigger, bearing in mind the angle and location of the wound. Now, I am sure that if Alec Dempster had considered for one moment that he would be required to give this sort of testimony, in a contentious internationally reported murder trial, he would most certainly have done such a simple thing as measuring Robin's arms. Instead, he was made to look somewhat foolish. Using Jim Doyle as a stand-in replica before the court, he attempted to prove the difficulty Robin would have had in reaching the trigger while holding the rifle to his head. The most cursory of glances would tell the least observant of people that the rather portly Jim Doyle bore no physical resemblance to the gaunt Robin Bain.

It is very noticeable to me that, despite all of Alec Dempster's training, his evidence was sadly lacking in detail. I put this down to the fact that the case was considered cut and dried at the time he did his examinations. For instance, he noted in evidence that he did not see any blood on Robin Bain's sweatshirt. Lodge's evidence, on the other hand, referred to heavy staining on the right shoulder and hood of the sweatshirt. He does not refer to either of the smears of blood on Robin Bain's left hand. These matters, which broadly confirmed the initial belief that Robin was the murderer as well as the suicide victim, were simply not noted.

The main premise of Dempster's eventual submission that Robin could not have committed suicide was that the left temple is the 'least preferred' site for self-inflicted rifle wounds. In addition, the angle of wound being from front to back was unusual and he had not come across it before. His experience was that wounds to the temple generally went across the head. The conclusion from this can be no more than that surely if this was a self-inflicted wound, it was not in the most common area of the head but in the least common area. Interesting information on this point is again in the police file, in the form of a report obtained by the Dunedin police from the Canterbury School of Medicine on 4 April, just a month before the trial. It is a report on suicides in the Canterbury region over the previous three years. It reports 175 suicides, of which 20 were by gunshot. Of those, seven were with the use of a .22 calibre rifle (most of the rest were shotguns); of those seven, one is noted as a wound to the chin, two as wounds to the temple (without specifying which one), three to the right temple and one to the left temple. The worst percentage then (allowing for the worst case that the two to the temple which do not signify right or left were to the right) is that 14%, or one in seven, of these self-inflicted wounds are to the left temple. Who is to say that Robin Bain did not fall within that 14%?

Michael Guest's very first question to Alec Dempster was very direct and to the point: 'With the certain limitations you referred to yesterday you do accept it was possible for Robin Bain to have committed suicide?'

Dempster's answer was: 'I consider it possible.'

I am not qualified to comment with any authority on how

a cross-examination should be conducted, but in view of the balance of the exchange between Guest and Dempster, I wonder whether or not Guest, having achieved this major concession, shouldn't have left it at that. Instead, an intricate and at times difficult to follow discussion took place in which, as Guest tried to push Dempster further into a corner on this issue, Dempster strained ever more strenuously to sustain his statement that 'in his opinion it was highly unlikely'.

The following couple of questions confirmed the possibility of suicide:

Guest: 'You embarked yesterday on a discussion of possibilities and probabilities?'

Dempster: 'Correct.'

Guest: 'You cannot completely rule out suicide?'

Dempster: 'I cannot completely rule out suicide.'

The only expert on this matter in the trial was conceding that suicide was possible, that it could not be ruled out. There is no book of rules on how to commit suicide, so I should think that the degree to which it is likely is hardly the point.

Another most peculiar confrontation between Guest and Dempster was in regard to the droplet of blood on the fingernail of Robin Bain's left-hand index finger which can be seen in photo 2.

In his evidence-in-chief Dempster proffered the opinion that this droplet of blood could not have got onto Robin's finger travelling in the direction that it is as a result of Robin Bain shooting himself. This obviously was part of the overall theory that Robin Bain could not have committed suicide. Guest's cross-examination of Dempster on this point alone takes up about four pages of the trial transcript, during which he attempts, without much success, to get Dempster to change his mind and concede that this droplet of blood could have got where it was as a result of Robin committing suicide.

I used the word 'peculiar' to describe this confrontation for the following reason: this blood was not tested at all to establish its origin! It could have been anyone's blood. It seems to me that all that was required to debunk Dempster's theory was to ask him whose blood it was, and in reference to the blood testing chart produced as an exhibit by the police, extract the concession that this could have been anyone's blood. Dempster's whole argument, like so many others in this case, would have fallen over because it was based upon a spurious premise in the first place.

To add to the degree of confusion surrounding all of this conjecture, when Dempster was re-examined later by prosecution counsel he was asked what position Robin might have been in when he died. Dempster answered, 'I can't say with any reliability what position he was in when he died. Standing, kneeling, sitting perhaps on the bean bag, I think those would be the possible positions.' This really only rules out lying down or standing on his head as alternatives. Dempster's uncertainty on this aspect makes it difficult to see how he could have been so forthright in his rejection of the likelihood of suicide.

A further farce, and one severely criticised in the report from the ex-CIB superintendent, was the police reconstruction of Robin's final moments. This was attended by Jim Doyle, Milton Weir, Mark Lodge, Kevin Anderson, police armourer Ngamoki, and the police photographer Trevor Gardiner, who recorded the series of simulated falls by Weir (acting Robin's part) on video.

The chart that was produced attesting to the results of this reconstruction lists nine various possibilities that these gentlemen had experimented with. Only two of them passed the criteria they set, which were: position of the body, rifle, spent shell, blood on the floor and blood on the curtain.

This reconstruction was seriously deficient in two ways. Firstly, it was carried out on 29 June, five days after David's arrest, and so the degree of objectivity is questionable. The results were assembled and compiled by the very same officers responsible for charging David; they were hardly open to the conclusion that it was suicide. Secondly, no independent expert was on hand to monitor the tests. The obvious person would have been Alec Dempster himself. It seems inexplicable that he wasn't asked to attend, unless of course one takes the view that the reconstructions were done, not to assess what might have happened, but rather to confirm what the police hoped had happened.

The reconstruction results are recorded as showing that suicide kneeling at the chair and murder kneeling at the chair were both positive in all respects except for the position the rifle was found in. They concluded, however, that in the case of murder the rifle was 'placed' by the offender, without considering that if it was suicide and the finder handled the rifle, then murder or suicide kneeling at the chair, as they put it, are equally likely. If the police had in fact retained an open-minded policy, the reconstructions actually show the possibility of either murder or suicide, and they would have continued to investigate other factors surrounding the case, such as Cottle's evidence and the testing of blood on Robin, more thoroughly. This again is confirmation, I believe, of my major contention, that David was arrested prematurely, and that everything the police did subsequent to his arrest was clouded by subjective judgement.

Perhaps the most damning evidence against the proposition that Robin had no involvement in the other murders and did not commit suicide are the two 'smears' of blood on his left hand and heavy staining on his sweatshirt. One smear was on the inside of his hand on the heel of his thumb, and the other was on the outside of his little finger running, according to Mark Lodge's diagram, from the joint nearest the finger nail to nearly the base of the finger.

If Robin Bain did nothing except come in from his caravan

to pray, as the police postulate, how did he get these two smears of blood on his hand? Drops or spots of blood, if tested and proved to have been his, might have spurted from the wound as he was murdered. But if it was murder, how could he have got smears of blood on his hands in two separate places, one on the outer surface, and one on the palm? This was never put to the jury either. So not only was the blood on Robin not tested to ascertain its origin, but also no account was taken of the fact that much of it could not have got there as a result of his own wound, and therefore it must have got there as a result of some other action.

Having now addressed all of the points which the judge considered to be the prime pieces of Crown evidence pointing to David as the murderer, it is worthwhile to put ourselves in the position of the jury.

The judge is directing the jury in his summing up. The jurors are untrained in law, unsophisticated as to the process of justice and courtroom tactics and, one presumes, diligent in their pursuit of doing the right thing. The judge referred to these twelve allegations as facts. Some of them were not facts, even according to what the jury heard in the trial. It may have been the duty of David's defence counsel to expose these half-truths for what they were, but the fact remains that the judge's statement that Robin was in completely blood-free clothes, for example, is simply not true. He wasn't. He had blood on his hat, his hood, his sweater and his trousers, not to mention of course his left hand.

My sympathy goes out to the jurors who were asked to provide a verdict in one of the most serious criminal trials in New Zealand's history. They could reasonably have expected in that natural Kiwi way to have been presented with the evidence in fair, reasonable and complete form instead of the misleading and partial 'facts' that the prosecution presented.

I suppose, in the adversarial system of justice that operates here in New Zealand, it is the responsibility of the defence to bring these anomalies to the attention of the court. It is not my intention in this book or anywhere else to castigate, criticise or blame individuals – with the best intentions, things don't always go according to plan in this life. What troubles me so much about this particular case is that most of the anomalies highlighted in this book have come from a close and detailed study of the police file itself, as supplied to me by Michael Guest. Not only did the police know that (for example in the case of the time of 6.44) they were providing seriously misleading evidence to the court, but one would expect that if Guest had read the file, then he too must have known. The question then is: did he know and fail to act for some reason, or did he simply fail to notice a series of significant and critical documents?

Perhaps the answer can be found in a statement he made on the 'Inside New Zealand' documentary, which he was paid, according to him, $7500 to participate in. During the programme, in a portion filmed just weeks before the trial actually commenced, someone came into his office with a reef of files, about ten centimetres thick. Guest asked what they were, and was told they were further discovery documents from the police on the Bain case.

He turned to the camera, shook his head, and said, 'Another four inches of papers. There probably won't be anything there, but we would be grossly negligent if we didn't flick through it thinking we might find something.'

I feel that this book would not be complete without my commenting to some extent on the defence. I am reluctant to do so, for it may well be taken to be a personal attack. It is not. However, my opinion is that Michael Guest and his inexperienced support group were entirely inadequate as a defence team for a person being tried on five counts of murder. I believe that Guest was very foolish to agree to the 'Inside New Zealand' documentary. I believe that despite having a 'good handle on the case', he was grossly underprepared in detailed analysis to conduct proper and complete cross-examinations. The lack of expert testimony called by the defence on such highly debatable issues as existed in this trial further exemplifies the hasty defence preparations. I believe that due to the lack of experienced members on his team he carried the burden far too heavily on his own shoulders, particularly with regard to tactics, which are critical in the cut-and-thrust of courtroom law.

The opinions I express here have been gleaned from discussions with a variety of extremely experienced and noted barristers. I am convinced that had Michael Guest enlisted the support of or, even better, joined forces with further experienced barristers, and set about from the time of David's arrest analysing in detail the police file, and constructing a defence based upon expert rebuttal of the Crown expert witnesses, David would be a free man. If the 'Inside New Zealand' programme revealed anything, it was that despite the incredible emotional commitment of the defence team, they quite simply were not adequately prepared or resourced to conduct a defence against the might of the Crown in such an important, complex and public case.

If in fact, he was as seriously limited in his legal aid funding as he suggested on that documentary, then that is a problem that needs to be addressed. However, my information is that the legal aid system entitles the defence to an expert to match every expert the Crown may call.

So was it bad luck or bad management? Take, for example, the Dean Cottle saga, which I accept a 'Perry Mason' scriptwriter could hardly have concocted: should the defence have made a far more serious effort to get Cottle on their side much earlier? Should they not have recognised far earlier that so much blood was untested?. Should they not have called on a pathologist of their own before they finally did, in Melbourne, only about four weeks before the trial? There are many such instances.

I have not covered some areas in the trial that the defence did very well. One of the objectives of this book is to demonstrate that for one reason or another the court did not hear 'the whole truth and nothing but the truth'. Perhaps I am being naive, in that that is just the way it is. If that be so, then I hope that change is in the wind. After all, we as citizens expect the criminals in our society to prevaricate, even on the stand. That is the nature of their occupation, so to speak. We do not expect it of anyone in our police, under any circumstances. My intention is not to blame Michael Guest, Bill Wright, Jim Doyle, the judge, the jury or any particular individual. That will ultimately be the job of a higher authority, I expect.

When the evidence is properly analysed, when the deceptions, distractions, courtroom tactics and dramatics are stripped bare, it is entirely clear to me that justice in the true sense of the word – the quality or fact of being fair, impartial and honest – has not been served on David Bain.

STRANGE HAPPENINGS

This case, a compelling and controversial mystery from the start, becomes more perplexing the deeper one gets into it.

In the first instance, David Bain's trial is unique in the annals of New Zealand legal history. Never before has anyone been tried for five murders here – it is the most serious criminal case against an individual ever brought before a New Zealand court.

It is unusual, too, that David had lost his entire family, and then the extended family members all turned hostile, leaving him entirely alone, with just a few dedicated friends and his lawyer as his only support. The family attitude remains to this day.

It is strange to say the least that a person who has been adjudged to have no psychological problems whatsoever is at the same time convicted of murdering his entire family without the slightest motive. An interesting document on this subject came to my attention. It was put out by the New Zealand police in December 1994, about six months after the murders and five months prior to David Bain's trial and conviction. It comes under the heading: '1992–1994 Murders where psychiatric condition of the offender has been possible cause.'

It lists 35 murders in total, the last one being David Bain; this five months before he was tried. In law, he was innocent until proven guilty. The reason given for his motivation in this document was: psychiatric disorder.

Another first, as I understand it, was the absolutely bizarre burning down of the Bain family home. Just days after David's arrest, he was visited in prison by his uncles, the executors of the will of Robin and Margaret Bain. They advised him of their intention, having made the decision in consultation with the police to burn the house down. This was David's house until or unless he was ultimately proven guilty. He had lost, just a few weeks earlier, his entire family. He had suffered the trauma and shock of finding them dead, and was now charged with their murders. The uncles say that David agreed to their proposal. How did they expect David to make any sort of rational decision at that time? Even more distastefully, the house was burnt down the same day as their visit to David. I doubt whether any New Zealander with a television set does not have some recollection of the pictures of the inferno when the fire department razed the home to the ground. This image is emblazoned on the minds of the people of Dunedin, the same people from whom, in less than a year, a jury would be selected. No stronger signal of the police and family's view of David's guilt could have been conveyed to the community. This offensive act truly set the scene for David's 'fair trial'.

The Cottle affair is also unusual in New Zealand legal history. Cottle, the prime defence witness, failed to show up to testify at the prescribed time, had a warrant issued for his arrest and finally arrived at the court voluntarily after the trial was over, at the luncheon adjournment between the final submissions of the Crown and defence. He was not allowed legal advice of any kind, then was questioned by the judge and counsel as to his reliability, finally being judged unreliable and sent on his way without giving evidence. Finally, he was fined

$200 for not turning up in the first place and Michael Guest was required to deliver his final address to the jury immediately after Cottle had been dismissed by the judge.

Another oddity in this case came in the form of an anonymous letter received by Michael Guest a couple of months after David's arrest. The thrust of this letter, which is certainly written by somebody who was familiar with David's family, is that a local Dunedin person who also knew the family well had been acting strangely and 'knew much more about the murders, eg: body position, rifle position, number of shots in each deceased and so on', than had ever been made public. It goes on to say that the writer could not for certain say that this person had anything to do with the murders, but was concerned enough to make this information known.

I cannot reveal any further details without exposing the identity of the person in question. I can say, however, that Guest, after consideration and some action, decided there was nothing in it and passed the letter on to the police. They took a statement from the person accused in the letter, and that was the end of the matter.

I should dearly love the writer of that letter to make himor herself known to myself, Colin Withnall or Stephen O'Driscoll. Absolute anonymity would be guaranteed. It is not that I place particular weight on the letter's contents, but it is another unsolved piece in the jigsaw.

Another first for New Zealand was the 'Inside New Zealand' documentary. Never before had legal counsel allowed a camera into its office and behind the scenes in such an intimate way. In fact, most barristers seem reluctant to comment at all on the workings and machinations of a trial, let alone be filmed in the process. Mike Guest's decision to enter into the arrangement is without precedent, and questionable from the point of view of the extent to which he may have been distracted from the important task he was responsible for.

Other bizarre twists and unresolved matters in this case relate to matters that the police themselves created. The question that continually befuddles people is, 'Why would they be so determined to get David, unless they were sure he did it?' I have my suspicions about what motivated those in charge of the investigation team, but have never concerned myself overly with the question. I have instead addressed myself to the issue of the evidence itself, and the discrepancies that exist between what the police knew to be true and what the court was told. However, it is intriguing to consider the following points, some of which I have covered already, and to ponder as to why they were as they were.

The first matter is a fresh one. It will be recalled that David made the 111 call at 7.09 am on that Monday morning. This was attested to by a print-out obtained by the police from the Telecom Malicious Call Centre in Hamilton. The anomaly here relates to the initial statements of the Telecom operator and her supervisor in Christchurch who actually handled the call. They were both interviewed on the following day by a detective from the Christchurch CIB, following a request from Dunedin CIB. Sandra Mary Bampton, the service assistant supervisor, says in her statement, 'I know the time on the print-out I gave you says that the time of the call starting is 7.10 a.m., but I believe we first started the call at about 6.45 or 6.50 a.m. This is because I had finished my previous day's work and my service assistant who starts at 7.00 a.m. wasn't there. Fran now also believes it was earlier.'

Fran Edwards, the operator who actually took the call, says: 'The caller was confused. Said, "My father is dead, my sisters and brother are dead. I can't breathe." He was very hard to understand. I think the call came in just after 6.30 a.m. I was talking to him for some time.'

A subsequent message from the CIB detective in Christchurch to the Dunedin CIB states: 'Statement from supervisor at Telecom. Note that they believe the call may have started earlier. She will make enquiries re this matter. The time on the print-out may just be *when it was transmitted*.'

It seems this issue was never resolved. Bampton was not called in the trial. Edwards was, but was not questioned by either side in relation to the issue of time. If it so happens that they are correct in their statements that the call was before 7.00 a.m., then the sinister missing fifteen minutes in David's memory is of course not missing at all.

I have already referred to the curious lack of records relating to the use of Cottle's cell phone. Another curious feature is the list of telephone numbers found among Laniet's possessions. Police enquiries were apparently unable to identify some of the subscribers referred to, yet enquiries carried out on my behalf resulted in this information being obtained.

Another oddity that has come to light in the course of my investigation and analysis is in relation to the photographic evidence. The police photographer was not called to give evidence in the trial. An edited version of the video footage taken by the police was shown to the court as evidence. Detective Sergeant Weir testified that the photographer was called in to the house immediately after the pathologist, who made his entry at 12.05 p.m. I have since requested from the police the original footage (something that the defence could have done right at the beginning) and although the tape provided is not the complete footage, I have established that the first footage taken on the police video camera was taken at 10.45 a.m., about an hour and a half before Weir testified that it was. Unfortunately, this tape, too, has been edited. It is my belief however, that the entire footage of the film taken prior to 12.05 would provide a number of answers to unexplainable matters, including the mystery of exhibit 172, the lens 'found' in Stephen's bedroom. The question is, 'Why is it that the jury were told that filming did not start until after 12.05 p.m. when the tape itself shows this to be untrue?'

Another extremely odd matter, again referred to in the

report I had done into the police investigation, is the fact that David was retained at the scene for so long. The report says in part:

> I am extremely surprised at the length of time David was kept at the scene. Clearly from the very beginning he was either the number one suspect or the number one victim. I am firmly of the view that all that was required was a short sharp interview . . . steps taken to ensure that no potential evidence was lost from David or his clothing and his removal.
>
> The lack of evidence on David, for example firearms discharge residue, would have been a powerful argument in his defence except that by the time it was done it was too late anyway, and therefore of no use to him.

I have already referred to the farce of the police reconstructions of the death of Robin Bain. Every reconstruction was done *subsequent* to David's arrest. I refer again to the report:

> The primary purpose of reconstructions is to duplicate an event which has occurred and to examine what happens during the duplication so as to draw conclusions as to what may have happened in the original event.
>
> It is highly preferable to conduct reconstructions prior to making an arrest. The reason is obvious, *namely that you usually rely on the results of reconstructions to give you evidence as part of the total evidence you rely upon to make an arrest.* [My emphasis.]

Nearly a year after David's arrest, the police did a reconstruction of the paper run. Incredibly, the officer doing the simulation *did not carry any newspapers* with him, and not unexpectedly, he arrived home at precisely the time needed to whip inside and turn the computer on.

They did a simulation of David doing the washing, mainly to establish how long the washing machine cycle took. They needed it to take as long as possible to sustain their theory that David could not have put the washing on when he got home because the machine was not going about 45 minutes later when the police made entry to the house, according to those police staff. They did this simulation on a weekend afternoon when the water pressure in that locality was considerably less than it is at 6.45 a.m. when David said he did the wash. The filling time alone was about thirteen minutes, roughly double what it would have been in the morning. In addition, they only put the machine through its longest cycle, at about just after 12 o'clock on the washing machine dial, whereas David said he flicked the dial around to about 2 or 3 o'clock. The shorter cycle was never timed.

The rifle they used to do 'ejection' tests relating to the shells ejected as each shot was fired was not even the same rifle as the murder weapon.

Robert Ngamoki was the police armourer. Part of his evidence was to be that the rifle was too long for Robin Bain to have reached the trigger and shot himself (despite the fact that no one had measured the length of Robin's arms). Guest demonstrated successfully to the court with a piece of stick that Ngamoki had *over-measured* the length of the rifle by about 8 inches (20 cm).

Another remarkable piece of testimony was that David's fitting and convulsing was a Hollywood, staged to fool the police. The senior ambulance officer made this suggestion in his testimony. Referring again to the judge's summing up; 'various other pieces of evidence including the fact that one of the experienced ambulance officers said in answer to a question, that he thought the shaking and shivering the accused did while they were there as being "put on"'.

The same ambulance officer's report states that David was

unconscious for three minutes. Was he putting that on too?

I have already dealt with the fact that while vital evidence was dissipating, disappearing and possibly being contaminated by overexposure to foot traffic, the crucial person who should have been examining that evidence, the pathologist, was left sitting on the street for hours. This, at best, seems to have been a gross oversight, and at the worst has extremely sinister implications.

I have already dealt at length with the fact that 'heavy blood staining' on Robin Bain's clothing was not even tested for blood grouping. It is obvious that if any of that blood belonged to Stephen, for instance, then the case against David disappears.

I have mentioned that clearly Robin Bain's head has been handled and moved after his death. Photo 23 clearly illustrated two things, which Alec Dempster could not answer but agreed with when I met with him. One, that if his head as depicted in the photos was in that position when he died, then the blood from the wound has run uphill and across the forehead. As Dempster agreed, blood does not do that. Also, the large stain of blood on the carpet to the left of Robin's head is removed by some inches from his head. Once again, as Dempster agreed, blood does not jump over open spaces. There is also a blood run on his forehead that has no origin and appears to be running in the opposite direction to the angle of his head. Dempster could offer no explanation for that, as clearly if that were the case it did not come from Robin's own wound. Also, there is a smudged area of blood on his right forehead, that appears to have been made by the palm of a hand.

Dempster put a microscope on the photo and agreed that it did indeed give that appearance. It was at about that stage that my meeting with him came to an end.

This list could go on and on – I have not even touched here on the issue of the lens and the timing evidence. Finding a suitable turn of phrase to summarise the discrepancies, omissions, deficiencies and untruths put by the Crown in their case against David is something I have struggled to do.

I have asked myself: Is it possible that the list of discrepancies, omissions and deficiencies in this case can be put down to chance? Or is this an example of what British judge Pitt Taylor described in the following excerpt from a treatise on the law of evidence, published early this century:

> . . . it must be remembered, that, in a case of circumstantial evidence, the facts are collected by degrees. Something occurs to raise suspicion against a particular party. Constables and police officers are immediately on the alert, and with professional zeal, ransack every place and paper, and examine into every circumstance which can tend to establish, not his innocence, but his guilt. Presuming him guilty form the first, they are apt to consider his acquittal as a tacit reflection on their discrimination or skill, and, with something like the feeling of a keen sportsman they determine, if possible to bag their game. Though both sportsmen and policemen alike would be horrified at anything unfair or "unsportsmanlike", yet as both start with the object in view, it is easy to unintentionally misinterpret innocent actions, to misunderstand innocent words, for men readily believe what they anxiously desire, and to be ever ready to construe the most harmless facts as preconceived opinions. These feelings are common alike to police, to counsel, engineers, surveyors, medical men, antiquarians, and philosophers; indeed, to all persons who first assume that a fact or system is true, and then seek for arguments to support and prove its truth.

Is this what happened to David, or is it possible that even more disturbing implications can be drawn?

ROBIN OR DAVID?

It is not my desire to expose the sordid happenings within the Bain family for the sake of it. But the need to do so is obvious. The whole reason for my involvement in this case is a desire to expose the truth, and in doing so I have to answer the judge's question to the jury:

'Who did it? Robin Bain or David Bain?'

Bearing in mind the implications of that poser, perhaps the most incredible aspect of this case is that not one scrap of evidence was put to the court as to the state of mind, life and times of Robin Bain himself.

No doubt, like all of us, he had his strengths and weaknesses, human frailties and personal virtues. Although it feels almost shameful to be exposing the life of a dead person, in this instance it is absolutely necessary, and should have been addressed, firstly by the investigating team, and then during the trial itself.

The police were made aware by Cottle's statement three days after the murders of a possible sordid hidden side in the life of Robin Bain. They did not aggressively follow up on this line of enquiry. Despite that, they still obtained some very telling evidence that they chose to ignore.

Let's look at what is known, partly gleaned from the police

file itself, and partly as a result of my own work over the past year.

On Tuesday 21 June, the day after the murders, the police took a statement from a 46-year-old woman who worked as a director of a well-known education facility. She stated that she had known the family for six years in Papua New Guinea from 1980 to 1986, and that she got to know the family well during that time. She saw them in Dunedin in 1990, but did not see them again until the January of 1994 when she called at the Bain home and stayed for an hour or two. She said, 'I was surprised Margaret looked so well when I arrived.'

Margaret told her that she was unhappy with Laniet, who had left home, but did not elaborate on details. Arawa was at teachers college and they were proud of her. David was changing courses at university and very involved in the dramatic society. They were proud of his achievements. 'Both boys were happy to see us; they were warm and friendly,' she told the police. She then says: 'The husband, Robin, was at home when we called. I was shocked in the change in his appearance. He looked cadaverous, white and gaunt. Knowing he was working fulltime surprised me. He looked like a man who couldn't do that. There was a big change in his appearance from when I saw him previously. He was very quiet. Said little. Seemed pleased to see us but very reserved . . .'

'Robin seemed depressed to me.'

A second statement taken the same day was given by a registered practising psychologist, who told the police that he had known Robin and Margaret since the early seventies.

He spoke revealingly of his impressions of them in the early days. 'Robin was a very introverted person who was sensitive, intense and serious,' he said. 'I spoke with Robin quite a few times and got the impression that their relationship wasn't great, almost a dependency rather than a good marriage. She on the other hand spoke of her husband as a naughty child. She was certainly the dominant person; she could belittle him in front of others. He would just take it and say nothing. I could tell from his face that he felt those comments deeply. I saw no evidence of any clinical signs of illness in those days,' he told them.

He went on to say that he saw them a couple of times following their return to New Zealand. He ran into Margaret in the street for a few minutes and she said things were terrible, and he was aware that they had separated, to all intents and purposes. He then said that he had seen Robin at the last Regent Theatre book sale and spoken to him for about half an hour. 'He was a very private person. He liked me and seemed pleased to meet me. I asked how the family was. He said something like, "It's a real battle bringing up children in this world".'

'I got the impression he wanted to come and speak to me about things. He didn't look good.

'He looked haggard, grey and depressed, much older than his age.

'I got the impression that he could be quite capable of doing a thing like this, killing his family out of a sense of betrayal on his wife's part and a sense of love as far as his children are concerned.' This from a long-time associate and registered practising psychologist.

Another statement was given on the Thursday, the same day as Cottle revealed the incest allegation.

The informant stated that Robin had boarded with his family before getting married, and he had seen a lot of Robin and Margaret up until the time they left for Papua New Guinea. He related that Robin owned a rifle and liked to go rabbit shooting.

He had met Robin again after the family's return from Papua New Guinea. 'When I first saw Robin I couldn't believe it as he was so drawn in the face and skinny as a rake. I thought he had a disease from the islands. He was dressed pretty shabby.

'The next thing I saw Robin at my father's 80th birthday. My father is a member of the male choir with Robin. That day Robin looked like a lost soul. I found out he had shifted to Taieri Mouth School with his daughter. This was the 7th of May. [Just six weeks prior to the murders.] My wife wasn't keen on having contact with the Bains, and my friendship with Robin was never really established.

'On the day of the tragedy I knew before it was announced it was going to be the Bain family. I don't believe Robin could have done this.'

I have previously told of how Alan Hunter, Laniet's flat mate, described Robin as having a possessive relationship with Laniet and being tense and crazy. He told the police of that incident.

Not long after I got involved with the case in January of 1996, I got to meet with Ross Stevens, the '60 Minutes' reporter, a couple of times. He had lived in Papua New Guinea for years and was a very close friend of Robin Bain's, knew the family very well, and had actually presented a TV documentary on the case just after the trial. Ross told me of an incident that had haunted him ever since the Bain deaths. The previous Christmas, about six months before the family deaths, Robin Bain had unexpectedly called at Ross's house in Wellington one evening, while Ross had dinner guests. He had not seen Robin since he had returned to New Zealand, and he too was shocked by his appearance. Robin, Ross said, had always been quite a sociable person as he knew him, and so he invited him to join the gathering. Robin declined. He was quiet and seemed withdrawn, Ross said. He and Robin went and sat in the lounge and chatted for a while, but it was awkward being removed from his other guests. After only a short time, Robin left, despite Ross trying to encourage him to stay and enjoy the company. Ross told me that later, and in particular in the light of what eventually happened, he felt Robin had wanted to talk to him. He wondered if, had the occasion been different, and had they been able to spend time together, in view of Robin's obviously agitated state of mind, the ensuing disaster might have been averted.

Yet another account of the clearly serious decline in the physical and mental well-being of Robin Bain, from a very close personal friend.

Further evidence that all was not well came from the Otago education authority, in a matter revealed on a '20/20' programme produced by Mike Turner and presented by Melanie Reid. They uncovered a letter confirming that, in the period just before June 1994, a complaint had been received from a family at Taieri Beach School about Robin. No details were available, but the psychological services branch of the education board had sent a person to see Robin regarding the complaint. I believe they also confirmed to the '20/20' team that Robin had not got the mid-year reports out on time. Now, I know that the board of trustees spoke highly of Robin at the time of his death. However, I place little weight on this as in almost every case of a disgraced school teacher in this country the relevant board has done the same thing, often very adamantly over a long period of time.

We know that Robin, by any standards, had been living a humiliating and decrepit life over his past few years. He drove a filthy old Commer van, and prior to getting the school house to live in just before his death he had actually lived in this van at the school during the week. On weekends he slept in the derelict caravan at the back of the Every Street house. This was filthy too, and littered with junk. He had no money to speak of; most of his earnings went to Margaret to support herself and the children. He was ostracised from the family and from the house and yet had to work to support both. This could well explain to a significant degree the depressed state of mind he was in at the time of and leading up to the tragedy.

In any crime, particularly a serious and horrendous one

such as this, motive is obviously a major factor. So of course is state of mind. I refer again to my CIB man's report, and quote: 'It is not necessary for the prosecution to prove a motive for these killings. However, in all homicide enquiries, the police treat establishing a motive as a key issue. Identifying a motive or motives dictates to a large degree how the enquiry is handled. In this case there was no obvious motive until Cottle made his statement.'

It seems to me that the ordinary person can easily understand this. Such events do not occur without a compelling reason – unless you're crazy, insane or seriously psychotically disturbed. If you try to rob a bank, you're doing it for the money. Simple stuff.

I have dwelt on Cottle's evidence already. The key point is not just the allegation of incest, but that Laniet was going home that very weekend to talk the whole thing out. She had not stayed at home for nearly a year. Her presence at home that night was the unusual feature, and I am certain, the precipitative factor – the trigger – in what happened the following morning.

In the time since my concerns about this case have been so publicly aired, and, perhaps even more to the point, since Cottle's evidence, previously suppressed, was made public as a result of the 'Holmes' appeal, some important information has come to hand, which entirely corroborates and confirms Dean Cottle's evidence. We have statements and affidavits from members of the community, the content of which so seriously undermines the credibility of certain parties involved in this case that I do not even want to consider the implications.

Firstly we have the owners of the local dairy across the road from the flat in which Laniet lived. They have revealed their information publicly on television and provided formal sworn statements through me to David's solicitor. They had become very well acquainted with Laniet and met Robin quite often when he would come into their shop with her.

The main thrust of their statements is to confirm that Laniet was a prostitute, that she would often chat to them about the state of her life, and that one particular day she told them point blank that 'she was having an affair with her father'. They said that they were surprised not to have been visited by the police or even seen any police personnel in the area after the murders, bearing in mind that Laniet's flat was directly across the road from their shop. They also asserted that on Sunday 19 June, the day before the murders, Robin Bain came into their shop with Laniet in the afternoon and was very insistent that he pay her account, which stood at about $20, in full. On that occasion she told them that she was going to spend that night at home. They further stated that they came forward to provide this information because the *Otago Daily Times* had reported, following the exposure of Cottle's statement, that the police said that Cottle's statement was entirely unsupported, and yet they had known all the time.

In a further remarkable revelation one of them goes on to say that he met Mike Guest at a party just after the trial and told him exactly what they have told me. He says that Guest seemed uninterested in what he had to say! Surely Guest could have used this information to back up Cottle's statement when he went to the Court of Appeal a few months later.

I also have mind-blowing information from an old friend of Robin's, whose family is well acquainted with members of Robin's family. In the first instance, this information reveals that Robin had 'serious personal problems' as a young man at training college in Wellington, and in particular these problems 'caused him to make it difficult to mix well with girls in society'.

The same informant then confirms what I had strongly suspected for a long time. Another unresolved matter on the police file is that more than one of Laniet's friends gave statements to the police saying that Laniet had a photo of a baby which she maintained she had given birth to in Papua New Guinea as a result of being raped. She says she gave birth when she was eleven years old and the baby was adopted out. You will remember that Cottle's statement alleges Laniet told him that her incestuous relationship with her father dated back to Papua New Guinea. The information provided by this long-time acquaintance of the Bains is that this baby was a result of 'the incestuous relationship that her father forced on her', and that this information was provided to our informant by a member of the Bain family. This informant goes on to say, 'Robin, knowing Laniet's impending release of the incest facts, could well have killed his wife and three children in order to keep these facts secret. He would trust David to keep the family secret because of his trust and pride in him, not for one minute thinking that he would be accused of the murders.'

One of young Stephen's closest friends has also given a statement to me saying that Stephen had said, 'There's something funny about Laniet and Dad; they carry on like Mum and Dad should.'

Clearly, something precipitated the dreadful tragedy. Some event, some happening or some revelation caused the killer to set about the cold-blooded execution.

The outstanding oddity about the events of that night and morning was that Laniet was home for the first time in nearly a year. On the Sunday night, Mrs Bain went out at about 11.30 to the cash machine at her bank. She withdrew $200 in cash, which was found at her bedside, and also transferred quite a significant amount of money from the joint account of Robin and herself to her own account. At the time of the deaths, Robin had $30-odd in his bank account, and Margaret had about $3000 in hers. To what extent this visit to the bank in the middle of the night is somehow related to the events of the following morning I cannot say with any certainty, but it indicates that something odd was going on in the Bain household during the night prior to the shootings. My information is that Laniet went with her and they also called at Laniet's Russell Street flat.

Another informant, a former PhD student, told me that, just weeks before the murders, he ran into Laniet at the university cafe. She was distressed and looking for David. She told him that it was urgent that she see David, and if he saw David could he make sure David got in touch with her as soon as possible. She said, 'I want to shift back home but I don't know if Mum will let me because I've fallen out with her. *But I can't stand what Dad's doing to me any longer.*' She wanted David to intervene between herself and Margaret so that she would be allowed back home.

It preys on his mind to this day that he left to go overseas the following day to lecture at a British University, and was not able to pass the message on to David. When he returned to New Zealand the family was dead and David was in prison awaiting trial. He wonders, with good cause, if, had he managed to get David to see Laniet, the entire tragedy might have been averted.

Obviously Robin was under extreme mental pressure, and he had an overwhelming and compelling motive. The secret of his unnatural hold on his daughter was going to be exposed. His time had run out.

He had the motive, but did he have the opportunity? He had been associated with firearms all his life. He had used David's rifle with David, and almost certainly had used it unbeknown to David. There is no other explanation for the spent shells, 20 of them, scientifically proven to have been fired by David's rifle, found lying on a dresser in his caravan. And Robin knew that David would be out on his paper run for about an hour that Monday morning. Ample time.

Yes, he had both motive and opportunity. But does this

possibility fit with the evidence? Is it not true that the police had an overwhelming mountain of evidence against David, and nothing, not a scrap to suggest the father's involvement?

When the police went to Robin's caravan, the light was on and the radio was going. At his bedside was the book he had apparently been reading, an Agatha Christie murder story about a series of family killings, *Death Comes as the End*. There is undisputed evidence that Robin always arrived at school dressed and ready for work. He did not even go into his house at the school on those occasions that he arrived at work from Every Street. He was found dead wearing track-suit pants, a singlet, a shirt, a brown jumper and a green woollen hat underneath the hood of the blue sweatshirt which was over the top of the jumper. He had not shaved. He was not dressed or prepared in any way to go to work that morning.

The blood recorded by Lodge as 'heavy staining' on his green hat, on the inside and outside of the hood of his blue sweatshirt, on the right shoulder of his blue sweatshirt, on the palm and finger of his left hand, and near the cuffs of his track suit pants, could not have got there from the fatal wound in his left temple.

I have no doubt that if the blood staining on Robin's clothing had been analysed for blood grouping, it would have been found to be the blood of deceased members of his family. The nature of these bloody stains on Robin's attire and body is such that they could not have got there as a result of finding the dead bodies. It could not have got there from his own wound in the process of him being murdered.

Only one possible explanation remains.

What is left of the 'mountain of evidence' against David when a different perspective is taken?

Only four real facts remain. A minute smudge of blood on the crotch of David's shorts was established to be the blood of Stephen or Laniet. Two spots of blood on the soles of his socks were established to be Laniet's or Stephen's. The fingerprints of his left fingers were detected on the rifle in a 'pick up' position, not a firing position. He had a light bruise to the right eye region, and a small recent skin abrasion on his right knee.

These four facts are each simply and innocently understandable, indeed not unexpected revelations if one attaches them to David's account of what he did that bloody Monday as the 'finder' of his slain family.

Everything else on the list of the police 'mountain of evidence' is nothing more than speculation and conjecture. Moreover, when the details are assembled they are in so many instances absolutely contradictory to one another, and simply do not stand the test of simple logic and common sense. For example, the police speculated that David wrote the fake suicide message on the computer to frame his father. Just hours later, he told the police that as far as he knew, his father did *not know* the whereabouts of the keys to his gun. If he was deliberately framing his father, wouldn't he have claimed that Robin knew where the keys were kept?

They speculated that he wore his own gloves to escape detection, which in itself is a contradiction. An even more inane notion is that he then, despite having all the time in the world, and supposedly having done the laundry to get rid of evidence against him, left these gloves, his own gloves, at the scene of the struggle with Stephen.

They speculated that doing the paper run between the first four murders and the last was a part of his master plan, designed to put an air of normality on the morning's proceedings. This again barely gets 1 out of 10 for likelihood or logic. If he was a practised professional Mafia hit man, perhaps he might have had the composure to do this. But a naive young man with no history of any psychological or mental disturbance, no background of troublemaking or unruliness? What makes this theory even more untenable is that he knew that his father got up at about 6.30 a.m., and yet he quite leisurely arrived home from his paper round fifteen minutes later, in, we are expected to believe, the full knowledge that his father might well come into the house to find four slain bodies about the place. Some master plan.

The police speculated that the spectacles were worn by David and dislodged during the struggle he had with Stephen. Unlike all of the 'heavy staining' on Robin which they never bothered to analyse, they did analyse the spectacles, and not an iota of evidence – no blood, no hairs, no tissues, no fingerprints – was found on the frame or lens to link them to the bloody struggle with Stephen, or to David having ever used them. This theory really starts to get into difficulty though, when it proposes that, the glasses having been dislodged and both lenses knocked out of the frame, one lens finished up under an ice skate boot under a bunk and David, without leaving any tell-tale sign whatsoever (remember he is supposed to be smothered in Stephen's blood at this stage) took the frames and the other lens and put them neatly on the chair in his own bedroom. It is a preposterous notion, entirely devoid of any supporting evidence and totally disdainful of logic or reason, that the same person who minutes later is going out with his dog on a paper round 'to put an air of normality on the morning's proceedings' would carefully place one lens and the spectacles frame on a chair in his own bedroom while ignoring the second missing lens.

According to the prosecution case, David 'must' have rushed into the house and turned on the computer immediately upon getting home so that it was ready for him to write the fake suicide message. We now know that he could not have done that because he was not home when the computer was turned on. But let's return to the theory. This proposition does not take into account that he would have printer's ink all over his hands. None was found on the computer. It does not take into account that the whirr of the computer fan would surely have alerted his father when he came into the lounge to pray.

They speculated that he did the washing to clean tell-tale bloody garments that he had worn in the process of murdering his family. But he did not wash his shorts, socks or tee-shirt, and clearly he sorted out the clothes in the laundry into darks and whites, and he told them in his first interview that he had done the washing that morning. Surely this cool, composed, cold-blooded executioner would, had he done washing as part of his master plan, not have mentioned anything at all about it. The police attempted to allege that his 'bloody' palm print was located on the washing machine. Under cross-examination it was conceded by Kim Jones, police fingerprint expert, that in fact it was a palm print only, and no confirmation existed that it was blood at all.

The speculation went on and on and on, and all the repetition took its toll on the court.

'A hundred witnesses can't be wrong.' I'm sure this was the prevailing mood in that court house by the time the Crown had finished presenting its 'case'.

IN SUMMARY

What, then, would a fresh appraisal of David's case reveal? Essentially I believe it will reveal a list of highly significant matters that were never put before the jury. I believe, as I have previously stated, that this list of 'new evidence' is so compelling, not only for the totally different perspective that it throws on the case, but also in that the 'mountain of evidence' against David falls into a crumpled heap and that, in fact, the real mountain of evidence suggests very positively that Robin Bain was the perpetrator.

The following are all matters that were not put before the jury at any time during the three-week trial of David Cullen Bain.

1. They were never made aware that, on the calculations done by the police themselves, the computer was switched on at 6.42, not 6.44 a.m. Further proper analysis conducted by Colin Withnall QC has proved that the computer was in fact switched on between 6.40.05 and 6.42.07, when David could not have been home.

2. They heard nothing of the evidence of Dean Robert Cottle. Since my involvement, seven new people, entirely unconnected, none of whom are known to Cottle, have

given statements corroborating his evidence to some degree or another, and in some cases expanding on it.

3. They heard nothing of the grave doubt now cast on the photographic evidence relating to the finding of the left lens, exhibit 172. Our findings are substantiated by photographic analysis conducted at Auckland University.

4. They heard nothing about the glaring anomaly that exists in regard to the time that David made the 111 call. The statements of Bampton and Edwards indicate that the 'sinister missing fifteen minutes' may not be missing at all.

5. They heard nothing at all of the state of mind of Robin Bain in the months leading up to the tragedy.

6. Although they heard that heavy blood staining existed on Robin Bain's clothing and smears and splatters were on his hand, they heard no explanation as to why this blood was never tested, and how it could have been where it was, if in fact Robin Bain was not involved in the other murders.

7. They heard nothing about the obvious fact that Robin Bain's head had been moved after his death, providing the strongest possible corroboration of David's account that he found his father dead, and also throwing grave doubt on the Crown 'no suicide' theory as it relates to the position of the rifle and the body.

8. They heard nothing of the ambulance officer's report that David was unconscious for three minutes after they arrived.

9. They heard nothing of the fact that no blood was found on the inside of David's running shoes, the significance of this being that the Crown theory about the sequence of the murders falls to pieces.

10. They heard nothing of the evidence that David had not been wearing glasses for the three days before the murders while his own were being repaired.

17. Robin Bain's old Commer van.

18. The back yard at 65 Every Street, with the caravan that Robin slept in.

19. Inside the caravan; there are 20 shells fired by David's rifle on the dresser.

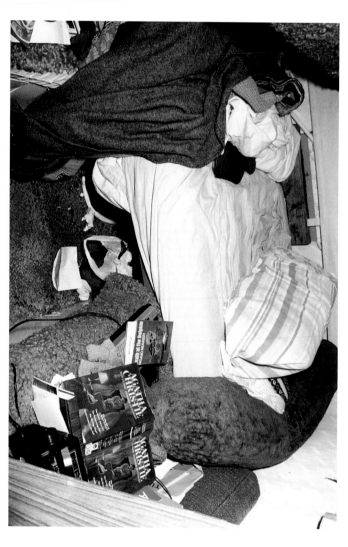

20. Inside the caravan. The Agatha Christie book which Robin had been reading is open to a page in *Death Comes as the End*.

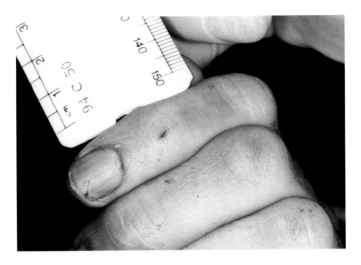

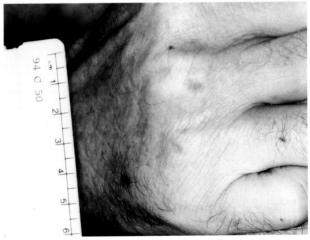

21. Above: the blood splash on Robin's fingernail, which the Crown said could not have got there through his shooting himself, and other blood on his fingers, none of which was analysed.

Below: the recent bruise and abrasions on Robin's hand.

22. Robin Bain. The computer is in the alcove behind the curtains to the right. The rifle is on the floor between Robin and the curtains, about 30cm from his left leg.

23. Robin Bain. The direction the blood has run from his wound and
the blood stain on the carpet clearly indicate that his head has
been moved.

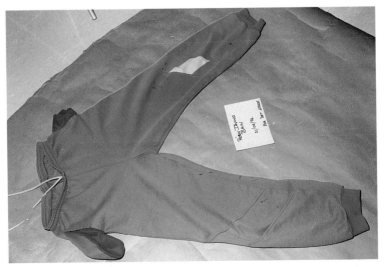

24. The trousers and sweatshirt that Robin was wearing. The blood stains on them are not consistent with the wound that killed him, and most of the blood was not tested for blood grouping to establish its source.

11. They were not made aware that when Weir testified that the video footage commenced soon after midday in fact he was not telling the truth. The police definitely took video footage prior to the plastic sheeting being laid out on the floor, which was done at 11.40 a.m.

12. They did not hear that David had always had untinted lenses in his glasses, whereas his mother had tinted lenses. The incriminating lens, exhibit 172, was tinted.

13. They only heard experts called by the Crown. In some matters, under cross-examination, Guest obtained significant concessions from these Crown expert witnesses. However, I have during my involvement found expert opinion that seriously takes issue with some of the most telling arguments put forward by the Crown.

The Crown in its summing up likened its case to the three points of a triangle. The first point, they said, represented the mountain of evidence against David. The second point was strong evidence that excluded Robin Bain from having killed other members of his family, and the third point was overwhelming evidence establishing that Robin Bain did not commit suicide.

The basic contention of this book is that David was arrested prematurely, at a time when although the police had every right to consider him a suspect, they also were aware of a substantial body of evidence that suggested a contrary conclusion. Proceeding with the arrest at the time that they did, I believe, led to an entirely subjective analysis of this body of evidence to the point where they ignored anything which did not suit their theory.

What have I discovered to support this claim?

Firstly, in regard to motive. On the day before David's arrest, the police were made aware by Cottle of a possible compelling motive for Robin Bain to have taken his family's lives and his own. Clearly, they didn't even have time to properly enquire into the matters raised by Cottle's statement.

Secondly, they had not commenced any reconstructions at all prior to David's arrest. Subsequently they conducted reconstructions to ascertain the possible outcomes on a variety of issues including:

- the sequence of events in the house
- the means of death of Robin Bain
- the washing machine cycle
- the paper run.

These should all have been done with a view to ascertaining the facts in order to arrive at a conclusion, not to attempt to prove a conclusion already made.

Thirdly, and of extreme significance, forensic analysis had hardly begun at the time David was arrested. This can be the only explanation, for example, as to why they didn't have the copious quantities of blood on Robin's body and clothing analysed. That is to say, had they tested the blood after arresting David, and found it to incriminate Robin, they would clearly have been in an embarrassing situation and so they preferred not to test it at all.

Add to this the fact that a firearms discharge residue test conducted in the proper manner at the appropriate time would probably have solved this case beyond doubt, and I lay my contention that this enquiry was conducted in a bungled and incompetent manner.

The disgraceful aspect is that the inaccurate, misleading conclusions that the police reached as a result of their own ineptitude were used against David in the trial. Of the three points of the Crown triangle, as I have already demonstrated, little remains intact.

The first point is the evidence against David. The two primary pieces of evidence against David I have dealt with extensively. Firstly, he could not have been home when the computer was turned on, and just as significantly, the time from when it was turned on until he did get home, somewhere between three and six minutes, was ample time for Robin to have typed in the message and killed himself.

Secondly, the conclusion that the glasses lens found in Stephen's bedroom had got there as a result of David wearing the glasses at the time he was alleged to have been involved in a struggle with Stephen is, as a result of my investigation, thrown into the gravest of doubt. I say this based on the following:

1. Expert analysis of the photographs has revealed that what Weir points out as being a lens is in fact a piece of plastic overlaying some white paper.
2. The position of the lens in photo 99 after surrounding objects have been uplifted is considerably removed from the position where Weir said he found it.
3. Absolutely no evidence exists at all to link this lens, or its mates the frame (exhibit 175) and the other lens (exhibit 176), found on the chair in David's room, to either the struggle with David or having been worn or handled by David.
4. If the lens had been where Weir says he found it, then it was in full view, less than 45 centimetres from Stephen's body, for three and a half days without being recognised by anyone, including other detectives who placed black arrow markers within inches of it, the police photographer and the scientific scene analysis personnel working at the scene.
5. Van Turnhout noted at 9.30 a.m. on the first morning of the enquiry, referring to the broken spectacles on the chair, 'there were no lenses in them [the frames]'. This strongly suggests to me that either two lenses were on the chair with the frames, or no lenses were there at all. It seems inconceivable to me that he would have seen the one lens beside the frames as depicted in the photograph and not written words to that effect.

The other evidence against David, being his fingerprints on the rifle, the small smear of Stephen's blood on his shorts and the injuries to his forehead and knee, are quite easily attributable to him being the finder of the dead bodies.

The second point of the Crown triangle, that evidence excluded Robin Bain from being the murderer of other members of his family, is thrown into doubt because the firearms discharge residue test was not done when it should have been and, more emphatically, by the unexplained and untested blood on various parts of Robin's body and clothing.

The third point was the evidence that excluded Robin's suicide. This can be answered by Alec Dempster's own words in answer to the first questions put to him under cross-examination, when he said: 'I consider it [suicide] to be possible.'

In addition to that, Dempster himself classifies the shot that killed Robin Bain as being a 'contact wound'. Bearing in mind that it was fired from in front of Robin, well within his range of vision, that seems an extremely unlikely scenario.

WHAT DO I THINK
HAPPENED?

Although I do not see it as a necessity in advancing David's case to prove step by step how these murders occurred, the long and intense analysis I have conducted over the past year has led to my own theory as to how it all occurred.

This theory is based strictly on what is known and I believe it is the only possible scenario that actually fits the evidence. Unlike the police, who selected the evidence to fit their theory, I have objectively analysed the evidence and arrived at conclusions as a result of what it tells me.

Statements from Cottle and others strongly suggest that for Robin Bain, that Monday was to be the end of the road, as he saw it.

To be exposed as a child molester and perpetrator of incest (and it may be that once the first crack appeared, more skeletons would have been revealed, as is often the case) was the worst possible outcome for him. He had been a religious missionary and school teacher, a husband and father. No more abominable disgrace could have befallen him, his immediate family and his extended family.

In his desperate state, a bizarre alternative, quite possibly sparked by the book he was reading, presented itself to him. The subject of that book was a family who fell apart and began to disappear mysteriously as a result. In true Agatha Christie style the answer does not come until the final pages. Robin was, it would seem from the photo of his caravan, about halfway through it. (An interesting aside to this thought is that Jim Doyle issued a directive for the CIB to investigate the possibility that David Bain belonged to the library, and if he did, 'to examine the selection of reading material to see whether or not it had any bearing on this case'. This after David had been arrested, of course.)

I believe that when Robin set out on this rampage of destruction he intended to kill David with the others, and then to set David up as the perpetrator and suicide victim: that is, he intended to set David up in exactly the same manner as the police case proposes that David set him up.

Whenever I canvass this proposition with anybody, their first reaction is one of incredulity that a father would do that to his son. And yet the whole country has come to accept that a son did it to his father. Is it then really so unlikely?

Let's consider it in the light of what we now know.

First of all, Robin's state of mind.

1. The single most horrifying thought for him is the impending disgrace.
2. He has been severely financially humiliated by his wife, and is consequently living a degrading and debased life.
3. He did not want to return from Papua New Guinea when they did, and his life had been a disaster in the time they had been back in Dunedin.

As a result, he may well have conceived that if he could eliminate his family and get away with it by implicating David, who owned the rifle, he could sell up, and perhaps return to his beloved Papua New Guinea where he had spent most of his adult life, with all of what funds they had to himself. If he failed to avoid detection, his secrets would remain hidden, and in a much less disgraceful way he would disappear from society, being locked away for murder rather than the socially unacceptable sexual deviation.

Now, let's put this to the test in the light of the evidence. Robin waits for David to go on his paper run. He obtains David's rifle, gets David's gloves and sets about his dastardly plan, formulated in the dark hours of the preceding night. He kills Laniet and Margaret. Laniet is shot three times in the head; she is the person slaughtered with a passionate hatred. John Douglas, the world-renowned FBI criminal profiler, when looking at the photos of these killings, and knowing nothing about the case, said to me: 'Whoever had the most reason to hate this girl is your likely killer.'

He then kills Stephen, in what turned out to be a debacle during which he removed the gloves and left them there. This unsettles him, and of course he gets blood all over his clothes and it transfers from his clothing onto the door frames as he goes downstairs to Arawa's room.

Having shot Arawa, he removes the bloody clothing. It is entirely possible that up till now he has moved around the house in his socks, and subsequently put on his shoes and clean socks. Now he has taken off the worst of the bloody garments he is wearing and washed his hands, in the process leaving blood stains around the laundry area as they were found by the police.

He then has to wait for David to return. He goes to check that the dead are truly dead. Perhaps he comes across the spectacles and decides to leave them broken in David's room. Another piece of the false trail. Of course, he makes sure not to leave any tell-tale prints or marks. He just bends them a bit, removes the lens, and puts them on the chair.

He now sits and waits in the computer room. From here he can see David coming home. He has to be ready to take him out as soon as he gets home before David discovers anything is amiss. He will do the final clean-up after David is gone. The blood on his hands has got there from handling the bloody rifle again while he waits.

He waits and waits; ten minutes, fifteen minutes, twenty minutes. As he waits in this dark room, with the four dead bodies of his family elsewhere in the house, despair sets in again. The horror of what he is doing overwhelms him. David is a good man, he reminds himself. He's my oldest son, the apple of my eye. *It's not David who deserves to die, it's me!* I'm the bastard. I've stuffed it up, David will carry on the family name.

He looks for a pen. There is none. He can't go around the house trying to find one in case David comes home. But he is a computer man, Robin, and he is sitting in the computer alcove looking out for David. He must get it over with now.

His penultimate act is to switch on the computer and write, 'Sorry, you are the only one who deserved to stay', not dreaming for a moment that this message, and the moment he happened to write it would conspire to see David charged with the murders.

He kneels at the chair, gun leaning beside him, makes his final peace with God, and it's over – over for him; but just beginning for the one 'who deserved to stay'.

EPILOGUE

Sunday 19 June 1994

On a grey Dunedin winter's day the mid-winter solstice celebration was attended by some staunch locals at St Kilda's beach, who participated in that peculiarly Kiwi custom of immersing themselves in the freezing southern waters.

David Bain dived in. His brother Stephen did too. It would be Stephen's final swim, and David's last one for a long time. Their troubled father was watching. Later that day he would go with his daughter Laniet to pay off her account at her local shop. She went to work, then, for a couple of hours at a cafe with her sister Arawa.

David joined them there to get a ride home having been at rehearsal for his latest production during the afternoon.

His very disturbed father was at home, as was his younger brother Stephen. Arawa went off babysitting for the evening. His mother had no dinner prepared for the family.

David and Laniet went down the road to get fish and chips for dinner. Dad, Mum, David, Stephen and Laniet had a meal together. Laniet had not shared a meal with her father and mother for a long time.

It was not a pleasant meal, though. The atmosphere was tense and acrimonious. After watching a video, the boys went off to bed about 8.30. David set his alarm clock for 5.30 a.m., read a book for a while and slept soundly after his busy day. Stephen did too.

Laniet remained with her parents. She told her father that she wouldn't be going out to Taieri the following morning with him. He was not happy. He was losing his grip on her; she was all he had left. His wife, the dominating influence, hated him. She didn't want him around, even, she just wanted his money. The conversation became bitter and Laniet was at the centre of the controversy. She had matured enough to stand up for herself. She couldn't take it any longer. Her mother, also, was very troubled. She too was depressed, because the untenable situation between herself and Robin seemed to have no end.

Tonight was different, though. What Laniet was telling them meant that finally, she and her husband had to face up to the disastrous mess that their lives were in. Laniet needed help. She had been abused for so long nothing less than professional counselling could make any difference. She was a seriously disturbed young woman, carrying a shame she could no longer deal with.

Margaret became angry. She turned on Robin. 'You are the devil. I've told you Belial has taken over your soul. Get out of this house.'

She was used to being in charge. She was much bigger than the gaunt, grey, depressed shell of man who masqueraded as her husband.

Laniet sobbed. She curled up, unable to move. A great realisation came over her, even though she didn't know what it was. A sort of load seemed to lift. Her heart didn't feel quite so heavy in a way she didn't understand.

Margaret consoled her. She was strong and practical,

despite her eccentricities.

Her daughter had clothes and personal effects at the Russell Street flat. She would need to get her to professional help too, without delay.

'Come with me,' she told her daughter.

At nearly midnight on Sunday night, Margaret and Laniet went to the bank cash machine to get some money that Laniet would need to attend to tidying herself up and sorting our her life. They also went to Russell Street, perhaps to pick up some gear, perhaps to tell her flatmates she was going home. Perhaps so that Margaret could lay down the law and make sure that they would leave Laniet alone.

Meantime, Robin, banished in disgrace, goes back to his filthy caravan. He tries to read a bit more of *Murder Comes at the End*. But he can't concentrate. He can't sleep. He cries. It's lonely and desolate out there, all alone. Very dark. The wind howls through the old trees. Whistles over the top of the house. His house.

His sons sleep soundly inside, another tense weekend between Mum and Dad behind them. They've got used to it by now though.

Arawa arrived home while her mother and Laniet were out. She saw the caravan light on, but wouldn't cross the path even to say goodnight to her father. She too sleeps soundly. She has training college as usual to attend tomorrow morning.

The car comes home. Robin hears it. Two doors slam. He can hear voices. It is Margaret, talking to Laniet. His Laniet. No, not his Laniet now.

Despair, remorse, self disgust. He hates himself. He cries and cries. He calls out for help. He prays. *'What have I done? Oh my God, what have I done?'* Belial. She's Belial. She's evil. *She's ruined my life. She's crazy. She's got my money. She's got my house. She's got my kids. She's got my Laniet. She's got my darkest secrets. She's got me where she wants me. My life is in her hands.*

She'll destroy me. They'll all support her. How can I expect them to understand what I've been through, why I am like I am? I do love them, I want the best for them. She's got them all, and she's got me too.

My dear old mother. Oh Jesus Christ, help me. My brothers, my young brothers. None of them deserve to have this disgrace, this shame, this horror.

My sons. David, the pride of my life, the apple of my eye. His life will be ruined for ever when she tells them about me.

God, how I hate her. And Laniet, you've taken her side, you've betrayed me. You've deserted me. You won't do this to me. You can't do this to me.

The wind dies as those long horrid lonely hours before daybreak pass remorsely by.

A calm seems to come over him. An overwhelming feeling of hatred. *It's their fault. I never wanted to be like this. They made me go like I have. They've done it to me. Arawa, she hates me. Stephen, he's his mummy's boy.*

David, the shame would kill him.

A totally irrational logic sets in.

Calm now. Think.

'Death Comes as the End.'

There it is.

That is the answer.

What time is it? I must work this out. 5 a.m. David will be out on the paper run soon.

It's cold. More clothes. My green woollen cap. My blue sweater.

Watch out now for David. There he goes, he's out the gate, and good, that mutt has gone with him. He could have been a problem!

I hate her. She's been the cause of all this. She made me do it. It's not my fault.

David is gone now; the way is clear.

This mess that we're in. There's only one way to end it. Death. No one's life will be worth it any more. That wife – she caused it all. It's her fault. She must go, and the rest of them with her.

Into David's room. *Out with the gun. Get the key from the desk. Right. Now the ammo. Must get the right ones. The low velocity bullets that don't make any noise with the silencer.*

This speculation on my part may seem graphic beyond necessity. It is quite intentional however to demonstrate my belief that the person who committed this atrocity must have been deranged, demented and filled with hatred at the time.

What actually happened next I cannot say for sure. The police cannot say. Only the deceased in that house actually know what took place. In what order it took place. I too could speculate. I could offer conjecture on what was worn. When it was taken off. Which direction people were walking in, and so on.

I would prefer, as the police should have, to look at all of the known facts and restrict my judgement as to guilt and culpability only on the basis of those facts.

The facts that we know for sure are:

David had no known motive. Nothing that has come to light has thrown any light on anything that may have set him off on this path of destruction.

On the other hand, in the light of all that is now known, and should have, in fact could easily have been known prior to any culpability being presumed, Robin Bain had an over-whelming motive, was in a degenerate mental state, and precipitative events in relation to those matters took place that very weekend.

As I write this page the horrific story of another man's murder in Raurimu is unfolding. A domestic violence expert is quoted as saying there is no single reason for anyone to commit mass murder. Perpetrators generally *had a mental illness*, there would be a *trigger event*, and the *availability of a weapon* would affect the death toll.

The police went to incredible lengths to put together their case against David, yet they did not even analyse the blood, the heavy blood staining, that was all over Robin.

The police misled the court on some critical matters of evidence brought against David. David's defence was ill equipped to combat the might and power of the Crown team.

The judge, inadvertently, maybe, put many matters to the jury that he qualified as being facts, which were not facts at all.

On the undisputed evidence that the police themselves gathered, including Denise Laney's, Tania Clark's, Detective Kevin Anderson's and as a result of a proper and correct analysis of that evidence, David was at least three minutes removed from the house, and maybe as much as six or seven minutes at the critical time that the computer was turned on by the killer. He could not have done it.

As a result of my year's work, of the expert assistance I have enlisted, of a true and objective examination of the facts, it is my belief that, but for a sloppy and incompetent police enquiry, David Bain would not have even been charged in the first instance, let alone convicted of these crimes.

Some matters may always remain unresolved. Why for example did Robin Bain, if he were the murderer, wear David's gloves and leave them in Stephen's room?

How did the glasses lenses and frames come to be found as they were?

Why did the police so assiduously press charges against David when so much conflicting evidence was unresolved on their file?

The answers to these questions may never be known. It is not within my scope or authority to determine the answers. I do not see that it really matters as far as it relates to David's innocence or guilt.

And so, after an exhaustive and exhausting year which has taken me around the world to the Privy Council, which has seen me meet and consult with, among others, John Douglas from the FBI, the Commissioner of Police, pathologists, detectives and ex-detectives, some of New Zealand's foremost members of the Bar, politicians, original witnesses, new witnesses, and a witness whose name was once suppressed; after the most passionate of discussions many times with David Bain himself, I feel able to answer the two questions that have haunted me from the start.

I have no doubt, in the light of all the evidence and a proper examination of the facts as presented in this book, that not only is David Bain's guilt thrown into the most serious doubt but his innocence is the only possible conclusion.

UPDATE

At the time of publication of this book, the legal team headed by Colin Withnall QC is preparing a submission to present to the Governor General, Sir Michael Hardie-Boys, applying for a pardon for David Bain.

It is expected that this application will be completed within the immediate ensuing months.

Extensive expert analysis both in New Zealand and overseas is currently in progress to support this application.

A public fund has been established to assist with the associated costs.

The fund is subject to audit under Law Society requirements, and has been authorised by the author and Colin Withnall QC.

Donations can be made to:

David Bain Appeal Fund
c/- O'Driscoll and Marks
Barristers and Solicitors
PO Box 639
Dunedin

APPENDIXES

APPENDIX 1

Dean Cottle's statement

23.6.94
1155 HRS
CIB OFFICE
DUNEDIN

DEAN ROBERT COTTLE STATES

Dean Robert COTTLE, that is my full name. I reside at [. . .]. I am presently unemployed and am aged 27 years.

I am making this statement to Detective Malcolm INGLIS about knowing Laniet BAIN.

I first met Laniet about 10 months ago in a bar in Dunedin. We got talking and got on well. After that meeting we got to know each other well and became friends. Laniet would talk to me and sometimes I would take her out for dinner. She did tell me that she had been a prostitute at some stage.

When I first started to see her I would see her maybe three or four times a week.

Towards the end of April I was seeing her less and it had been about three or four weeks since I had last seen her.

But in the times we had together she used to tell me things. She was a nice girl and we got on well.

About the family, she told me that her father Robin had been having sex with her and this had been happening for years. That he was still doing this as I believed it. She told me that she wouldn't go to bed until 3.00 a.m. and knew this. She didn't want it coming out what had happened to her, I wasn't to tell anyone.

It was one of the reasons for her leaving home. She was also fed up with everything. Her mother was hassling her and they used to sit around and each take turns at talking to God.

She first moved into a flat in Kaikorai Valley off Nairn Street. There were no-hopers in there and I told her she should get out of that address.

She moved out of that flat and into the Russell Street address. It could have been the start of March. She used to go up to stay in Alexandra with the family. She also told me that her sister Arawa had been involved in some prostitution.

I presumed that she had told her sister what she had been doing. I asked what her sister had thought of that and she had replied not much as she had done a couple of jobs herself. I didn't push it anymore and let it drop.

She was also involved with cannabis but I'm not interested in that.

I decided on Friday 17th of June to give her a ring and see what she was up to. I phoned the family home as I knew that she was moving out of Russell Street and I thought that she had moved home. I spoke to her mother and she gave me the phone number to get hold of her. I had told her that it was a friend trying to get hold of her. I phoned the number and they answered Taieri Beach School. I presumed that it was her father that answered the phone and I was surprised as I didn't think she would be back with her father.

He told me that she was in town somewhere and he thought that she would be back at about seven.

Later that day I was driving through town and saw Laniet coming out of a coffee shop. It was in the afternoon, it was the coffee shop that is on George Street past Frederick Street heading north on the right hand side. It has a big noticeboard and is dark with students using it.

I stopped and spoke to her on the footpath for about 5–10 minutes. She told me that she was going to make a new start of everything, that her parents had been questioning her about what she was doing. She said that she was going to tell them everything and make a clean start of things. I said that if she wanted to talk to give me a ring or if she wanted to go out for dinner. She had always been very scared of her parents finding out what she was doing. I thought by saying this she was going to tell her parents about prostitution.

I also presumed that she was going to talk about the incest because she said everything. That was about all we said, I don't think it would have taken any longer than five minutes. I didn't see any friends that she could have been with.

She didn't talk much about the rest of the family but it seemed quite normal that she got on with her brothers and sister well. That she was closer to Arawa.

I never met David. I only ever saw him once when I picked her up outside the Trustbank Theatre in King Edward Street. She said that's my brother. She only did those shows to keep everyone happy, she didn't like doing them.

Ever since I have known her, all she has wanted to do is go back to Papua New Guinea. She really liked it over there.

The night she told me about what her father had done to her, she also told me before this that something had happened to her in Papua New Guinea. She didn't say what but I presumed she meant something sexual. After that she started crying and told me about what her father did to her.

Just thinking back on it, I'm not sure if it was Friday. I think it was Friday but if you check their phone you will see a call from me. She seemed quite a level headed girl to me.

I have read this statement [and it is] true and correct.

'D R COTTLE'

Witnessed and taken by:

'MNT INGLIS'

Det 6145

APPENDIX 2

Summing-up of Williamson J.

Madam Foreman, Ladies and Gentlemen:

Introduction

Who did it? David Bain? Robin Bain?

The real issue in this trial is whether you are satisfied beyond reasonable doubt that David Bain killed his mother, sisters, brother and father.

On the one hand, the Defence have said to you that you cannot be so satisfied. While it has no obligation to prove the identity of the killer, the Defence says that it was probably Robin Bain.

It points primarily to these facts:

1. There is no evidence of motive for David, whereas Robin as a proud school teacher being excluded from his home, did have a motive.
2. David could not have turned the computer on at 6.44 a.m., if Mrs Laney is correct that he was at the gate at 6.45 a.m.
3. Since the red sweat shirt which he had been wearing on his paper run was located in the washing machine, David's evidence about putting the washing on after he had come back from the paper run must be correct.
4. The murder rifle was near Robin Bain and pointing at him.
5. The larger of the two magazines was near his right hand and may have been used by him to reach the trigger to shoot himself.
6. The message on the computer itself makes sense only if it had been typed by Robin and addressed to David.
7. It would have been physically possible for Robin to shoot himself.
8. There are other ancillary matters such as Robin's enquiry about the rifle the week before; the empty cartridge cases and firearms code in

the caravan; and the alleged organising of the school reliever.

They are the major points put by the Defence.

On the other hand, the Prosecution says that the case against David Bain is overwhelming and that his guilt is the only reasonable conclusion on all of the evidence.

It points particularly to the combination of the following facts:

1. The rifle and ammunition was David's and the key to the trigger lock was in an unusual place where he had hidden it.

2. His bloodied fingerprints were found on the murder weapon.

3. His blood-stained gloves were found in Stephen's room.

4. David had fresh injuries to his forehead and knee. There is no explanation for them and the nature of them indicates that it was he who had the fight with Stephen.

5. The glasses (with a missing lens) and fitting his general glass prescription were found on a chair near where he was in his room when the police arrived, and, significantly, the left side of the frame was damaged and the missing lens was found in Stephen's room quite near his body.

6. Blood-stained clothing, including the green jersey with matching fibres to those found under Stephen's finger nails, was washed by him; and his 'Gondoliers' sweat shirt with blood on the shoulder had been sponged.

7. Blood found on the top of the washing machine powder container, porcelain basin and various light switches, must have come from his touch.

8. Droplets of blood were found on his socks as well as blood which had caused the luminol observed part sock prints in other parts of the house.

9. The computer had been switched on at 6.44 a.m. and that you would conclude, on all of the evidence, that this time was just after David had returned home from the paper run, that is if you accept evidence, including his own, that he was at the nearby corner at 6.40 a.m. and that it would take 2 to 3 minutes to reach 65 Every Street.

10. David's partial recovery of memory may have enabled him to suggest explanations for some of the blood on him but it does not explain other vital items such as the fingerprints, the clothes, or the glasses. It con-

firms, however, the Crown says, that David confidently denies matters that he cannot remember although they have happened.

11. If David heard Laniet making gurgling noises, then she must have been alive at that time and consequently he was by her bed before the last fatal shot was fired. Other comments of his such as that his mother's eyes were open when he went in and, to his aunt, that they were 'dying, dying everywhere', tend to confirm that he remembers, in part, being there before the deaths.

12. Not only does the expert pathologist say it is unlikely Robin Bain shot himself because of the angle of the gun shot wound, but Robin Bain, the Crown says, could not have killed the others because:

(a) No one else's blood was found on him.

(b) There was no blood at all of any type on his socks or shoes.

(c) His fingerprints were not on the rifle, although if he had shot himself, he would have been the last person to have gripped it firmly.

(d) No gun powder traces were on his hands.

(e) If he had been the wearer of blood stained clothing and was intent on suicide, why would he have bothered to change his clothes and to be in completely blood-free clothes when he shot himself?

They are the main points that have been made and argued before you on this vital issue. A decision about it involves you in reaching a conclusion upon all the evidence you have heard after weighing up those arguments about the competing points. It is a decision on the facts and consequently one entirely for you, not for me.

General Matters

It has been my duty to preside over the conduct of this trial, to rule on questions of procedure that arise, (and, as you are aware, they have arisen from time to time in this trial), and now it is my task to direct you about the law that actually applies to the case. I must ask you to accept what I say about the law as authoritative because that is my province, that is my job. But a decision on the facts, is for you as the jury and for you alone. If therefore I appear to you to indicate any particular view on the facts which does not accord with your own view, you must disregard mine because decisions on fact are for you as the jury and not for me. The verdicts are for you.

You must, of course, come to your verdicts solely upon the evidence that has been given in the Court. If any of you have heard anything about this case or any person involved in it before you took your place on the jury, or you have remembered something that you had heard before, please dismiss those things from your mind because the law requires that an accused person be judged only upon the evidence given in Court.

Counsel for the Accused drew your attention to some media comments and correctly told you to ignore them. Judgments in criminal trials cannot properly be based upon gossip or rumour; or 'what the taxi driver said'; or hearsay or media speculation. It has to be based upon evidence at the trial. You, of course, must consider the whole of the evidence you have heard, weigh it all up, bearing in mind the submissions that have been made to you by Counsel, and then reach your verdict in accordance with directions as to the law that I will explain. You decide, for example, just what you make of the witnesses; which witnesses you accept, which you reject. You can accept some parts of what they have said and reject other parts. Those decisions are for you. In particular, it is for you to assess the witnesses' demeanour and to judge their reliability, their credibility. In considering the evidence and assessing its weight and worth and the inferences you draw from it you will, of course, apply your collective common sense and knowledge of human nature because you are here as representatives of the community to apply your fair and wise judgment.

I ask you, as Counsel have done, to put aside any feelings of prejudice or sympathy one way or the other and to arrive at your verdict conscientiously and dispassionately. Some words by their very nature suggest emotional reactions. Mr Wright, on Friday, referred to 'cold-blooded' and to 'executions', whereas the Crown, of course, need to prove intentional killings by an unlawful act and nothing more colourful than that. Mr Guest spoke of a 'pale Accused emerging from dungeons after 11 months of imprisonment'. Whereas, as normal, the Accused has been held in custody awaiting his trial and has not been subject to any sentence of imprisonment. Counsel also said, 'don't hang him' and that 'his life was in your hands'. Well, of course, there is no capital punishment in New Zealand. So don't allow emotional words and reactions to affect your decision. It is a decision that has to be made in a calm, dispassionate manner based on the evidence.

The other preliminary but important matter I wanted to mention is the onus of proof. The burden or onus is on the Crown which has brought the charges. It rests on the Crown from the beginning to the end. There is no onus on an Accused at any stage to prove his innocence. He does not need to give evidence. In this case he has chosen to do so but he still carries no onus. The law is that the Crown must prove each charge beyond reasonable doubt before you can bring in a verdict of guilty. You must be satisfied beyond reasonable doubt of the Accused's guilt and that means you must, on the whole of the evidence, be satisfied of the three essential elements of murder which I will explain in a moment, namely, he killed the person named in the indictment; that he did so by an unlawful act; and that he intended to do so. It is not a matter of being satisfied beyond reasonable doubt of every single fact in the case but rather of the Accused's guilt at the end of and on the whole of the case.

Reasonable doubt means just what it says. There has been reference during the course of the case to a standard of proof of certainty but as I have just mentioned, the standard is beyond reasonable doubt. It does not require proof to absolute precision or to mathematical certainty. It does require proof beyond reasonable doubt. It follows that before you can convict any Accused on any charge, you must be satisfied beyond reasonable doubt from the evidence of that person's guilt. If you are so satisfied, it is your duty, in accordance with the oath you took at the commencement of the trial, to find the Accused guilty. If you are left with a reasonable doubt, then equally it is your duty to acquit. You apply that to each of the charges. On your return to Court, after your deliberations, you Madam Foreman will be asked to announce the jury's verdict which must be unanimous, that is, it must be the decision of each of you.

I have dealt with then the important preliminary matters, most of which apply to every criminal trial and I ask you to keep those in mind during your consideration of this case.

Indictment

I will turn now to the indictment. That is the official document that you will have with you in the jury room in which the charges are set out. It contains 5 counts, or charges.

They are separate ones. For reasons of efficiency and common sense, they are being tried together in one trial but the evidence against the Accused on each charge has to be considered separately. There may be evidence which relates to more than one charge but it is necessary to consider each charge separately. It would be wrong, for example, to bolster up the case on one charge by a conclusion in relation to the other, or to reason that if the Accused is guilty of one he must be guilty of the lot. In this case, in fact, no distinctions have been urged on you as between the 5 charges. It has really been accepted, in the way the case has been handled by both the Prosecution and Defence, that the one issue, the one dispute, applies to each of these 5 charges.

Charges

Now, each charge is that the Accused, David Cullen Bain, on the 20th of June 1994 at Dunedin, did murder a stated member of his family. Charges of murder require proof of three essential elements:

First, a homicide. Homicide is defined, in our law, as a killing of one human by another directly or indirectly by any means whatsoever. So it must be proved in this case that David Bain killed the person named in the charge by some means.

You must be satisfied on the way this case has been presented, that the Accused shot each person at reasonably close range and that those actions were the cause of that person's death.

As with all elements of the charge, it is a matter for you to decide if the Crown has proved particular elements to the required standard. In this case, of course, the Defence have accepted that each person was killed by a bullet from the exhibit rifle but while that admission is not really contested, it is a matter for you to be satisfied about. It is your decision.

The second element that must be proved is that the homicide was culpable or, in other words, blameworthy. For the purposes of this case, it is sufficient to explain that homicide is culpable when it consists of killing a person by an unlawful act. To deliberately use force on a person, to shoot them, is clearly an unlawful act. It is an assault unless, of course, that action was justified or excused by some other provision in our Crimes Act, for example, when a person is acting in self-defence. Such a justification is not suggested in this case. So, on this second element you have to be satisfied that each person was killed by an unlawful act.

Those are the first two elements then, a homicide or killing and proof that it was culpable.

The third of the elements in murder relates to murderous intent. The Crown's case against the Accused is based upon the simple intent that the Accused meant to cause the death. It hardly needs any explanation from me. You have to decide on all the evidence whether the killer actually meant to cause death. The Crown says to you, what other reasonable inference can you draw from evidence other than that he actually shot each victim in the head at close range?

The element of intention must be judged at the time of the shooting. A later loss of memory for that vital time would not affect the position of guilt. As Professor Mullen confirmed in his evidence, I think, from his colleagues' research, that such a loss of memory is not an unusual feature for those who have witnessed or perpetrated violent, horrific events.

It is not necessary in a case such as this for the Crown to prove motive in order to establish the charge of murder. Motive really means the reason or the emotion that has prompted a particular act. Intention, on the other hand, includes meaning to bring about a particular result or being aware or believing that that result will happen. It includes particularly the means to the end with the consequences along the way. I know these words are hard to understand, but if I can give an illustration it may assist. It has got nothing to do with this case, of course, but a person may blow up an aircraft in order to get insurance money for some goods on the aircraft. The motive or object may be to get the insurance money but the means of doing so include an intention or the inevitable consequence that the crew and the passengers in the aircraft will die. That illustrates the difference between motive and intention. What the Crown must prove is intention.

Automatism

[...]

Insanity

Insanity in law is a rather special concept. It is not the same as the medical concept. It does not include every abnormal behaviour or aberration of the mind. Killing a person or killing a number of persons is abnormal but it does not follow that the killer must be legally insane. In law, everyone is presumed to be sane until the contrary is proved. So the onus of proof of insanity is upon an Accused who must establish that upon the balance of probabilities.

As you are well aware in this case, Professor Mullen's is the only medical evidence. In view of that clear evidence and the approach of the Defence in this trial, you can really properly dismiss automatism and indeed medical insanity from your consideration.

The issue remains whether you are satisfied beyond reasonable doubt that David Bain fired the fatal shots.

Evidence

Now, the material upon which you have got to base your decision is the evidence which must be considered in relation to each charge. That evidence consists of:

Oral Testimony – First of all, of the oral testimony that you have heard over the past 3 weeks. It includes the depositions that were read to you by the Registrar. As I have already explained during the course of the trial, those depositions may properly be placed before you as evidence in certain situations. Such evidence may not be as good as that given by witnesses in Court because you don't have the opportunity to actually see and hear it being given and to assess those witnesses for yourselves, but once depositions have been read to you by consent, they properly form part of the evidence in the trial. They have the same effect as if given by any other witness.

Exhibits – Secondly, apart from the oral testimony and depositions, there are all the exhibits which have been produced and which you will later have with you in the jury room. The live ammunition will, as usual, be kept in safety, but if you want to examine any of that, just let the Registrar know. Those exhibits form part of the case and as you know, they consist of a large number of items, the photographs, the clothing, the bullet fragments, the shell cases, the rifle, the numerous other items including the written statements made by the Accused to the police.

Statements – The oral and written statements made by the Accused prior to the trial are not sworn testimony. You have heard the manner in which those statements were made to Detective Sergeant Dunne and Detective Sergeant Croudis and some to David's relatives. These oral and written statements are properly part of the material for you to consider. The truthfulness, the accuracy, the weight that you give to those statements is for you. You can attach different weight to different parts. You don't have to accept it totally or reject it totally. You can attach more importance to some parts. Again, those decisions are factual ones and entirely for you.

Some reference was made in evidence at one stage to the Accused being silent when asked particular questions or later, on legal advice, refusing to answer some questions that were proposed. His silence is not evidence against him. Indeed, as you will have noticed, the warning that is given to any Accused by a police officer expressly advises that person that he is entitled to remain silent. It would be quite wrong to reason because he was silent or because he refused to answer questions he must have something to hide or be guilty of the offences charged. At times during the trial Counsel said that the opening for the Defence was the first time that the Accused had had an opportunity to put his side of the matter. There may be some emotion in those statements but they are also slightly misleading. An Accused, of course, has an opportunity to make a statement to the police and may give evidence and make submissions at a preliminary hearing. He is not prevented in law from doing so. The fact that he elects, on advice, not to do so, is quite normal and may, of course, be done for very good reasons. He cannot be criticised for not taking that opportunity. The important point I wanted to make is that silence or failure to answer or to give explanations is not evidence against an Accused.

Circumstantial Evidence – As a jury you are entitled to draw inferences from the facts that have been proved in evidence. Inferences are not guesses. Rather, they are logical, reasonable, fair deductions from facts which have been proved. It is important in this case as it is indeed in most criminal cases, because the Crown here is asking you, for example, to draw the inference from the combination of a number of different circumstances, that the Accused did shoot each of the victims, although he may be now blanking it out of his mind. It is for you to decide whether that is the appropriate and reasonable conclusion to come to from all of the evidence that you have heard but you cannot, of course, speculate or guess. Evidence by way of inference is often referred to as circumstantial evidence. It is evidence of facts from which a jury may infer the existence of the vital fact in issue. Circumstantial evidence is often contrasted with direct evidence such as eye witness evidence. Usually circumstantial evidence derives its force from the fact that it consists of a number of items all pointing to the same conclusion. it is really a process of reasoning. Because crimes, if premeditated, are usually committed by stealth or in secrecy, it is not uncommon that there is no direct evidence and that proof of those crimes is by way of circumstantial evidence. Sometimes when facts are just taken one by one, item by item, they don't have a very strong probative value but when they are considered together, they do. So you must weigh then the combined effect of all of the circumstances which have been proved in this case to decide whether you are satisfied beyond reasonable doubt of the Accused's guilt on the crimes charged.

Accused's evidence – In this trial you have had the advantage of having seen and heard the Accused himself giving evidence and being cross examined. He did not need to do that. The fact that he gave evidence does not change the situation about that one little bit. The onus, as I have said, remains with the Crown. By calling evidence, the Accused undertakes nothing at all. As Counsel indicated in their addresses, it is often said that where an Accused gives evidence or calls witnesses it can possibly have three effects – first, you might conclude that the evidence was absolutely truthful and reliable and an answer to the Crown's case. If you were to accept in this case the Accused's evidence that he did not kill any of the victims, then of course that would be the total answer. But such evidence can have another effect. Secondly, although you may not accept it as the total truth, it may leave you with a reasonable doubt as to just what the true position was and in that case the Crown would have failed to prove its case to the required standard.

The third possibility is that you may find the Accused's evidence unreliable, not credible, and reject it as having any probative value. If that is your view, then you should not automatically conclude that the Accused must be guilty. In that case you have to set it completely aside and go back to the rest of the available evidence and decide on the basis of that evidence has guilt been established?

Lies – In this case the Prosecution has urged that the Accused has either blocked these killings out of his mind or he has just lied to you because he told the police at the time that he had not seen any of the victims other than his mother and father, but the evidence, the Crown says now proves, and indeed the Accused accepts, that he did enter the other bedrooms and see his brother and sisters.

Before you could take any lie or lies into account, you have to be satisfied that the Accused did tell a deliberate lie or lies. The mere fact that a person tells a lie is not in itself guilt of the crime charged. You have to ask yourselves, what prompted him to do so because an Accused may lie for various reasons, for example, to protect someone else, to avoid embarrassment, even panicking or confusion or matters of that kind. A lie, however, may be relevant to credibility, that is whether you believe the evidence given in Court by an Accused but you should guard against what might be said to be a natural tendency to think, oh well, if he told a lie or lies, he must be guilty of the offences charged.

Fingerprints – Another matter in the evidence to which I should refer is that of fingerprints. The Crown here relies, in part, on fingerprint evidence and, in particular, the evidence of the bloodied fingerprints on the rifle. Evidence of that kind has long been recognised as a proper method of identification. If fingerprint evidence is accepted so that you are satisfied that the fingerprints obtained from that rifle were fingerprints of the Accused, then that evidence can be sufficient, without more, to identify the Accused as the person who placed those fingerprints on the rifle.

In this respect the Crown relies upon the evidence of Kim Jones, the senior police fingerprint technician. For reasons he described in his evidence, he said that he has no doubt that the prints found on the rifle in blood were made by the 4 fingers of the left hand of the Accused and he produced you will recall, in support of his opinion, the photographic comparison and he pointed out the points of similarity which are all marked.

In the end the decision of whether you are satisfied beyond reasonable doubt that the fingerprints found on the rifle are those of the Accused is a matter for you and not for Mr Jones. You, of course, are entitled to give weight to his expert opinion but it is for you to decide whether you accept that as proof. You make the decision depending upon your assessment of Mr Jones, his level of expertise, the manner in which he gave evidence, particularly when cross examined. Ultimately you may conclude the evidence of fingerprints on the rifle has not been seriously challenged; but rather the Accused says that he cannot now remember handling the rifle.

Experts – In general terms, expert evidence is available to a jury to help them in their consideration. It is not for the experts to actually make the decisions in the particular case. Their evidence needs to be weighed up just like all other evidence. Clearly, Mr Ngamoki made a mistake in recording the length of the rifle and adopted a less than wholly accurate method of measuring the distance and angle of shell ejection. As far as his opinions are now relevant to any issue in this trial, you would have to be cautious before accepting them.

Doctor Dempster may have impressed you as a very competent and experienced forensic pathologist, but while giving respect to his opinions, the decisions ultimately, I emphasise, are for you after giving such respect and weight as you think fit to the opinions that you have heard.

Charts – [. . .]

Hearsay – One other item of evidence that I should mention is what is called hearsay evidence. The evidence of Kyle Cunningham is in that category. It is hearsay because he was telling you of statements made to him by another namely, Robin Bain. The best evidence of that, of course, would be from Robin Bain. When you are weighing hearsay evidence you have to consider carefully whether you are satisfied the witness has accurately reported the statements made to him and you have to consider whether in the view of the general nature of that evidence it has any particular significance in the trial.

Those are the points that I wanted to make to you about the evidence and the approaches that you must take to the evidence. I realise that I have been speaking now for an hour. What remains for me is to summarise to you briefly the cases that are put for each side but I will adjourn now for a five minute break.

Summing-Up Resumes: 10.35 a.m.

Case for the Crown

On Friday you heard two very detailed and thorough addresses which highlighted the main arguments for each side. It is part of my task as the Judge in summing up to deal with those arguments and to summarise the position. I am not going to repeat what has been said to you because I know that will be reasonably fresh in your minds. I intend merely to summarise the principal points made as I noted them at the time. If I don't mention to you a particular fact which you believe is important, please don't conclude from the fact that I haven't mentioned it that there therefore it is not important. Make up your own mind about any point. I emphasise that it is your judgment in these matters which is decisive.

For the Crown Mr Wright started, you will recall, by referring to what he said were three corners of a triangle. He said the first was the mass of evidence indicating the Accused's involvement; the second corner of the triangle was strong evidence that excluded Robin Bain from killing other members of his family; and the third part of the triangle was overwhelming evidence establishing that Robin Bain did not commit suicide.

He said to you that, just why it happened it is not possible to ascertain; that these events are so bizarre and abnormal that it is really impossible for the human mind to come up with any logical or reasonable explanation for them. He went on and said to you that although the evidence about the luminol sock foot prints in the house was tested at great length, there now can be no doubt that the prints were made by the Accused and so much of the evidence that you heard does not matter any longer in the sense that you need not worry about it; that, indeed, it need not have been called, since all the Accused now says, supports other evidence that those foot prints were his and that he went into those rooms and got wet blood on his socks.

During his address Mr Wright suggested to you that these killings were part of a plan by the Accused but that two things went wrong with it for him; first, Stephen came awake and fought so that a quick second shot must have been delayed and secondly, the police did a lot more thorough careful job in investigating this matter than ever the Accused could have expected. Counsel argued, in a general way, that the Accused had become a person increasingly disturbed during the days before this event; that he was anti his father; and that his behaviour became unusual and almost obsessional about some rather strange matters. As to the first thing that Counsel claimed went wrong, Mr Wright said, that you would conclude from the evidence, that Stephen must have become alerted to the fact that he was being approached by someone with a rifle and that he struggled; that you would conclude from the evidence that Stephen, no doubt lying in his bed because that is where the bullet was found on the pillow, put up his right hand to push the gun and thereby placed his fingerprint on the silencer and at the same time putting up his left hand in the gesture indicated by the pathologist; that the first shot, instead of going into his head, went through his hand and across the top of his head causing the loss of an amount of blood; that then a fight took place with the assailant using gloved hands, indicating some deliberation and planning in handling the gun and then pulling Stephen's sweat shirt tight around his neck during the course of the struggle in a manner which partly incapacitated him; that the blood coming from Stephen's head, got onto the gloves; that the gun had jammed or was not operating correctly; the gloves were removed so that the trapped bullet could be released and finally a shot fired through the top of the head of Stephen to kill him. Counsel argued that it must have been during that struggle, not only that Stephen got those unusual injuries, but that the Accused suffered the bruising to his forehead and the fresh injury to his knee and that the glasses he had been wearing, while his own good ones were being repaired, were damaged and the lens fell out. So that is the way the Crown described how those events, those very important events had taken place. Mr Wright asked you to reach such conclusions from all of the evidence you had heard about what had happened in Stephen's room.

Further he said the evidence established that the gun must have misfired again in Arawa's room and he suggested to you that after the Accused had missed her with his first shot, which went into the wall, and he reminded you that since the Accused would no longer have had the glasses on the likelihood of a missed shot was greater; that ultimately he shot Arawa when she was kneeling.

Counsel suggested to you that after these events had happened, the Accused put the washing on, including in it the green jersey which he had been wearing; that the jersey then had blood on the right shoulder coinciding with the marks on various places in the house, doorways or architraves; that some of it must have soaked through his green jersey shoulder onto the white Gondoliers shirt and that the Accused then sponged it as it seemed to be only a minor amount of blood. Mr Wright argued that because of the nature of those circumstances, the shirt could well be in the category where the Accused didn't put it in the wash because he thought at the time that he had sponged the marks off; that when they were wet it looked as if they were gone but, in fact, they were diluted and could be seen later in the pattern that Doctor Cropp referred to.

Counsel contended that the Accused went and did the paper run because that was part of an essential element of the whole plan and that the Accused must then, on return from the paper run, have gone to the alcove in the lounge and switched on the computer at 6.44 a.m. Counsel said that you would be satisfied about that time because of all the evidence about the paper run being carried out a lot earlier that day and because the Accused himself had said that at 6.40 a.m. exactly he was at the corner of Heath and Every Street and it would have taken two to three minutes, at a moderate walk, to go from there to Every Street. So the argument Mr Wright put to you was that the evidence would confirm that it was the Accused who switched this computer on at this significant time. Counsel then said to you well, he must have waited there in that alcove, put the message on the computer, waited with the rifle as his father came, as he would have expected him to, and then shot his father through the head at close range; that he then went down to the wash house again; washed his hands when some of the blood got flicked about; and then went to ring 111 as you have heard.

Mr Wright suggested to you it is those later actions which really explain the 25 minute (approximately) gap between when the Accused got back from the paper run and when he rang the emergency services whereas he said to you, on the other hand, the evidence given by the Accused just does not explain that delay.

Counsel went on to point out to you various other portions of evidence including the fact that one of the ambulance officers, one of the experienced ones, said in answer to a question, that he thought the shaking and shivering the Accused did while they were there was being 'put on'.

That is the way Mr Wright argued the case. He said, look at the total picture and you would conclude, not only from those items but also from the mass of evidence, that there was proof beyond reasonable doubt. He asked you not to chop the cases up into little segments but rather to consider the overall effect of the evidence and he dealt with those 10 basic facts; including that the rifle and the ammunition were the Accused's; that the fingerprints and blood were on the rifle; and that his bloodied gloves were found in Stephen's room. Counsel said to you that, if the father was supposed to have been the killer, why, if he was going to commit suicide afterwards, would he have gone and hunted out, without disturbing other items, the gloves found in Stephen's room and used them in the way that the killer must have. Mr Wright also referred to the fresh injuries on the Accused's face and knee; the lens from the damaged glasses in Stephen's room; the droplets of blood on the Accused's socks; the computer time; the fact that the trigger lock had a key in a porcelain container which was placed there by the Accused and was not lying obviously for anyone to pick up; that the Gondoliers sweat shirt did have blood on the right shoulder in a manner which looked as though it had been sponged; and that, he argued, the washing machine, if put on when the Accused had arrived home from the paper run for its full or near full time, would have still been going when the police arrived and they did not hear it. It was suggested to you the only conclusion you could draw was that the washing machine was put on earlier.

Counsel said that there were very curious matters in the Accused's explanation of what he says he now remembers and that you might find it difficult to accept some of those matters as being correct. He said if you took that view you may well think it is really unbelievable that these things happened in the way the Accused has suggested to you that they did because his explanation to you, he said, requires him to have done some very strange things. He pointed to the following. He said that to believe the Accused, you would have to accept that the Accused came home in the dark from his paper run, went into the house, went into his room where he had to hang up a paper bag behind the door, took off his shoes, put the transistor away, and did all this without putting the light on when the light switch was just behind the door; that he did not apparently stand on the bullets and other equipment and trigger lock and so forth that were on the floor in that area; that he just went downstairs to the wash house and picked up a green jersey, which he asked you to believe was there with blood on it to the degree where the blood smeared onto him and various blood marks were left on other places within the wash house: all coming from the green jersey. He reminded you in detail of that evidence and the significance of it including the blood in the porcelain basin. Further he submitted to you that it was very significant that the bruising on the Accused was reasonably fresh and must, on the evidence, have happened in the early hours of that morning at some stage.

So far as the message on the computer was concerned, he made various arguments which you will probably remember well enough. He said that the words used in that message are very strange and they suggested it could not have been from Robin but David; that the very nature of those words, when you study them, gives a clue as to who was the real author. You will remember the two points he made. He said the Accused was the one who talked about the deceased being taken away and that the word in the message 'stay', in 'deserved to stay' fits the stay and take away concept the Accused had talked about. He also contended it was a strange use of the word 'deserved' rather than 'deserves' if in fact it was Robin talking to David about a future event.

Mr Wright also argued, in relation to the first part of his triangle, that the washing machine, even with allowances for a limited use of the wash cycle at all, would have taken a longer time than that between David Bain arriving home and the police arriving. The presence of the red sweat shirt had not been referred to I think at the time of Mr Wright's address and he did not appear to deal with that item during the course of his address. The presence of it in the washing machine may have been suggested by him to have been the result of being placed there at a later time, perhaps put into the machine after Robin Bain's shooting just in case there were any marks on it and while the sequence of the machine was finishing but it was not a matter he dealt with in detail because it was raised more graphically at a later time.

On the second part on the triangle Counsel said that when you looked at the case so far as Robin Bain was concerned, the most startling feature was that there was not one piece of evidence that Robin Bain had been into the rooms of the deceased on this particular morning and he said if Robin had been the killer; intent on killing the others and later committing suicide; it is strange that there was no blood on him from Stephen, Laniet, Arawa or any of the others; that there were no finger prints in any significant place from him and, in particular, that his fingerprints were not on the rifle when, if you were to accept the defence view, Robin must have been the last person to have gripped it or held on to it.

Further, Mr Wright submitted to you that there was no real evidence of Robin Bain arranging a relieving teacher; that while such a suggestion had been made to the other teacher at the school there was no evidence of it and that the teacher explained why a relieving teacher may have been arranged for a period. So far as Robin Bain's diary was concerned, he said have a look at it, look at the nature of it and you would conclude that one diary amongst others does not lead to the inference that he was deliberately not writing down future events after 20 June; that the diary really dealt with matters that had happened on particular days. he said also that Cunningham's evidence, when heard in full, did not take on the significance that Counsel for the Accused earlier claimed for it; that really it was a conversation about the destroying of possums around the school and little else. Of course, he also emphasised the point that why would Robin Bain have changed his socks and his jersey and all of his clothes if he intended to kill himself after shooting the others. He said the normality of Robin's actions in bringing in the paper and acting as usual just don't fit in with those of a murderer, followed by suicide.

Counsel then came to the third part of his triangle. He said you would accept, after looking at all the evidence, there was no real evidence here of a suicide and he asked you particularly to accept Doctor Dempster's opinion. He said to you that Doctor Dempster stated that while it was physically possible, suicide was highly unlikely. I think it may be useful if I were to deal with some of that evidence. There is a mass of evidence and, as I say, because I select to read one portion, that is not to say that the other portions of evidence are not important. Doctor Dempster said about suicide:

'I have had regard to the material I observed on the curtain, the position of the body, the weapon itself, the site of the entry wound and its direction in considering whether it could have been self inflicted. I considered it unlikely that this death was self inflicted on the basis of the anomalies in terms of the location of the weapon, location of blood spots, the location of the entry wound and its direction through the head.'

You recall that indeed those points the doctor made were the very ones that Mr Wright relied upon when he was making his submissions to you but Counsel went on to argue that it is not just a question of Doctor Dempster's opinion but that this is a case where you will also have to have regard to the evidence that there was no suicide note; no fingerprints on the silencer or any other part of the gun (in particular, he referred to the silencer, as Robin would have had to have held the gun there with at least one of his hands); that it was unlikely although not impossible that a shell case ejected from the gun, if he had shot himself, would have gone through the gap in the curtain and landed where it was found; and further, that when you look at the position of the magazine near his right hand, the fact that it is standing on its edge, is explainable logically only by it being put there rather than having fallen out of his hand because if it had fallen, it would have fallen on its side. His argument was, don't consider each point just by itself but look at the whole and when you add those points to Doctor Dempster's opinion, then suicide was not remotely possible in this case. They are the arguments he made.

After dealing with those three parts of his triangle he went on in his address, you will recall, to deal with the Accused's statements and his evidence. He contended that this loss of memory, genuine or feigned, does not mean that the Accused did not murder the five persons. He emphasised to you what Professor Mullen had said that if you have lost your memory 'you don't know what you don't know'. Mr Wright pointed out that on 20 June, the Accused had said quite firmly to the police that he had never been in Stephen's, Laniet's or Arawa's rooms that morning but that is not true because the Accused now admits he was in those three rooms. The Accused now says that he did not kill any persons but Mr Wright says,

'Is that true or is it partly that he has forgotten or that he just blocked out those events from his mind?' He asked you to form the conclusion that David Bain just has a convenient memory; and that there were clear differences in the statements he made to the police and in his evidence. Counsel pointed to the ownership of the important green jersey, now said to be Robin's but earlier said to be Arawa's; the raised voices that had never been mentioned earlier and the washing machine and sequence of events. Mr Wright argued to you that this memory return really provides a way of explaining to some degree the blood that could be sheeted home to him. He, you will recall, submitted that loss of memory does not excuse, even if genuine.

Finally the point emphasised by Mr Wright was what he called a strange feature of the Accused's own evidence. You will recall he said the fact that the Accused said that he hear Laniet gurgling was very significant. Counsel argued that if you had regard to Doctor Dempster's evidence and the Accused's evidence, that you must conclude that the Accused was in that room between the first one or two shots and the final fatal shot. Mr Guest, of course, immediately said that that was not accepted and he submitted to you that the evidence of Doctor Dempster did not go as far as saying that Laniet could not have been making gurgling noises after the final shot. Since both Counsel have referred to this matter, it seems appropriate to read the relevant portions of the evidence in full so that you can then consider them.

The Accused, in his evidence, said this:

'At that stage I noticed the bullets and the trigger lock on the floor and the casing for the bullets. I went back out and into mum's room to find out what was going on. I was asking, calling her and asking what the story was and it was then that I – when I opened the curtain she didn't respond at all. So I went in further and saw the blood on her face and her eyes were open and she didn't say anything at all. Saw the blood on mum's face and saw that she was dead. And then I think I went through into Stephen's room and over to Stephen. In Stephen's room I can only remember seeing Stephen and the – he was covered in blood. His face was red. He looked as if he had blusher all over his face and down his neck. In his room I can't remember seeing anything else, just him. I touched him. I got down beside him and touched his shoulder to see if I could wake him. But he didn't move at all. And then I left the room. I can't remember walking through anywhere but – *The next thing I remember is being in Laniet's room and I could hear her gurgling.* I could see blood all over her face and on the pillow. I can't recall if I touched her. I went right up beside the bed. I must have left the room at that stage, I don't recall it. I was – the next thing I remember is I was down in Arawa's room.'

So that is the Accused's evidence about this passage. Doctor Dempster's evidence must properly start with his description of the wounds to Stephen because, in particular, he said that the head wounds to Laniet and Stephen, you will recall, were the same or similar. So far as Stephen was concerned then, he said:

'The second bullet wound was situated almost exactly in the midline of the top of the head, right on the top of the head (indicates on diagram). This diagram shows the location of the entry of the bullet and its direction through the head which is directly downwards and slightly backwards. This bullet passed between the cerebral hemispheres. There is a very narrow space between the 2 cerebral hemispheres and this bullet was so symmetrically placed that it passed down this gap then passing through the portion of brain which joins the 2 cerebral hemispheres and through a portion of the midbrain known as the Ponds. This injury I believe would have been immediately fatal. He would have been incapable of any voluntary movement. It is always possible of course after an individual is shot in the head that a few reflex movements may occur.'

That is what he said about that injury to Stephen. About Laniet he said, again referring to these head charts:

'The 2 charts demonstrate the location of the 3 bullet wounds, the wound I have just described is the lower spot on the left side of the deceased's face just below the base of the skull. The 2nd wound is located above the ear and that is the wound which in photo 10 from which some brain material can be seen protruding. The third wound was inflicted in the top of the skull and it is also angled downwards and slightly backwards. The direction of the 2 bullet wounds to the side of the head extended into the side of the head and slightly backwards but passed more or less directly across the direction of the head. They had been fired from a position on the left side of the body. Their direction is shown in the final diagram. The first wound in the scalp over the top of the head (indicates on diagram) this wound here with the arrow pointing to the top of the head. In my opinion that wound would have been fatal. Once again this bullet wound passed between the 2 cerebral hemispheres, through the corpus callosum and into the Ponds. It is almost an exact replica of the wound, the fatal wound, suffered by Stephen. The 2nd wound to the cheek (indicates) this one here, the lowest of the wounds, I don't believe that wound would have been fatal, and I believe that Laniet would possibly have been capable of voluntary movement after that wound had been inflicted. The 3rd entry wound is the wound which is located relatively high up on the skull above the left ear. That wound had passed through major important structures in the brain also and had destroyed most of the basal ganglia and also would have in my opinion been fatal and incapacitated the deceased from the time it was fired. I examined the main airways of Laniet. The main airways contained a large amount of heavily blood stained and mucoid frothy liquid. The airways and air spaces in the lungs were also distended with similar material which is largely a result of the lungs developing pulmonary oedema or becoming waterlogged and also due in part to some blood from the injuries to the base of the skull finding its way into the airways. It indicates to me that Laniet has survived for some time after the first of the injuries which on its own is unlikely to cause immediate death or the wound which is least likely to cause immediate death would be the wound on the left side of the cheek, the lower most of the the 2 wounds on the left. The ingestion of blood into the lungs is partly ingestion of blood into the lungs and partly due to fluid being formed in the lungs but I would have anticipated that Laniet would have been making audible gurgling or similar noises as this material accumulated in the airways.'

So that is the evidence that was given about this point upon which you must reach your conclusions.

Mr Wright's argument was that this evidence of the Accused's, which Counsel said, in effect, was a slip during the evidence, revealed that the Accused must have been present before Laniet received the fatal final shot or shots. He has also referred to other matters as indicating similar conclusions; such as, the mention of the mother's eyes being open, and the evidence of the aunt, Mrs Clark, that the Accused had said to her:

'dying, everyone dying and can't stop them and taking them away and it was all jumbled and mixed but it was all those sorts of words and he said, dying everywhere and then he mentioned Schindlers List, just like Schindlers List and back to black hands and so on again. During this time I was down in front of David and watching him and he then kept saying, you know, everyone dying, dying, you know, dying all around, dead, dying and I aid to him, did you see them dying David? He just stopped and he opened his eyes and he looked straight at me and said, no, I only saw Mum and Dad and they were already dead.'

Those then were the arguments presented for the Crown.

Case for Accused

For the Accused, Mr Guest immediately said to you that you would not be happy about the final major argument made by the Crown; that Doctor Dempster had not actually said, in so many words, that the gurgling must have finished as soon as the fatal wound and Counsel argued that this gurgling could have continued on afterwards. He asked you to make up your own minds on the evidence but suggested that the evidence did not go anywhere as near as the Crown's argument tried to claim. He said then to you that the Crown had put theories about the skin off the Accused's knee at the start of the case, and seemed to have given that away; that they had theories about the ejected shells which they didn't seem to continue with and had been dropped during the case; that the paper run theories they had could not be supported. He suggested to you, you could put all the present theories in the same category as the earlier ones and eventually place very little weight on them.

Counsel also immediately dealt very briefly with the 10 points that the Crown had mentioned. He said the fact that the Accused owned the rifle didn't prove anything; that the fingerprints could have got on that rifle by the Accused picking it up at some stage which he does not now remember; that the clothes could have been washed by the father; that the glasses were not so significant as the Crown tried to say because the Accused didn't remember wearing them at all and there was no evidence from anyone else from the Crown he had been wearing those second or alternative glasses that he said belonged to his mother. Mr Guest, in replying, also said if David was the killer wouldn't he have hidden those glasses or thrown them somewhere else when he was on the paper run? He said to you that the droplets of blood on his socks relied on by the Crown did not really take it any further; that if the Accused was in the bedrooms after these events, he could well have got the blood on them so they do not take the matter any further.

Counsel dealt for some time with the paper run times. He urged that point upon you as being powerfully against the Crown's case. He said to you that there was evidence from Mrs Laney that the Accused was at his gate at 65 Every Street at 6.45 a.m.; that it must have been him that she saw and therefore he could not have been the person who turned on the computer; that in effect it must have been turned on by somebody else, namely, the killer.

Since that evidence has also assumed a particular significance, I should perhaps remind you of what the evidence generally is about timing for you to consider. The witnesses whose evidence was read to you, you recall, gave various times. Those times related to when they had observed or heard indications of the Accused delivering the papers at various points along the run. There is a chart that was produced as a schedule summarising that evidence. Mr McConnell, the distributor of these papers, in his evidence said that at 5.40 a.m. on this morning:

'I went past the bundle of papers I had dropped off for David BAIN and noticed the bundle hadn't been picked up.

'I didn't think it funny that David BAIN hadn't picked up his bundle of papers as he usually starts at 6.00 a.m. but occasionally he starts later or sooner.'

Further he said:

'If he started at about 5.50 a.m. this morning he would have finished at about 6.30, 6.45 a.m.'

Mrs Laney said:

'I am an enrolled nurse at Karitane Rest Home, Every Street, Dunedin.

'I live in Dunedin.

'I have been working at the rest home for about six years.

'On Monday 20th June 1994 I was working at the rest home and I was supposed to start work at 6.45 a.m. but I was a bit late.

'As I drove to work I came up Every Street from Somerville Street, Dunedin.

'I drove past 65 Every Street, Dunedin.

'As I did so I noticed a person going past the partially opened gate at 65 Every Street, Dunedin.

'As I saw this person I thought I must be running late as I normally see him down by Heath Street, Dunedin.

'I looked at the clock in my car and it read 6.50 a.m.

'I know the clock is 4 to 5 minutes fast as it was about 6.45 a.m. as I drove past him.'

Other evidence that might bear on this is the evidence of the Accused who said:

'That morning I ran most of the paper run but walked the streets we have heard about in evidence. The time I got back to the house I can't recall the exact time but I know that I was at Heath Street at 6.40 exactly. I told an officer it takes 2 or 3 minutes to get home, that is an approximation I can't tell you exactly how long it takes.'

And then there was the evidence of Detective Constable Thomson who told you of test runs that had been carried out by Constable Peters, without the newspapers but simulating placing them, took 47 minutes on the first occasion and 50 minutes on the second. So far as Heath Street to Every Street, he said that he had walked that route himself:

'To cover the distance at a moderate walk it took me 2 minutes and 15 seconds on the first test and the second it took me 2 minutes and 16 seconds.'

That is the evidence that bears on that matter. As I say, judgments about that evidence are for you.

Mr Guest argued that if you accept Mrs Laney's evidence and it was 6.45 a.m., and the person at the gate she saw was the Accused, then he could not have switched the computer on at 6.44 a.m. He went on then to say the key to the trigger lock did not mean much because it was in a small container; that if Robin Bain searched about he could have found it; that the blood stains on the sweat shirt could hardly have come from the Accused sponging them because surely if he carried out this exercise and saw blood on his sweat shirt, he would have put that into the washing machine as well. He said also the washing machine evidence the Crown relied upon fell to the ground when you consider that the red sweat shirt that the Accused had worn on the paper run was one of the items found in the washing machine and must have been put in there by the Accused after he had returned from the paper run.

Counsel then went on in his address to say, you have heard a lot of evidence in 3 weeks but there just isn't evidence, he emphasised, of any valid motive for these crimes; that David Bain was not shown to have had any motive that would explain them. David Bain, he said, according to his friends and relatives, is a person who, in his character and nature, would be far away from being a killer. Rather, that he is a person who has normal sort of music, sport and social interests. Counsel said to you that there was no evidence here of insanity or indeed of any significant abnormality which could explain to you why David Bain might kill other members of his family. Counsel asked you to accept that David Bain had told the truth and therefore to acquit him.

Mr Guest continued to say to you again and in more detail (and I am just summarising it) that if David Bain had been the killer then why would he walk on the blood; why would he not hide the glasses and the clothes; why would he have waited months before saying he was in the rooms; why would he have rung 111? He said it was unreasonable of the Crown in its argument to you to on the one hand to be relying upon what they said were mistakes or problems that had arisen for David Bain and yet claiming he was cunning and clever and calculated in other respects. Counsel made numerous points to you about the witnesses. He said that overall they would support the view that David Bain told the truth to the police rather than pretend or, as Counsel said, doing 'a Hollywood' or lying or carefully calculating what he was saying and doing. Mr Guest reminded you of a number of matters including the fact that the Accused does not need glasses, he says, to carry out a number of actions and, in particular, that he didn't need those damaged glasses which were found in his room.

Mr Guest accepted that the luminol prints must have been the Accused's but not that they were in the position where the only conclusion you could draw was that the Accused must have put them there because he was the killer. The blood on the towel he said did not support the concept of a calculating killer covering up his tracks. He argued that the time that would be necessary for David to have killed these persons after the paper run was just insufficient in that the Crown really had not proved what had happened. He emphasised to you that if the Accused had killed before the paper run then you would have to believe that he did so quite calculatingly and that upon coming home from the paper run he waited for his father in a deliberate way and then shot him; that after that he put the sweat shirt which he had been wearing on the paper run into the washing machine. Counsel submitted that you couldn't really, given that sequence and the nature of those events, conclude that the Accused was responsible for the killings.

As to Robin Bain, Mr Guest submitted to you that he did have a motive; that he was a proud school teacher who had been rejected by his wife and family and that under the pressure of those over months and months, he had just snapped. Later Counsel pointed to various alternatives that Robin Bain may have had in his mind and sequence that he may have followed in killing these persons. He put to you possible versions of how Robin Bain could have killed his wife but been heard by Stephen or others and then got into the awful dilemma of having to kill others as well. He said that Robin Bain could have been acting in a possibly deranged and unthinking state while doing these things, including taking the green jersey off and perhaps trousers; putting them in the washing basket; changing his clothes and washing his hands and going upstairs in completely clean gear.

Mr Guest spent some time, you will recall, giving you a reconstruction of how he said Robin could have placed the rifle on the chair and placed his head against it and shot himself and he asked you to accept that that was more than just a possibility. So far as those demonstrations are concerned, I think I should give you a warning to be careful about them. It is important to have regard to the evidence in that respect and in particular to the angle of the shot. You recall that was a point that Doctor Dempster emphasised and took care about in arranging the demonstration before you. I draw your attention to this particularly because the demonstrations that Counsel has performed you will recall he kept putting the gun to his head in this position at the side of the head. It is necessary to look at the entry wound to explain. If you will please look, say in the big book at photograph 36, you can see the wound there on Robin Bain and the position of it. Also in the other book of photographs the first page or photograph 2 perhaps more clearly, you can see the position of that entry wound. The wound was in the position shown in those photographs. It was not further back on the temple. It is an important point only because that is one of the features emphasised by Doctor Dempster so that any demonstration must have regard to the exact location of that entry wound as well as the track of the bullet through the head. You will recall Doctor Dempster referred to that on this original exhibit and not just the direction across the head but also the level of the shot; in other words, that it didn't go up or down significantly but went straight through on that angle. It is the angle of the shot and the level of it that have to be both taken into account when any demonstration is done that may indicate whether suicide was likely or unlikely. I mention this only because you have had, during Counsel's address, so many demonstrations of possible positions that the rifle could have been placed in relative to the head that it is important when considering both those demonstrations and Doctor Dempster's evidence that you have regard to the proven facts so far as the entry wound and the angle and level of the shots.

Overall what Mr Guest was arguing, by his demonstrations and what he said to you was that you couldn't accept Doctor Dempster's assessment of the likelihood of suicide; that you should not accept that but rather you should reject it and conclude that Robin Bain shooting himself was a real physical possibility. He emphasised to you that was a decision for you and it was not for Doctor Dempster.

Counsel urged you to the view that ultimately you would be left in the position where David Bain had given evidence on oath that he did not do it; that he had not succumbed to any challenge in cross examination by the Crown and that you should accept his evidence. He said and you will recall he posed to you a large number of questions as to why David Bain would have done various things if he in fact had committed these crimes or why, if he was the calculating person that the Crown tried to make out, he hadn't committed the crimes in some other way; or without making the mistakes that the Crown were now saying they relied upon. Counsel said to you, if David Bain was the killer that the Crown said, why wasn't he making more of a case against his father in evidence? Why wasn't he saying things which would have implicated his father to a greater degree. Finally, after making all those points to you and emphasising on a number of occasions the particular points concerning Mrs Laney's evidence and the red sweat shirt evidence, Mr Guest said that you should accept David Bain's evidence in Court, or at the very least, you should conclude that there was and is a reasonable doubt and acquit him on all charges. That concludes the summary of the cases presented to you by both Counsel.

Conclusion
In view of the way in which this trial has been conducted, the only verdicts truly open to you are ones of guilty or not guilty.

If during the course of your deliberations you wish to have your memory refreshed about what a particular witness has said, then the procedure is that you tell the Registrar, and you would be brought back into Court and I would read the relevant portion of the evidence to you. The reason why that procedure has to be followed rather than just handing you over these volumes of 450 odd pages of evidence is that the Accused and Counsel must be present when any information is given to a jury and indeed some abbreviations are used which, if you are not familiar with them, make it difficult to read.

When the attendants are sworn, I would ask you to retire and consider your verdicts.

Jury retires: 11.45 a.m.
Jury returns with questions: 5.23 p.m.